D0569946

# BAMAKO SOUNDS

# Bamako Sounds

. . . .

## The Afropolitan Ethics
of Malian Music

Ryan Thomas Skinner

A QUADRANT BOOK

*University of Minnesota Press*
*Minneapolis*
*London*

**QUADRANT**

Quadrant, a joint initiative of the University of Minnesota Press and the Institute for Advanced Study at the University of Minnesota, provides support for interdisciplinary scholarship within a new, more collaborative model of research and publication. http://quadrant.umn.edu.

Sponsored by the Quadrant Global Cultures group (advisory board: Evelyn Davidheiser, Michael Goldman, Helga Leitner, and Margaret Werry), and by the Institute for Global Studies at the University of Minnesota.

Quadrant is generously funded by the Andrew W. Mellon Foundation.

Publication of this book was made possible in part by a grant from the AMS 75 PAYS Endowment of the American Musicological Society, funded in part by the National Endowment for the Humanities and the Andrew W. Mellon Foundation.

For supplemental audiovisual material, chapter study guides, book reviews, and links to related online resources, visit http://z.umn.edu/bamakosounds.

Chapter 5 was originally published as "Money Trouble in an African Art World: Copyright, Piracy, and the Politics of Culture in Postcolonial Mali," *IASPM@Journal* 3, no. 1 (2012): 63–79; reprinted by permission.

Copyright 2015 by the Regents of the University of Minnesota

All rights reserved. No part of this publication may be reproduced, stored in a retrieval system, or transmitted, in any form or by any means, electronic, mechanical, photocopying, recording, or otherwise, without the prior written permission of the publisher.

Published by the University of Minnesota Press
111 Third Avenue South, Suite 290
Minneapolis, MN 55401-2520
http://www.upress.umn.edu

Library of Congress Cataloging-in-Publication Data
Skinner, Ryan Thomas, author.
    Bamako sounds : the Afropolitan ethics of Malian music / Ryan Thomas Skinner.
    Includes bibliographical references and index.
    ISBN 978-0-8166-9349-8 (hc : alk. paper) — ISBN 978-0-8166-9350-4 (pb : alk. paper)
    1. Music—Moral and ethical aspects—Mali—Bamako. 2. Music—Moral and ethical aspects—Mali. 3. Musicians—Mali—Bamako—Social conditions. 4. Ethnomusicology—Mali—Bamako. 5. Group identity—Mali—Bamako. 6. Group identity in the performing arts—Mali—Bamako. 7. Mandingo (African people)—Mali—Bamako—Ethnic identity. 8. City and town life—Mali—Bamako. 9. Bamako (Mali)—Social conditions. I. Title.
    ML3917.M35S55 2015
    780.96623—dc23
                                                          2014025344

Printed in the United States of America on acid-free paper

The University of Minnesota is an equal-opportunity educator and employer.

21  20  19  18  17  16        10  9  8  7  6  5  4  3  2

# Contents

# A Sense of Urban Africa

THIS BOOK IS ABOUT THE MORALITY AND ETHICS of musical identity and expression in a West African city: Bamako, Mali (Figure 1). Bamako is a city that incorporates multiple scales of place: national, local, translocal, and global. It is Malian, the multiethnic capital of a modern nation-state; Mande, the metropolitan center of a cultural heartland; Muslim, an urban locus of the Islamic Ecumene; and African, a continental city in a postcolonial world.[1] Bamako residents encounter these registers of place to varying degrees and in a variety of forms in their everyday lives, but such encounters, in all their diversity, always entail an ethical stance: an active positioning of the self vis-à-vis national, local, translocal, and global polities. These situated, value-inflected encounters constitute what I call an "Afropolitan ethics." For the group of professional musicians with whom I have worked over of the past fifteen years, such ethical stances are the frequent subject of musical performance and interpretation. Music, whether performed live on stage, broadcast on the radio, or streamed over the Internet, is a privileged mode of moral expression in Bamako today. In this book, I present Malian artists and their audiences as a key demographic through which an Afropolitan ethics may be examined and elaborated, exemplifying broader trends in Africa and its diaspora.

By employing the term "Afropolitan," I invoke a perspective on contemporary African urbanism that acknowledges the worldly orientations of the continent's peoples and recognizes the prescriptive and volitional moorings that bind individuals to local lifeworlds. In the words of African historian and culture critic Achille Mbembe, Afropolitanism is

the awareness of this imbrication of here and elsewhere, the presence of the elsewhere in the here and vice versa, this relativization of roots and primary belongings and a way of embracing, fully cognizant of origins, the foreign, the strange and the distant, this

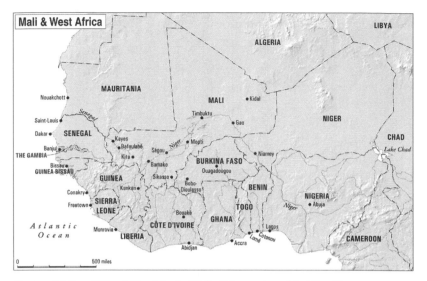

*Figure 1. Mali and West Africa. Map by Philip Schwartzberg, Meridian Mapping, Minneapolis.*

capacity to recognize oneself in the face of another and to value the traces of the distant within the proximate, to domesticate the un-familiar, to work with all manner of contradictions—it is this cultural sensibility, historical and aesthetic, that suggests the term "Afropolitanism." (2010, 229)

Rejecting the undifferentiated universalism that the term "cosmopolitan" connotes (a critique that I elaborate in the conclusion of this book), Afropolitanism locates Africans' global routes and local roots within a postcolonial and diasporic geopolitical framework. It represents particular urban African perspectives on the world that respect the specificity of cultural provenance and practice, reflect the common concerns and interests of continental and diasporic peoples, and respond to the essentialisms and injustices that continue to provincialize African peoples and inhibit their access to the international community. Through ethnography, social history, and close listening, this book elaborates the concept of Afropolitanism through the lives and works of Bamako artists. It shows, through thickly described case studies, the social and musical means by which artists reconcile local concerns with global interests and assert

Figure 2. Sidiki Diabaté in the studio. Photograph by the author.

themselves within an uneven postcolonial and diasporic world as ethical Afropolitan subjects.

To understand the ethics of Afropolitanism in Bamako, this book addresses multiple modes of self-identification and expression within the individually coherent and collectively co-present moral spheres of urban culture, profession, aesthetics, religion, economy, and politics. Take, for example, the life and work of artist Sidiki Diabaté (Figure 2). Raised in the bustle of Bamako, Sidiki belongs to a renowned clan of Mande "griots," or *jeliw* (sing. *jeli;* the *w* indicates the plural), musical artisans practicing the time-honored art of musical panegyric and storytelling known as *jeliya* (literally, *jeli*-ness; the *ya* indicates the abstract noun).[2] Within this tradition, Sidiki's family has performed the *kora* (a twenty-one-string Mande harp) for generations (see Skinner 2008a; a family history of music to which I return in chapter 3). His grandfather and namesake was a founding member of the Ensemble Instrumental National in Mali, and his father, Toumani, is a Grammy Award–winning virtuoso on the world music circuit. Sidiki is a devout Muslim and proud of his African roots. In his music, he also reaches out to the diaspora, beyond his artisanal birthright, as a producer of hip-hop. Sidiki's moral personhood is the convergent product of his Mande heritage, Islamic faith, diasporic aesthetics, professional identity, and family history, with its postcolonial expressions of musical nationalism and globalization. These are the *moralities*—the salient local moorings and social imperatives—that locate and orient his being-in-the-world. Sidiki's *ethical* subjectivity—predicated on personal interest, choice, and agency—emerges from an irreducible investment in and negotiation of the multiple moralities that anchor his identity, a multiplicity that is the product of a particular urban African experience in the world, of his Afropolitanism.

Throughout West Africa, music has long been a privileged medium of moral and ethical identification, canonically expressed in the verbal arts of praise song, epic narrative, and didactic lyricism, but also represented in the forms and styles of instrumental performance and dance. Socially privileged, music takes on a distinct and at times contested ontology among contemporary artists and their audiences in Bamako, who, in the course of performance, traverse the generic boundaries of "tradition" and "modernity." As members of a profession historically tied to state sponsorship and presently bound to commercial enterprise in local and global culture industries, artists are not (or not only) restricted to the secret societies or clan-based artisanal professions that once exclusively delimited musical practice in Mande society. They do, however, draw heavily on such traditional culture in their modern musical expressions, particularly when moral and ethical concerns are most salient (about which more in chapter 2).

Precisely because of their status and identity as modern musicians, Bamako artists have incorporated a variety of musical genres into their Afropolitan art world. Drawing on local, regional, and diasporic sounds, artists perform the music of *jeliya, wasulu* (a popular music form derived from hunter's music), *zigiri* (a musical expression of ritual Islamic praise), *takamba* (a genre of musical praise and celebration from northern Mali), hip-hop, reggae, jazz, and Afropop—not in isolation, but in a complex mix of urban music making. In this way, I describe Bamako's music culture as not only multigeneric but also *inter*-generic, as artists create and combine a great diversity of sounds within an equally rich social environment. Thus, an artist like Sidiki Diabaté may begin the day performing as a *jeli* for a life-cycle ceremony, lay down a hip-hop track as a sound engineer at an afternoon studio session, and finish the day sitting in on a gig as a freelance artist at a local nightclub. When asked about these different musical identities, on stage with his *kora* or behind a mixing board in the studio, Sidiki refers to himself as a "musician," an artist free of the constraints of convention, even as he affirms his status and identity as a *jeli*. "In my family, you are born into *[jeliya]*," he says, "but when I'm here [in the recording studio], I'm a musician, not a *jeli*."[3] The Afropolitanism of artistic practice in Bamako emerges from this generic movement and subjective multiplicity, not from any single venue, style, identity, or form of expression.

## Moral Positions and Ethical Projects

In each chapter of this book, I emphasize a salient social position through which artists and their audiences imagine a diverse range of ethical projects in the contemporary Bamako art world. Thus, I present urban social space, professional identity, musical aesthetics, popular piety, the economy of culture, and (post)national politics as the existential grounds on which much performative and productive agency takes place among professional musicians in (and out of) Mali today. This list of artistic social positions is not exhaustive, but it is, I think, broadly representative of the ethico-moral lives and works of many of the artists who call Bamako their home in the world. In presenting these modes of artistic being sequentially, I do not mean to suggest that they represent isolable and exclusive categories of sociomusical existence; rather, I hope to progressively demonstrate, from one chapter to another, the co-presence, interconnections, and tensions of the multiple moralities and varied ethical projects that make up the complex lifeworlds of my Afropolitan interlocutors.

By "social position," I mean the distinct point of view, way of acting, and mode of thought of subjects aligned by affinity (of gender, race, class, kinship, profession, and so on) and located within a varied and stratified social space. A social position is the structural framework for what Pierre Bourdieu calls *habitus*, those "schemes of perception, appreciation and action [that] enable [socially positioned subjects] to perform acts of practical knowledge based on the identification and recognition of conditional, conventional stimuli to which they are predisposed to react" (2000, 138). Phenomenologically, a social position represents a mode of being-in-the-world, a culturally modeled means of engaging with, experiencing, and evaluating the human artifice—the "human world" of Merleau-Ponty's thought ([1962] 2002, 403–6)—in all its variety. In this way, social positions are often encountered as givens in social space, even as they are achieved and confirmed in practice through modes of being. Such givenness shapes our sense of a stable, sustainable, and essentially *moral* world, of the immanent rightness and goodness of things as they are.

In this book, I argue that *all* modes of being, insofar as they model systems of social constraint and socially embedded agency (Bourdieu 2000, 138); of prescribed adherence to the mores and lifeways of a given society; of custom and convention (consonant with the Latin root of "morality," *mor*); of value-oriented "stance" (Berger 2010), are potentially moral. This does not mean that one necessarily perceives a social position as inherently "right" or "good," particularly if one encounters a social space as an outsider. Indeed, from the stranger's vantage, social positions are also potentially immoral, shrouded in foreignness, the exotic, and the absurd. (I have more to say about this moral ambiguity, occasioned by cultural difference but also the coexistence of different and sometimes opposed modes of being within social space, in subsequent chapters.) Yet, for cultural insiders, social positions act as normative moral frameworks for agency in society. They are akin to Hegel's concept of *Sittlichkeit*, the idea, as Theodor Adorno explains, "that the norms of the good are directly anchored and guaranteed in the life of an existing community" (2000, 12; see also Eagleton 2009, 125). Importantly, the "life" Adorno describes appears more as a collection of fragments than a coherent whole (see Adorno [1951] 2005). In other words, "the good life" cannot assume a reductive and singular moral compass; as social positions multiply within social space, so too do moralities.

As John Miller Chernoff observed in an earlier study of West African music culture: "Relying on their sense of appropriateness, [Africans] may participate equally in what we might think of as exclusive kinds of identities, perhaps being both nationalistic and tribalistic, Animist and Christian or Muslim, traditional and Westernized" (1979, 156). In Bamako today, artists are urbanites, working professionals, aesthetic critics, religious practitioners, entrepreneurs, and citizens; they are these, and they are much more. Each of these social positions presents an intentional orientation toward the world, conditioning what it means to live in the city, establish a career, make good art, deepen one's faith, earn a living, engage in (or oppose) civic life, and so on. As Georgina Born and David Hesmondhalgh have argued, in their postcolonial critique of the musicological disciplines:

Rather than conceiving of individual subjectivities as fully self-transparent and coherent, then, and in contrast to the apparent "unities" of collective experience, we should adopt the insights of poststructuralism and psychoanalysis and develop an awareness of the multiple musical identifications or subject positions to which individuals are susceptible as producers and consumers. (2000, 33)

With an interest in elaborating these "multiple musical identifications" in Bamako, this book asks: How do conventional forms of sociality emerge from living in and accommodating to the built environment of the city? How does one reconcile the co-presence of conflicting musical identities that, in positioning themselves in terms of given-ness and choice, tradition and modernity, produce different notions of social and economic value and musical expression? How do culturally informed aesthetic values adapt and respond, in the space of production and the course of performance, to global imaginations? How do popular religious practices, bound up with an urban African sense of place, confront (and conform to) transnational orthodoxies? How do postcolonial subjects make claims on, contest, and negotiate normative political and economic systems? And, what does it mean to make "Malian music" in a country fragmented by political dispute and internecine conflict?

Part of what I hope to accomplish in this book is to identify and elaborate certain salient modes of being and the moralities they encode as existential frameworks for the *habitus* of musical artists in Bamako today. Thus, I consider the complex amalgam of place, profession, artistry, piety, economy, and politics as social positions that give existential substance to this particular urban African "art world" (Becker 1982). This move "beyond culture" (Gupta and Ferguson 1992) to a more socially varied and morally multiple anthropology, resists reductive analysis, emphasizing social pluralism over cultural relativism. By this I mean that in any given context in which multiple modes of being are at play (as they always are), all moralities are not equal. Sometimes this is a question of foregrounding one social position over another, as when Sidiki says, "In the studio, I am a musician, not a *jeli*"; while at other times claims to social positions may themselves be contested: Does your clan name give you the right to perform this music? Are you the right kind of Muslim? What does your claim to intellectual property mean in the informal marketplace? Who defines "patriotism" in a time of internecine conflict and crisis? My point is not, however, to deny commensurability, or the concept of culture as an anthropological hermeneutic.[4] My argument is that while music culture in Bamako does encompass multiple moralities, articulated through multiple modes of being, it remains both coherent and dynamic. It is precisely this sociospatial coherence and dynamism, in which artists performatively negotiate the possibilities and constraints of a plurality of social positions in urban social life, that I call an "Afropolitan ethics."[5]

Read as a whole, the case studies presented in this book reveal a particular conjuncture of morally inflected social positions and ethically oriented subjective agency observed in the lives and works of Bamako artists. This articulation of the conditional and agential exemplifies what Raymond Williams calls a "structure of feeling," or a paradigmatic patterning of social disposition and activity in a given social space, or "culture" ([1961] 2001, 64–88). As Stuart Hall explains, one discovers such "patterns of a characteristic kind . . . not in the art, production, trading, politics, the raising of families, treated as separate activities," but in the way this "complex of practices" incorporate "the underlying patterns which distinguish [them] in any specific society at any specific time" (Hall 1980, 60). In this book, I use the term "Afropolitan" to qualify the structure of feeling shared and experienced within a community of artists and their interlocutors in Bamako, Mali. Before elaborating further on this Afropolitanism, however, I will say a few words about the "sensuous human praxis . . . through which men and women make history" (63) in places like Bamako today.

In her seminal treatise on existentialism, *The Ethics of Ambiguity* ([1948] 1976), Simone de Beauvoir argues that subjective agency, intentionally directed at the world, is both socially emergent and contingent, or "positioned" in Bourdieu's terms. She calls such agency "projects," resonant with Hall's history-making praxis and what anthropologist Michael Jackson identifies as the culturally relative self-making impulse to claim the right to call the world one's own (Jackson 1998, 20). Projects are the means by which people act to consciously (re)produce the human artifice; they are vital acts of "natality," constituting what Hannah Arendt calls the *vita activa* of the human condition ([1958] 1998); they, simply put, make being be (de Beauvoir [1948] 1976, 71). As such, projects move us from a discussion of social position and modality to one of subjective agency and intentionality, but this should not be read as a facile distinction between structure and practice. De Beauvoir writes, "If it is true that every project emanates from subjectivity, it is also true that this subjective movement establishes by itself a surpassing of subjectivity. Man can find a justification of his own existence only in the existence of other men" (72). In other words, existential projects are inherently intersubjective and are, thus, contingent on the intentional interests and actions of others. For de Beauvoir, as for Bourdieu, there can be no pure intentionality, no purposeful thought or action that is uncoupled from social space, unconditioned by social position.

Yet, projects can never be fully contained by the structures (positions and modes) of society. The socially emergent character of existential projects makes them "ambiguous," insofar as they remain open to the possibility of indeterminate outcomes, irreducible to any individual interest or desire. It is our ability to give purposeful shape to this horizon of possibility, subject to context and circumstance, that defines an "ethics." As de Beauvoir writes, "There is an ethics only if there is a problem to solve" (18). The "ethics of ambiguity" is, thus, the ability to meaningfully act upon social space—to solve a problem—without denying the intentional agency of others or one's own intentionality. "To will oneself free," de Beauvoir writes, "is also to will others free" (73). By contrast, to deny one's own freedom, or to refuse the right of others to act upon the world, is to "[harden] in the absurdity of facticity" (71), what Jean-Paul Sartre calls the "bad faith" of an excessively moralistic society (Sartre [1956] 2001).[6]

## Toward an Afropolitan Ethics

These ethico-moral concerns are consonant with Achille Mbembe's important account of postcolonial subjectivity (1992), a rendering of African modes of identification within a particular structure of feeling—the postcolony—at the end of the twentieth century:

The postcolony is made up not of one coherent "public space," nor is it determined by any single organizing principle. It is rather a plurality of "spheres" and arenas, each having its own separate logic yet nonetheless liable to be entailed with other logics when operating in certain specific contexts: hence the postcolonial "subject" has had to learn to continuously bargain [marchander] and improvise. Faced with this plurality of legitimizing rubrics, institutional forms, rules, arenas, and principles of combination, the postcolonial "subject" mobilizes not just a single "identity," but several fluid identities which, by their very nature, must be constantly "revised" in order to achieve maximum instrumentality and efficacy as and when required. (5)

Like Mbembe, my attention is drawn to the bargaining, improvisation, mobilizations of identity, and intersubjective revisions that characterize the ethical projects of African subjects in the world today. And, like Mbembe, I perceive popular culture as a particularly rich space through which such projects articulate and develop; though I do not entirely share his conception of popular culture's statist "promiscuity" and aesthetic "vulgarity" in contemporary Africa (see also Ivaska 2011; about which more in chapter 6). Following Mbembe's more recent work (Nuttall and Mbembe 2008; Mbembe 2010), I am also interested in locating postcoloniality, "that [condition] of societies recently emerging from the experience of colonization" (Mbembe 1992, 2), within a broader sociospatial configuration of continental urbanism, itself part of an emergent global southern modernity (to paraphrase Nuttall and Mbembe 2008, 24–26). Thus, I return, as a gesture toward the chapters that follow, to the concept of Afropolitanism.

For Mbembe, Afropolitanism emerges from a decentered and dynamic idea of Africa. It is Africa conceived as a site of passage, and reproduced through circulation and mixing (2010, 224). It is what he calls an "interval," or "an inexhaustible citation susceptible to multiple forms of combination and composition" (226). Presenting an archaeology of this African interval, Mbembe invokes prehistory, stating that the continent has always been characterized by itinerancy, mobility, and displacement (227); that is, Africa, present and past, possesses, for him, an irreducible heterogeneity based on movements and migrations, appropriations and accommodations, imitations and inventions through the millennia. This idea of Africa leads Mbembe to a vision of African renaissance. He moves from a critique of what he considers to be an earlier politics and aesthetics of "loss," especially in the literary canon of Négritude, to one of reimagination and renewal (224)—a "new dawn" suggested by the title of his book, *Sortir de la grande nuit* (French, "Out of the darkness," an homage to the late Frantz Fanon). This renewal is profoundly syncretic and incorporative, building on Africa's inherent social and cultural diversity, from which new subjective potentialities—new ethical projects—may emerge, on the continent and within its proliferating diasporas.

Mbembe's account of Afropolitanism is essentially ethical, urging us to attend to the varied conceptions, emergences, and orientations of existential projects in the modern African world. It is in this way that he is able to speak of the Afropolitan's radical breaks with the past, predilection for syncretism, and desire for renaissance and reinvention. I find this perspective compelling and rich in its capacity to account for and elucidate a wide range of urban African social life. Others, however, would beg to differ. Indeed, the idea of Afropolitanism has received a great deal of critical attention in popular media of late, variously recommending and rejecting its use as an empirical marker and conceptual tool in a (broadly defined) African world (for an overview, see Eze 2014, 239–41). In most definitions, Afropolitanism refers to a concurrence of the urban and global in (and out of) contemporary Africa, to a mode of identification emergent from what AbdouMaliq Simone has called "the worlding of African cities" in the twenty-first century (2001b). For some (such as Mbembe), Afropolitanism intersects with themes of continental renaissance, creativity, mobility, circulation, and exchange, bound to an ontological rejection of extant modes of (post)colonial being-in-the-world (see also Gikandi 2010). For others, Afropolitanism reinscribes reductive and stereotyped ideas of "African-ness," now coupled with the aestheticized subject positions and commoditized cultural styles of a diasporic and urbane African elite (see Tveit 2013 and Dabiri 2014; compare Tuakli-Wosornu 2005).

Cognizant of this critical discourse around an emergent (and contested) keyword in the Africanist lexicon, my approach to Afropolitanism emphasizes a broader field of social practice, whose scope, scale, and, ultimately, location is continuously being negotiated, expanded, collapsed, claimed, and contested. This is why I follow Mbembe in presenting the Afropolitan as a "site" of existential practice, or, in the terms employed here, an ethics of urban African being-in-the-world. Afropolitanism is too fractious, too elusive to operate as an essential (and essentially moral) mode of identification. The term does, however, effectively bring together multiple subjective valences that conditionally converge to produce an affective presence, or what I call (via Raymond Williams) an urban African structure of feeling. In this way, the Afropolitan is as ethical as it is multiply moral, as intentional as it is irreducible.

To call the urban artists whose lives and works I discuss in the pages that follow Afropolitan in this broader ethical and moral sense is to attend to both a mode of identification and the polity of which it is an intersubjective part. It is to observe an urban African context—Bamako—that encompasses the many social positions and existential projects city dwellers claim and create every day. It is to this Afropolis that I turn in chapter 1, but, before I do, I will say a few concluding words about this Afropolitan sense of place. By calling Bamako an Afropolis I invoke an anthropology of African urbanism that considers the ways in which cities like Bamako are rooted and routed in the world (see, for example, De Boeck and Plissart 2004; Ferguson 1999; Larkin 2008; Meintjes 2003; Perullo 2011; Simone 2004; Shipley 2013; and Whitehouse 2012a). Yet, recent theoretical accounts of the modern African city have tended to favor narratives of displacement over emplacement, of imaginative ethics over established moralities. "Cities," Achille Mbembe and Sarah Nuttall argue, "are subjects *en fuite*. They always outpace the capacity of analysts to name them" (2008, 25). In their study of the "elusive metropolis" of Johannesburg, Mbembe and Nuttall identify this excess of signification in the "multiplicity of registers" that continually (re)produce the urban African experience. Like Johannesburg, Bamako appears similarly "elusive," as registers multiply within and beyond its urban landscape. As I observed at the outset of this introduction, Bamako is Malian, Mande, Muslim, and African; and it is still more than all of this.

My argument in this book is not to deny such Afropolitan (or more broadly urban) elusiveness, but to assert that people in cities like Bamako routinely operate across multiple scales of place and modes of being to cultivate intersubjective coherence in their everyday lives (what Loren Kruger calls "urban *allusiveness*," 2013, 17). Put differently, I echo the questions posed by anthropologist Bruce Whitehouse in his insightful study of dignity and belonging among migrant urbanites in an (which could be any) African city: "Why is it that, even as lives are becoming increasingly mobile, the process of identity construction for many people has become increasingly circumscribed by territorial boundaries? If globalization is associated with deterritorialization, how do we explain concurrent processes of reterritorialization around the world?" (2012a, 23). In the pages that follow, I examine the musical means by which artists creatively and critically reposition and reorient themselves within a complex but no less coherent moral community; in a world that is lived, conceived, and perceived from an urban African perspective; in a city saturated with speech, song, instrumental jams, public broadcast, and punctuated cacophony. It is to these Bamako sounds that I now turn.

# CHAPTER 1

# Representing Bamako

## A Sense of Place

I first met Issa and Lassy through one of those moments of serendipity that crop up (or so you hope) in the course of long-term fieldwork. I had entered my second month of research in Bamako, feeling overwhelmed by the density of a project not yet distilled by time. I was sitting at a cyber-café in Bolibana, the Bamako neighborhood on the Niger River's left bank, close to the city center, where I lived during my year-long stay in 2006–7 (Figures 3 and 4). I don't remember to whom I was writing, but the email undoubtedly lamented the unfamiliar sameness of a place that I knew so well but had changed so much since my last extended stay five years prior. At that time, in the early 2000s, cybercafés were few and far between; by 2006, they were everywhere, with more and more people maintaining correspondence and doing business on the Internet, foreshadowing the online social networking that would flourish in the coming years.

Behind the desk by the entryway, Mohamed, the café's manager and technical troubleshooter, clicked on an mp3 file. A hip-hop track came on over the computer speakers, the volume turned up. Amid the din of computer fans, café conversation, and my own thoughts, I heard a police siren, a simple keyboard riff, and an autotuned voice singing on the vowel sound *uh*. I continued to type. Then, the beat dropped with a record scratch, and I heard a chorus, chanting and singing in Bamana, the local lingua franca. "Bolibana! Come on! Let's go!" I stopped writing. "Bolibana! Conviviality is here!" I began to listen. "Bolibana! Solidarity is here!" Who was this? "Bolibana! Don't you know about it?" I wanted to know. The track seemed to call out from the core of my research, where music and place come together to articulate localized forms of audible aesthetics and sociality.[1] I took this as a sign to more actively explore my immediate surroundings and, I hoped, track down the artists who had composed this rap about the Bamako neighborhood where I lived, Bolibana.

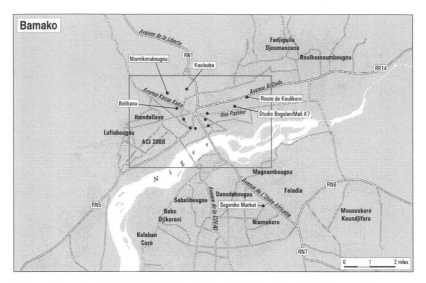

*Figure 3. Bamako. Map by Philip Schwartzberg, Meridian Mapping, Minneapolis.*

This chapter begins with my mediated and live encounter with this community, from which more general ethnographic and theoretical reflections on the city of which it is a part—Bamako—emerge. Throughout, I emphasize representations of urban culture—in film, public writing, and music—that elucidate, inscribe, and resound the moral and ethical production of space. Drawing on Mande social thought and an account of social space inspired by the work of Henri Lefebvre (1991), this chapter explores how *Bamakois* (Bamako residents) experience and express the civility and wildness of everyday urbanity, in which the "civil" and "wild" are popularly understood to signify communal solidarity and socioeconomic precarity, respectively. To navigate the city is to move in and out of civil space, in an out of the intimate, genealogical, and customary— the conviviality and solidarity about which Need One wants us to know. Wildness is understood, thus, as a mode of psychosocial exclusion, incoherence, and distance, which urban artists represent as a source of both anomie and, at times, inspiration. This ambivalence evokes, I argue, a particular Afropolitan ethics, in which encounters with wildness—whether in the form of endemic poverty, political corruption, or foreign cultural influence—entail individual agency and, to varying degrees, choice about how to avoid or embrace wild realities, reconcile them with established

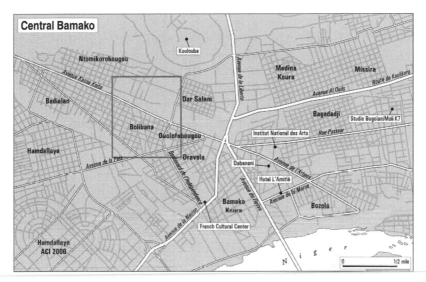

*Figure 4. Central Bamako. Map by Philip Schwartzberg, Meridian Mapping, Minneapolis.*

civilities, or, at the limits of ethical possibility, succumb to them through acts of desperation.

As evidenced in this chapter, such ethical practice, expressed through public representations of space, is an everyday feature of artists' lives and figures prominently in the themes and styles of their work. Yet, as we shall observe in the final section of this chapter, this ethics of sociospatial practice is strongly gendered. Through image, text, and sound, Bamako is represented to its audiences, again and again, as a city divided. This division manifests, much like Hannah Arendt imagines the ancient Greek polis ([1958] 1998), as a rupture between the public and the private, between an urbanism defined by masculine agency and a domesticity that celebrates familial intimacy as it prescribes female subjugation. Thus, urban civility becomes expressly tied to ideals of feminine morality, bound to the household. *"Badenya duman tunbɛ!"* Need One affirms. "Conviviality," but, literally, "mother-child-ness" *(ba-den-ya)*, "is here!" At the same time, urban wildness appears as a problem of masculine subjectivity, in which widespread un(der)employment and the concomitant erosion of patriarchal authority present manifest threats to male personhood. There, among the young men in the wilds of the postcolonial city, the public sphere of the polis is increasingly experienced as a space of privation—of what

Giorgio Agamben calls "bare life" (1998)—contrasted with the idealized (feminine) humanity of the hearth and contested through strategic acts of (masculine) moralization and ethical practice, written on, resounded in, and displayed upon the social space of the city.

## Life at the End of the Road

An idiomatic translation of *boli banna,* which in Bamana literally means "the running has finished," would be "the end of the road." It implicitly refers to West African warrior Samory Touré's surrender to the French colonial army in the late nineteenth century, which some say took place in Woyowayankɔ, to the west of the city.[2] Yet, for the roughly 20,000 souls who today live in this urban district, Bolibana is simply "home," where the road ends (Figure 5).[3] With its own food market, corner boutiques, roadside restaurants, barbershops, soccer fields, pharmacies, mosques, schools, newsstands, petrol stations, mechanics, carpenters, welders, tailors, and roving hawkers, Bolibana, like most Bamako neighborhoods, is largely autonomous (which is not to say "self-sufficient," being bound up with municipal, regional, and transnational circulations of people, capital, goods, and services). Its communal residences—characterized by large, extended families, usually encompassing at least three generations who live and labor side by side in rectangular mud-brick or cement compounds with earthen floor open-air courtyards where goats and chickens mingle with residents—gives Bolibana (like many districts in Bamako) the traditional air of a rural village, despite its apparently modern urban setting.

Back at home, I asked my friend Chaka, who was a big fan of Malian hip-hop (with various beats and flows playing from the headphones that dangled from his ears), to ask around about the group Need One. Mohamed at the cybercafé told me that they had recently released the track "Bolibana" to local radio stations and television. "Bolibana" quickly found its way onto the Internet and was being widely circulated on computers and cell phones, via Bluetooth connections, throughout the city. The next day, Chaka came over to tell me that he had found Need One. The group's hangout was just down the street, beside a barbershop stall no more than 100 yards from where I lived (compare Weiss 2009). In fact, on the day that I went to Mohamed's cybercafé and heard their song, I walked by and greeted these youths. A group of six or so young men sat, chatting and smoking around a charcoal stove, boiling a pot of tea outside

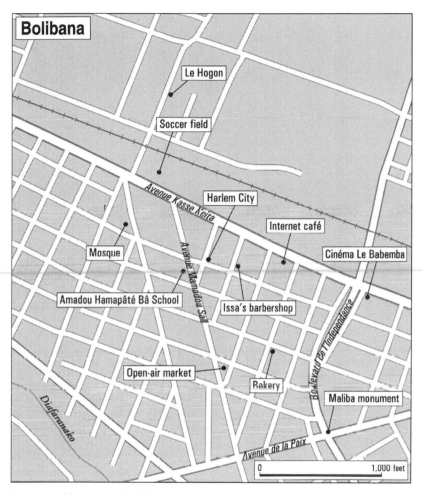

Figure 5. *Bolibana. Map by Philip Schwartzberg, Meridian Mapping, Minneapolis.*

a colorful container-like *salon de coiffeur*—the barbershop that belonged, I soon discovered, to group member and neighborhood hair stylist Issa Cissoko, aka Isolmo (Figure 6). From a portable cassette player came the soundtrack to their streetside gathering: hip-hop. This was their neighborhood *grin*, or conversational club; a social space produced at the intersection of this urban soundscape, sociability, and setting; a locus of social life in Bamako, where thousands of such groups can be found on the front stoops, along the roads, and in the parking lots of every neighborhood; a

*Figure 6. Issa's Barbershop. Photograph by the author.*

ubiquitous intersubjective presence in the city that gave tangible meaning to Need One's lyric, which I was about to hear for the first time, *"Badenya duman tunbɛ!"* ("Conviviality Is Here!").[4]

In West Africa, as elsewhere, greeting is a public sign of conviviality, and in Bamako one does a lot of greeting. Leaving home, you do not cross the threshold without hearing *"K'anw b'u fɔ"* ("Tell them we greet them"), to which there is only one response, *"U n'a mɛn"* ("They will hear it"). Conveying words of welcome is a part of the antiphonal phenomenology of walking the city (de Certeau 1988). There is the call, *"I ka kɛnɛ wa?"* ("How's your health?") And, the reponse, *"Tɔɔrɔ si tɛ!"* ("No problem at all!"). But the counterpoint is never far off. Arriving at the cybercafé, I find the power has been out all morning. *"Problème b'a la de!"* Mohamed says. "Now there's trouble!" (compare Olukoju 2004). Actually living in a neighborhood like Bolibana quickly dispels any idealized notion of the persistence of rural tradition and social coherence in the midst of urban modernity in Africa today. As urbanist AbdouMaliq Simone writes, "The sense of generosity and moral responsibility evinced in African cities remains substantial." However, "while a vital energy is mobilized to make do, the insides of associations, households and institutions seem now to live with a nearly constant sense of edginess" (2001a, 104). Indeed, signs that would indicate a more rustic and convivial residential life—communal living, household gardens and livestock, and public sociability, which, among the *grinw*, involves lengthy conversation and copious amounts of tea—are, by and large, tactics of "getting by" in the face of unrelenting poverty. From this perspective, families live together to better manage scarce resources. Gardens and livestock are kept to avoid food shortages and generate extra income. Neighbors spend hours together talking and drinking tea because, for the time being, they are out of work. City residents insist on greeting each other to keep their humanity intact.

A few days later, I invited Lassy and Issa over to my place, a rented two-room apartment in a large family compound, for tea and conversation. I explained to them my interest in their group, Need One, and the current Malian hip-hop scene more generally. Their enthusiasm was palpable, if oblique. "No problem," they told me (*"Problème t'a la"*); a common retort in Bamako, where problems (financial, familial, and physical) are ubiquitous. (One might just as easily exclaim, *"Problème b'a la de!,"* like Mohamed when the lights go out at the cybercafé, but finding solutions means keeping opportunities alive.) "We'll talk," they said (*"An bɛna baro kɛ"*); the principle means by which sociability is maintained and social mobility is pursued in Bamako (see Schulz 2002).[5] When Lassy and Issa arrived later that evening, I found them talking and joking with my neighbors in the courtyard while wrestling with children who scurried playfully around their legs. Of course, everybody knew each other here. In a sense, they were coming to greet me as a new member of the neighborhood. I let the two rappers into my living room, welcoming them with pious words (*"Aw bisimala"*) and friendly handshakes. We sat around a coffee table with shot glasses of sweet green tea and a sense of mutual interest. Lassy and Issa brought along a copy of the music video for "Bolibana." So, with greetings exchanged and tea served, I plugged my DV camera into my laptop computer and we watched the clip together.

## "Bolibana"

The video begins with Lassy Keita, aka Basta Killa, calling his partner, Issa, on a cell phone (yet another ubiquitous technology by mid-decade; five years earlier, the only person I knew with a *portable* was my globe-trotting host, Toumani Diabaté).[6] "Hey my man, what's up?" They plan to meet up in town. The volume increases as a keyboard and voice trace a simple repeating melody. An image of nighttime traffic resonates with the sound of a police siren. In the distance, two anonymous SUVs pull out of a parking lot. The beat drops. Need One and their posse are gathered in front of an overpass, now in broad daylight, throwing their hands up as they praise their hometown, Bolibana.

## Chorus

| | |
|---|---|
| *Bolibana! A'ye na! Anw ka wa!* | Bolibana! Come on! Let's go! |
| *Bolibana! K'i ka na! Anw ka wa!...* | Bolibana! I said come on! Let's go!... |
| *Bolibana! Badenya duman tunbɛ!* | Bolibana! Conviviality is here! |
| *Bolibana! Sinjiya duman tunbɛ!* | Bolibana! Solidarity is here! |
| *Bolibana! Teriya duman tunbɛ!...* | Bolibana! Friendship is here!... |
| *Bolibana! A'ye na! Anw ka wa!* | Bolibana! Come on! Let's go! |
| *Bolibana! K'i ka na! Anw ka wa!...* | Bolibana! I said come on! Let's go!... |

The aural and visual dimensions of the clip convey a particular sense of Afropolitan place. In Need One's Bolibana (the neighborhood and the track), hip-hop thrives. "This is our reality," they tell me. "This is Malian rap. . . . This is Bolibana." The soundscape of backbeats, samples, record scratches, and verbal art couples with the gendered and generational cultural style of Afro-diasporic youth culture. Young women are dressed in tank tops, short skirts, and tight jeans. Some wear shades beneath their freshly coiffed hair. Young men are clothed in sports jerseys and baggy pants. Some have gold necklaces hanging upon muscular frames. Cyphers form around breaking and swaying dancers, performing tough and sexy gestures. Heavy shoulders, bent elbows, and extended fingers accent lyrical flows. There are signs of the postcolony as well. The video takes place in a parking lot outside of the Babemba cinema complex, near an overpass connecting the Boulevard de l'Indépendence to the road leading to Koulouba, Bamako's "hill of power" (seen at a distance) and seat of presidential authority.

## Lassy's Flow

| | |
|---|---|
| *Ɛ-iyo, Bolibana, Bolibana,* | Hey-yeah, Bolibana, Bolibana, |
| *e t'o kalama?...* | don't you know about it?... |

| | |
|---|---|
| *N'i t'o kalama, ne bɛ k'i la,* | If you don't know about it, I'll tell you, |
| *k'i lab'o kalama.* | I'll help you get to know it. |
| *I jasigi. I k'i basigi.* | Be calm. Be cool. |
| *I tulo majɔ. I tulo mada.* | Pay attention. Listen. |
| *Teriya ni hɔrɔnya,* | Friendship and dignity,[7] |
| *u bɛ Bolibana.* | they're in Bolibana. |
| *Balimaya ni sinjiya,* | Kinship and empathy, |
| *u bɛ Bolibana....* | they're in Bolibana.... |
| *Nɛgoya, o t'anw fɛ yan.* | Egotism, we don't have it here. |
| *Juguya, o t'anw fɛ yan....* | Cruelty, we don't have it here.... |

As the rap unfolds, images and lyrics cut to and comment on neighborhood sites and scenes. As we watch, Issa and Lassy draw my attention to the venues, describing them like local tour guides. There's the Platinum Club, a nightclub formerly located above the Babemba cinema; Rokia's grilled chicken stall and the Niamey pastry shop, good places to eat and meet up with friends; the cinema, where you can catch all the latest releases from Hollywood, Bollywood, and Nollywood; a young couple walking and whispering under streetlights and neighborhood children outside their homes, chanting "Bolibana!"

*Issa's Flow*

| | |
|---|---|
| *Adamadenya bɛ ne kan yan.* | Humanity is with me here. |
| *Teriya fana bɛ ne kan yan.* | Friendship is also with me here. |
| *Sinjiya fana bɛ ne kan yan.* | Empathy is also with me here. |
| *Hɔrɔnya ni teriya,* | Dignity and friendship, |
| *u bɛ Bolibana yan.* | they're here in Bolibana. |
| *Balimaya ni sinjiya,* | Kinship and empathy, |
| *u bɛ bolibana yan....* | they're here in Bolibana.... |
| *Rokiaba bɛ yan.* | Big Rokia is here. |
| *Syɛ mɔlen bɛ yan.* | Grilled chicken is here. |
| *Dun ka fa saba tila.* | You're sure to eat your fill. |
| *Wallahi n t'o jɔrɔ.* | I swear I'm not worried. |
| *I jija i ka ko fɛ....* | You've got to love your place.... |
| *Bolibana so* | The house of Bolibana |
| *kɛra baroso ye....* | has become a house of talk.... |

Lyrically, "Bolibana" draws attention to the phenomenological tension between communal civility (conviviality) and urban edginess (precarity) in contemporary Bamako. On the one hand, moral concepts and kinship terms are invoked to characterize the district: Dignity and friendship, they're in Bolibana; Kinship and empathy, they're in Bolibana; Humanity is also here. Issa raps, "The house of Bolibana has become a house of talk" *(baroso)*, a space of conviviality.

*3-D Fariman's Flow*

| | |
|---|---|
| *Ɛ-iyo, Bolibana, na n ka cɛ.* | Hey-yeah, Bolibana, come here my man. |
| *I dabali kana ban na . . .* | It shouldn't surprise you . . . |
| *N'i ka taa Plati la,* | If you go to the Plati [Platinum Club], |
| *anw manw sigilen,* | our guys are in place, |
| *Bamana ta Plati la.* | at the Bamana Plati. |
| *Dɔw bɛ taa Niamey la.* | Some go to the Niamey [pastry shop]. |
| *Dɔw bɛ taa ciné la . . .* | Others go to the cinema . . . |
| *E ka so ye ne ka so.* | Your home's my home. |
| *Ne ka so ye e ka so.* | My home's your home. |
| *Kɔngɔ tɛ mɔgɔwsi faga yan.* | Nobody dies of hunger here. |
| *Bolibana bɛ bɔ kɛnɛma! . . .* | Bolibana is getting out! . . . |

On the other hand, vital threats to family and community are implied by frequent references to what is supposedly absent from, or not part of neighborhood social life: egotism, we don't have it here; cruelty, we don't have it here; nobody dies of hunger here. Lassy tells us to be calm, to be cool. Issa swears that he's not worried. The track, thus, portrays urban African subjectivity as a problem of existential control, of life on the edge, caught "between the world one calls one's own and the world one deems to be not-self or other," what anthropologist Michael Jackson calls "the driving force" of human social life (1998: 18).

## Civility and Wildness

In his essay on "associational life in the informal African city," AbdouMaliq Simone argues that

the reliance upon reciprocity, sharing of resources, social coopera-tion, familial or community obligations, highly codified moral prescriptions and open-ended information flow may be vital elements to preserve a sense of coherence under conditions of scarcity or social vulnerability. But there is also a need to be opportunistic and provisional. (2001a, 105)

Simone points to an experiential disjuncture between "morality" and "ethics," in which moral spaces of family and community exist in tension with ethical choices made "under conditions of scarcity or social vulnerability." Later I develop this dialectic conception of ethico-moral being-in-the-world by attending to its manifestation in the human artifice of the city. I begin with the most salient sociospatial point of reference for Bamako artists like Need One: the conviviality of a Mande sense of place. Then I turn to the "opportunistic and provisional" precarity of city life to define the principal ethical terrain of urban subjectivity: the abstract space of the Afropolis.

In Need One's "Bolibana," we encounter a rich lexicon of moral community taken from the annals of Mande social thought. In line after line and verse upon verse, we hear of the conviviality (*badenya*), empathy (*sinjiya*, literally "mother's milk-ness"), friendship (*teriya*), kinship (*balimaya*), and humanity (*adamadenya*, literally "children of Adam-ness") that collectively index what Simone calls "a sense of coherence," or, in Heideggerian terms (1962), a culturally conditioned ontology of being-with-others (*Mitsein*) as a fundamental mode of being-in-the-world (*Dasein*). This centripetal morality of living among one's kith and kin anchors subjects within a space of shared belonging, custom, and intimacy. And yet, Need One's artistic practice—their musical being-with-others—is not so firmly bound to hearth and home. "Bolibana is getting out!," 3 D Fariman exclaims. As a circulating product of creative agency, "Bolibana" also signifies a centrifugal ethics of subjective action; the track is, in other words, an outward expression of undertaking and initiative the Mande call *waleya*. Venturing to act beyond the coherence of moral community is a matter of personal interest and desire and can be existentially risky. Will this endeavor succeed or fail? In either case, what are the consequences? I have more to say about the precarity of subjective action in contemporary Bamako later. Here, I want to emphasize the specifically Mande sense of personhood (*mɔgɔya*) that emerges from Need One's "Bolibana," rooted in the intimacy and solidarity cultivated at home and routed through the deeds and works undertaken out there, in the world.

This dual, ethico-moral mode of being can also be mapped onto physical space. In an earlier reflection on space in Mande social thought, I outlined the conceptual division of society "between 'civil space,' centred on family compounds *(luw)* of which the city *(dugu)* is composed, and 'wild space,' referring to 'the bush' *(kungo)* that lies beyond the boundary *(dankun)* of the city and its surrounding fields *(forow)*" (Skinner 2010, 19; see Johnson 2003; see also Bagayogo 1989). As sites of spatial production, these categories represent the strategic, prescriptive, and formal ordering of the world that Henri Lefebvre calls "conceived space." As forms of social design, such structural constraints (buildings, routes, borders, fields, and so on) also suggest patterns of dwelling, use, and practical activity (housekeeping, construction, commerce, farming, and so on) that shape the habitus of "lived space." These are the sociospatial loci of civility in the Mande world. Beyond this archetypical human artifice lies, again drawing on the Lefebvrian lexicon, "abstract space"—the alien, uncultivated, and menacing "wilderness" of ante/antisocial space (1991, 37–52). Within this model of Mande cosmology, spaces of civility (the city) and wildness (the bush) represent the social and material contexts through which the morality of heritage and intimacy and the ethics of innovation and distinction articulate.

As an active ethico-moral dialectic, the subjective agency of movement into and out of civil and wild spaces (re)produces stability, friction, dynamism, conflict, consensus, and creativity in Mande society. At stake in these acts of departure, innovation, and (re)integration is the moral and ethical personhood *(mɔgɔya)* of the social actor. Hunters are the canonical agents of ethical action in Mande society as they deploy their knowledge of the wilderness to brave its dangers, procure its resources, cultivate its lands, and, thus, expand the scope of the civil (see Cashion 1984; Cissé 1964, 1994; Hellweg 2011). As ethnomusicologist Lucy Durán and cultural theorist Chérif Keïta have observed, Malian musicians have usefully appropriated the hunter identity to negotiate, contest, and reconfigure cultural constraints on musical practice associated with caste and gender (see Durán 2000 and Keïta 2009; I discuss such socioprofessional constraints and possibilities in greater detail in chapter 2). Yet, before an ethical action has been achieved, it remains ambiguous and potentially threatening, occupying an interstitial social space, mapped physically onto the borderlands *(dankun)*, between societal reinvention and ethico-moral breakdown. It is not enough, in other words, to wear the hunters' garb; one must also hunt.

Figure 7. Bolibana family compound. Photograph by the author.

In urban Africa, these spaces of interstitiality appear to be less and less the transient exception and more and more the intractable rule (Agamben 2004) as spaces of social civility become more circumscribed, more isolated, more tenuous. As Brian Larkin observes of the continent as a whole, "contemporary Africa is marked by the erosion of accepted paths of progress and the recognition of a constant fight against the insecurity of everyday life" (2008, 169). For Bamako residents, the interior of the family compound (dukɛnɛ) and surrounding neighborhood (kinda) are spaces of refuge from the dissociative commotion of the modern city (dugu) (Figure 7). Gathering and socializing (through conversation, tea drinking, domestic labor, and shared meals) in the open-air courtyard of the compound or underneath shade trees outside residences are critical to the psychosocial welfare of individuals who reaffirm moral sentiments of family and community—expressed by the notion of sigiɲɔgɔnya, or "communal togetherness" (literally, "the state or act of sitting together")—in the socially civil spaces of the neighborhood commons.[8] Such convivial spaces and sentiments of civility are contrasted to the bustling central city (*dugukɔnɔ*) that resembles more and more the wilds of the bush (*kungo*) where open sewers breed disease, congested traffic threatens lives, and markets bustle with predatory peddlers ready to swindle or "eat" (*ka dun*) their customers through suspect sales.

In the space of urban African modernity described by Simone and represented by Need One, we encounter, thus, an emergent ethics of urban wildness, what Gauthier de Villers calls *l'ethique de l'informel* (2002, 27), in which everyday interdictions, breakdowns, shortfalls, and inconsistencies must be intelligently confronted and negotiated; for as the Mande proverb states, *"mɔgɔya ye hakili ye"* ("Personhood is intelligence"). In Bamako today, intelligence is a matter of "getting by" and "making do" (French, *se débrouiller*), a tactical mindset for which the proverbial slogan on the street is, *"N'a ma ɲagami, a tɛ se ka ɲɛnabɔ"* ("If it's not mixed up, it'll never work out"). For Michel de Certeau, tactics are "the space of the other," "a guileful ruse," and "an art of the weak" playing "on and with a terrain imposed on it" (1988, 37). In this sense, we may situate the cultural morality of Need One's public praise of place ("Bolibana") within a broader tactical—which is to say ethical—space of Afropolitan urbanism. Beyond the conviviality, solidarity, and friendship of their hometown is an opportunistic and provisional social and professional terrain that includes circulating tracks online and via Bluetooth connections without concern for copyright infringement (about which more in chapter 5), drawing on networks of neighborhood solidarity to make sure there's enough food to eat ("Nobody dies of hunger here"), sharing in a common struggle with the psychosocial burdens of endemic poverty ("Egotism and cruelty, we don't have them here"), and always looking out for opportunities to pursue social mobility, as when a foreign ethnomusicologist stops by and shows interest in your work. "No problem," they said. "We'll talk."

There is, in other words, an in-the-mix ethics that values keeping things in play (opportunistic and provisional) in order to work them out. It is this playful, guileful, and tactical ethics of African urbanism that John Miller Chernoff captures in his ethnographic (auto)biography of a barmaid in Accra, *Hustling Is Not Stealing* (2003). "Bolibana is getting out!," Need One insists, affirming the observation that "in spite of the poverty of a city like Bamako, it remains . . . a space of hope" (Diarra, Ballo, and Champaud 2003, 46). As ethical expressions of sociospatial production, this hope of urban betterment (against all odds) cannot be separated from the moral imperative to root oneself in a civil sense of place. "Your home is my home," the rappers tell us. "My home is your home." Maintaining this ethico-moral balance serves to mitigate the potential for risk and failure in the wilds of the modern Afropolis. "I swear I'm not worried," Issa proclaims, speaking from a grounded sense of moral certainty. Yet, despite such assurances, fears of civil dissolution, frequently voiced in terms of a breakdown of traditional social norms, are rampant in Bamako today. Thus, much ethical energy has been devoted to the defense and preservation of civil space in the city. The principle threat to such civility is what I, following Lefebvre, call the "abstract space" of the Afropolitan wilderness.

## The Court(Yard)

"My ear to the ground, I heard tomorrow pass by." It is with these words, the cadence to Aimé Césaire's surrealist ceremony of terrestrial transcendence, *"Les pur-sang"* ("The thoroughbreds," Césaire 1983), that filmmaker Aberrahmane Sissako closes his film *Bamako* (2006), itself a surreal impression of everyday life in urban Africa. Does the Négritude poet's verse represent a hopeful sense of renaissance, of an "awakening" born of an earthly (African) potential (see Dayan 1983, 423), or is it a "nostalgia for the future," a mournful memory of an African modernity that never came to pass (see Piot 2010)? In the film, Sissako does not allow us the privilege of a definitive answer. In a continental city subjected to the (neo)colonialism of "civilizing missions" and "structural adjustments," from the imperial past to the neoliberal present, *Bamako* bears witness to the persistence of local entrepreneurship, communal solidarity, and grassroots politics. Yet, the film also confronts its audience with the indignity and misery of privatized redundancies, clandestine migration, preventable illness, and premature death. Such are the irreconcilable (even surreal) ambiguities of a polity embedded in abstraction, of a city in which the boundaries between the civil and the wild are no longer evident.

This, as Sissako represents it, is Bamako, the modern-day capital of Mali and an emblem of urban Africa. The film takes place almost entirely in the domestic space of an open-air courtyard. It is, in Lefebvre's terms, a "lived space," composed of "inhabitants and users" (1991, 39) and conceived as an ideal-typical locus of urban African civility. It is also, in reality, Sissako's childhood home, a fact that engenders an ethos of *badenya* within this otherwise anonymous mise en scène. Indeed, Sissako's original title for the film was *La Cour*, a reference to both the courtyard setting and the fictional court proceeding that takes place within its walls (about which more later). The lived civility of this generic-yet-intimate Bamako courtyard takes many forms: A toddler scurries about the premises (signaled by the chirp of a squeaking shoe), minded by a host of adult kin; a young woman tends to a young man (her husband, brother, or cousin) who suffers from a debilitating disease (AIDS, malaria, Ebola, or another "tropical" [read: "African"] malady); a wedding party enters, fronted by a *jelimuso* (female griot) who announces the marriage procession with a strident "calling of the horses" *(sow wele)*, a canonical genre of public verbal art that draws attention to civil subjectivities (in this case, a bridal pair). There is also a woman, Saramba, who runs a cloth-dying business inside the compound. Her labor is doubly symbolic in the film. On the one hand, it produces a locally representative palette of color (ochre, indigo, green, and red) that frames civil space in an array of clotheslines and hanging fabric (Maingard 2010). On the other hand, Saramba herself embodies a local African economy that the film presents as an alternative to exogenous economic interests.

In *Bamako*, we are confronted with these alternatives, side by side. There, in the midst of everyday household activity, a trial is underway, in which international financial institutions (the World Bank and International Monetary Fund) stand accused of systematically underdeveloping Africa and exacerbating the suffering of its people (compare Rodney 1974). The prosecution—African civil society—calls on a series of witnesses who testify to the abjection of life on the frontiers of globalization. There is Madou Keita, who tells of his perilous journey through the Sahara en route to an impossibly distant Europe, Samba Diakité, a dispirited former schoolteacher whose testimony is consumed by a silence that embodies public sector redundancy, and Zegué Bamba, a Senufo farmer whose dramatic lament (which the film does not translate or subtitle) gives voice to what James Ferguson calls "the art and struggle of living" within the "dense bush" of "global modernity" (1999, 251–52). Their stories bear witness to the flourishing of "abstract space" in the Global South. In Lefebvre's Marxian language, this "neo-capitalist" conception of space, "in thrall to both knowledge and power, leaves only the narrowest leeway to [lived spaces], which are limited to works, images and memories whose content . . . is so far displaced that it barely achieves symbolic force" (1991, 50). Abstract space is the social and material apotheosis of alienation and estrangement. It is the wilderness of a globalized capitalist modernity.

Even as this dramatic theater of moral contrast plays out in the court(yard)—pitting the local, lived, and civil against the global, abstract, and wild—a series of subplots creates as space of ethical intrigue that foregrounds the choices people make to negotiate urban African wildness. At the center of these narratives is Chaka, a solemn middle-aged man whose marriage is falling apart after he was laid off from his job.[9] We first encounter Chaka in the film's opening scene, as he walks alone at dawn through barren city streets, his only company being a group of workers tying bits of wood and metal beams to a scaffolding that rises without any apparent construction attached to it (compare Melly 2010). When not sleeplessly wandering the city or tending to his only child, four-year-old Ina, Chaka spends his time learning modern Hebrew from a slim, worn paperback and accompanying (equally worn) cassettes. As he explains to Falaï, a videographer documenting the ongoing trial, "One day, there will be an [Israeli embassy] in Mali, [and] I will be its security guard." Falaï responds with bemused laughter, but, seeing the seriousness of Chaka's claim, apologizes, his laughter unabated. Falaï has found a career niche, entrepreneurial and aesthetic, filming "the dead"; not only are funerals abundant in Bamako these days, the deceased are, as he puts it, "more true" as subjects ("Les morts sont plus vrais"). His work embodies what Achille Mbembe calls the "necropolitics" of globalized governmentality, "in which vast populations are subjected to conditions of life conferring upon them the status of living dead" (2003, 40, emphasis in the original; I return to Mbembe's concept of the necropolitical in chapter 6). These present-day "wretched of the earth" (Fanon [1963] 2004) become the future subjects of Falaï's urban videography, a macabre archive of an abstract space Mbembe terms "death-worlds" (see also Piot 2010, 18–19).

Chaka's wife, Melé, presents another approach to Afropolitan ethics in the abstract. A Senegalese woman from Dakar, Melé has married into the domestic sphere of la cour and thus occupies the precarious social position of an outsider. Among the women, she remains distant and is sometimes looked upon with suspicion and scorn. When Melé calls Beï (a young brother-in-law) to tie her blouses in the morning, she appears to others as a seductive threat, whose beauty indexes potential infidelity. Her position as a domestic interloper is further exacerbated by a swiftly dissolving marriage. Early in the film, she informs her mother on the phone, "I'm coming back to Dakar." Later, when she tells Chaka of her immanent departure (essentially, a notice of divorce), he says, simply, "But without Ina," their daughter. She leaves, in other words, as an outsider, a foreigner, without the rights of a mother, without the bonds of *badenya* (mother-child-ness). Melé also works on the social margins. She is a nightclub singer. While Chaka roams the city streets, Melé entertains into the night, performing Afro-Cuban standards for (mostly) male patrons at Bamako's Akwaba club. There, she is as much an artist as an escort. The film begins and ends with Chaka walking, Melé singing. In the final scenes, Chaka leaves the family compound to take his life with a gun he stole from a slumbering police officer. Melé cries as she sings the Ghanaian highlife standard "Naam" shedding tears for a life torn asunder by the abstract, the wild.

Earlier, in the midst of this existential descent, a reporter who has been recording the court proceedings summons Chaka for a statement. "Before, you said that 'the greatest consequence of structural adjustment is the destruction of the social fabric.' The passage was completely erased. Could you repeat it?" "What happened?" Chaka asks. "With all of these different cassettes, I got confused," the reporter admits. "I must have recorded over it." Chaka pauses. "Don't bother. No one will listen."

## Writing Culture

In our encounters with Need One's "Bolibana" and Sissako's *Bamako*, we have observed two pronounced psychosocial modes of representing (and producing) urban space: conviviality and precarity. Neither mode, as I have noted in both cases, is absolute. There are symbolic traces of the wild (egotism, cruelty, hunger) embedded in Lassy's and Issa's neighborhood panegyric, and there are scenes of civility (local entrepreneurship, care for the sick, life-cycle ritual) manifest throughout the disquieting abstraction of the court(yard). Yet, considered generically, the two artistic works do communicate distinctive sentiments: of celebration, on the one hand, and anxiety, on the other. Here, I draw out and focus on the experiential middle ground of sociospatial life in Bamako, emergent at the interstices of the convivial and precarious, the celebratory and anxious, the civil and wild. It is the space of venturing out into the city, the (Afro)polis, "the space of appearance in the widest sense of the word" (Arendt [1958] 1998, 198). It is the space of being present in and perceiving an urban public, the Afropolis of Bamako. It is, in Lefebrvian terms, a "perceived space" of embodied and interpretive spatial practice (1991, 38), a phenomenology of being-in-the-world and with-others within a common urban architecture.[10]

To be sure, it is an ethical space, in the midst of the city, beyond the bounds of established civility (the family compound), but it is not so starkly immoral as the dystopian cityscape of *Bamako* would have it. Morality appears in the urban wilds of the city in generic forms of language, of countless spoken greetings, proverbs, prayers, benedictions, and praises exchanged at any given moment among itinerant urbanites, from all walks of life. *"K'anw b'u fɔ,"* I am told as I walk out the door ("Say we greet them"). *"U n'a mɛn,"* I respond ("They will hear it"). Such moralizing speech, in all its variety, is itself a part of a broader aural dimension of perceived space in the city, including (among other forms of meaningful resonance) outdoor radio and television broadcast, streetside tea conversation, ambulant Sufi chants, amplified music, and periodic calls to prayer. I examine the ethics and aesthetics of such forms of public aurality (secular and religious, live and mediated) in chapters 3 and 4 of this book. Here, I draw attention to the visual presence of vocal morality, in the form of public iconography (image and text) on walls, and placards, and public transportation. Though principally cultural and religious in content, articulated in terms of Mande and Islamic mores, such writing and related imagery frequently foreground aesthetic, political, economic, diasporic, and more broadly "global" social positions, often in a complex mix of moral signification. Such writing represents, I argue, in the spirit of an Arendtian existentialism, intersubjective "islands of security" in the city though commonly shared idioms that create, when viewed and read, "something which *inter-est,* which lies between people and therefore can relate and bind them together" (Arendt [1958] 1998, 182; emphasis in the original).

Outside of my compound in Bolibana, on the wall by the entryway facing the street, is the word "KEITALA." "Keita" is the family name *(jamu)* of the property's principal residents. It is a noble *(hɔrɔn)* name, shared by ancestors of Mali's greatest king, Sunjata Keita, who founded the Mali Empire in the thirteenth century. The suffix *-la* is locative. This is the Keita's home—*Keitala*—an inscribed statement binding moral sentiments of heritage, intimacy, and place. On the wall of the same compound, facing an adjacent street that leads to the Rue Kassé Keita thoroughfare, is another sign that reads "HARLEM CITY." Harlem City is the name of a bar and eatery run by Ablo Keita, one of the residents of Keitala who has worked at the bar that adjoins his home since he was a young man (beginning as a dishwasher, then moving up the ranks as a waiter, barkeep and, now, owner; Figure 8). For Ablo, the "Harlem" reference signifies a

*Figure 8. Harlem City. Photograph by David Novak.*

specific kind of Afropolitanism. "Modibo (aka 'Franky') Keita gave it that name in the 1980s," he explains. "It represents négritude. It symbolizes respect for the black race and African authenticity. . . . It's a sign of the bar's African-ness."[11] At Harlem City, the diasporic signifier thickens in a tavern soundscape that includes the latest in Malian popular music, as well as Afropop classics (from the 1970s, '80s, and '90s) and African American soul (especially James Brown). Juxtaposed with the domestic sign, "Keitala," "Harlem City" signifies an Afropolitan social space in Bamako, at the intersection of tradition, kinship, and diaspora.

Down the street, at Rue Kassé Keita, I hail a cab, or, rather, several cab drivers hail me, a *toubab* (white person) whose fare into town usually carries a privileged premium. Written on the side of the taxi is the phrase, "SEUL LE TRAVAIL LIBERE L'HOMME" ("Only work can liberate man"). The (reasonable) fare negotiated, I enter the vehicle with a flurry of greetings. As I told my housemates on my way out the door, "They will hear it," an expression of what my Bamako friends and Hannah Arendt describe as the humanizing "faculty to make and keep promises" that provides continuity, durability, and a modicum of certainty in public life (Arendt [1958] 1998, 237; see also Skinner 2010, 27–28). "How's your health?" "No problem." "Yours?" "Can't complain." "Your family's well?" "They have no troubles." "And your business?" "It's getting better, little by little." I give him a destination. "*Bon,* let's go!" We pass by the Babemba Cinema, called out in Need One's "Bolibana" with a name meaning "the great ancestor" *(ba bɛnba).* We proceed toward the city center and downtown marketplace where shops bear names of "good meeting" and "positive agreement" *(bɛn ka di),* "friendship" *(teriya),* and "personhood" *(mɔgɔya).* On our way through the older neighborhoods, a fast-food joint praises God *(Alhamdulillah)* and an auto parts store claims a space of good sociability *(ambiance,* a French term associated with musical liveness in Bamako, about which more in chapter 2). "I'll get off here," I tell the driver. We stop, and I pay him. *"K'anw bɛn"* ("May we meet again"), he says. *"Inshallah"* (*"God willing"*), I say.

Driving through the city, everyday speech and public writing produce a punctuated ethos of morality in "the ocean of uncertainty" that is the Afropolis,[12] a wild space of risk, possibility, hope, and anxiety, to which an urban poetics, spoken and written, intermittently responds. Perhaps the most striking presence of such moralizing discourse can be found in and on the city's public transportation vehicles. The "Sotramas," as the ubiquitous green vans are called (for the *Société des Transports Maliens,* the now-defunct organization that regulated them decades ago), embody an uneasy confluence of the civil and wild. As cheap modes of transportation (costing between 25 and 50 cents for a crosstown trip), Sotramas attract a large and varied clientele. Riders are seated on makeshift wooden benches that line the perimeter of the gutted vans, with upward of twenty people packed in during the morning and afternoon commutes. The vehicles themselves are old and worn, kept running day after day through the mechanical ingenuity of their drivers. They break down frequently, and (when traffic allows) they travel much too fast. Accidents are frequent and so too are the injuries. Yet, Sotramas are also intensely social spaces. As the van fills with clients, space is made for the new arrivals; children are seated in laps of perfect strangers (made less "strange" through the antiphony of public greeting); luggage is carried in and distributed to whatever space remains beneath, above, or between the riders. Material wildness is mitigated by social civility.

From the outside, the vans announce themselves through the screeches and groans of their engines, the routes called out by their attendants *("Hamdallaye!" "Magnambougou!" "Faladie!")*, and the words and images painted on their frames. Some of the inscriptions are exalting ("GOD IS GREAT"); others are edifying ("PATIENCE IS GOOD"). Some inspire calm ("THE SOFT AND GENTLE ONE"); others inspire hope ("AFRICA UNITED"). Many of the messages are cautionary. "VANITY IS BAD," reads one. "PEOPLE ARE NOT GOOD," reads another. One vehicle warns, "WATCH OUT MY FRIEND, THEY ARE CROOKS." Another announces, ambiguously, "PERSONHOOD TODAY." (Is it good or bad?) There are also pictures, of a face superimposed on the map of Africa; portraits of prominent preachers, politicians, and cultural heroes; iconic images of global culture; and serene scenes of rural life. Such words and images are often juxtaposed in complex compositions on vehicular surfaces, together with decals and ornaments that produce even more layers of symbolism. On the hood of a van, on either side of a text (in French and Arabic) that gives thanks to God in the year 2011, are two identical stickers of Osama bin Laden, themselves flanked by painted images of American flags and propulsive fire. Above these external signs, lined up on the dashboard, is a collection of cassette tapes, including recordings of Islamic preachers, Malian pop divas, and hunter's panegyric. Still higher in the interior, suction-cupped to the windscreen, are two miniature Malian flags, above which, draped over the central rearview mirror, is another American flag, framed in decorative lace (Figure 9). With this mix of visual signifiers, the audible metaphor is not so much cacophony as it is polyphony (compare Ferguson 1999, chapter 6). In other words, these multiple moral signs are not, from an ethical standpoint, contradictory, but complementary; they produce a varied civil space to which (most) urbanites can relate and find meaning. "If it isn't mixed up," *Bamakois* say, "it will never work out!"

Such symbolically dense pictorial and textual signs, inscribed on the surfaces of public transportation vehicles, act as media in the sense described by Brian Larkin; they "carry messages (signals)" amid the material "interferences" and "breakdowns" (noise) of public urban space (2008, 10). In Bamako, the signals this iconography produces communicate formulaic expressions of Afropolitan modes of being (cultural, religious, political, economic, diasporic, and so on), rendered as a variable and mixed urban pastiche. In Arendtian terms, these images and texts engender, at intervals paced by traffic, mobile sites of *inter-est*. They are fragmented moral ephem-

*Figure 9. Public transport iconography. Photograph by the author.*

era through which Bamako residents appear to each other in a common public through shared (though not uncontested) social positions. This artwork represents, in other words, moral points of reference (what Arendt calls "islands of security") for an always already ambiguous and precarious Afropolitan ethics. Yet, to whom do these moral references point? Who are the Afropolitans interpellated by this urban iconography? And, what does this say about the subjectivity of ethical agency? In the section that follows, I respond to these questions by returning to my encounter with the hip-hop group Need One, examining the (un)ethical and (im)moral subjectivities represented in a music video we produced together in Bamako: an Afropolitan hip-hop parable titled "Sabali" ("Patience").

## Engendering Ethics

Not long after our first meeting, Lassy and Issa approached me with an urgent request: they wanted me to participate in the production of their debut album. This recording project had become a frequent topic of discussion at the neighborhood *grin*, and I knew that, for them, the stakes were high. These young rappers were trying to establish careers as artists in Mali, but they faced, among many other challenges, a hostile industry in which producers are perceived to be untrustworthy and exploitative. My presence offered new hope, and greater expectations. Famed rapper Djo Dama of the group Tata Pound had told (but not, he insisted, "promised") Issa and Lassy that he would personally finance the production and promotion of the album, but things were moving slowly, too slowly. With the exception of a single studio recording session, financial and material support was not forthcoming. Issa and Lassy were hard-pressed to release the album before *les vacances*, the summer months when the urban youth would be watching music programs, attending street parties, and buying cassettes. "We trust you," they said to me. "You can help us."

I could not make the argument that I lacked the means or experience to assist. I had far greater access to capital than they did, and, as far as experience goes, in Mali that is always a matter of negotiation, of one's ability to make do and get by in any given situation. I was experienced if I was willing to play the part, to go with the flow. "Alright," I said. "I'll help you." For the album to have a chance at success, Need One would need a music video for promotion. I had a camera and tapes. Tata Pound agreed to a "featuring," which meant that Djo Dama and Dixon, two members of the hip-hop trio, would each rap a verse on the track (the third member, Ramses, was in New York City, mining material for a solo album). I also agreed to play my *kora* on the track, and I paid for the remaining studio time. Then, with recorded track in hand, Need One, Tata Pound, their posses, and I got together over a long weekend to film the clip.

The track begins with Lassy's flow.[13]

*"Sabali"*

| | |
|---|---|
| *Anw bɛ taa kɛ cɔgɔ di?* | How will we get there? |
| *Anw bɛ na kɛ cɔgɔ di?* | How will we arrive? |
| *Anw kan ka duwawuwɲini,* | We need to seek benedictions, |
| *ka tila ka barikaɲini.* | and also seek blessing. |
| *Fanenidenw cayara.* | Fathers are too often insulted. |
| *Babagadenw cayara . . .* | Mothers are too often injured . . . |
| *Aw bɛɛ ye kɛɲɛkɛdenw!* | You are all delinquent children! |

| | |
|---|---|
| *Aw bɛɛ ye galakaɲimidenw!* . . . | You are all disrespectful children! . . . |
| *Dɔw bɛ taalen tunga la,* | Some [young people] have gone abroad, |
| *nafolo tɛ sɔrɔ la!* | but no fortunes are found there! |
| *Dɔw bɛ jagokun daminɛ,* | Some go into business, |
| *jagokun tɛ yiidi voilà!* | [but] that business does not prosper! |
| *N'i y'a segesege,* | If you look carefully, |
| *ko wolofaw duwawu t'u ko sa!* | they don't have their dad's blessing! |
| *Wolobaw duwawu t'u ko sa!* . . . | They don't have their mom's blessing! . . . |
| *Ne y'a fɔ, i tɛ malo!* . . . | I said it, you have no shame! . . . |

As Lassy lyrically chastises those "who don't respect their parents," calling them "delinquent" and "disrespectful," a young boy dressed in slacks, a shirt patterned with graffiti tags, and white sandals steps out onto a veranda. He listens to loud music (presumably hip-hop) through earphones. Holding his hands to his ears, he waves his elbows and shuffles his feet. Sitting underneath the grassy overhang is the boy's father, dressed in a white cap and a long shirt. The old man calls the boy over to run an errand for him. The boy acknowledges his father but continues to listen to his music and dance as the elder speaks. When a coin is presented to the boy, he lets it fall to the ground. The old man raises a reed fan to strike the boy, but the boy runs off, leaving his flustered father behind. Later in the verse, a girl walks out into an open-air family courtyard where her mother sits beside a small wood stove. The girl wears a pink sun visor, pink T-shirt, denim miniskirt, and knee-high black boots. The mother, by contrast, wears a blue headscarf and matching robes. The mother watches silently as her daughter approaches and gestures to her, as if to say, "Can't stay Mom, gotta go!" The mother puts her hand to her mouth in disbelief as her daughter charges off with a dismissive wave of her hand.

Need One crafted theses scenes under the direction of Tata Pound member Djo Dama. As he explained to me, both sketches are intended to contrast the brazen behavior of the youth with the demanding domesticity of their parents. The boy and girl are dressed in fashionable Western clothes while their parents wear traditional robes and headwear. The father and mother engage in everyday domestic affairs, while the boy and girl antagonistically go their own way. "I said it," Lassy raps, "you have no shame!" The youths' actions mirror each other in a farce of inter-generational conflict, with Western pop culture pitted against local mores and traditions. Yet, by invoking the idea of "shamelessness" (malobaliya), Need One implicitly genders their critique of Bamako youth culture, a subjective stance made apparent in the video's subsequent scenes.

Shame (malo) in Mande society emerges as a response to an individual's perceived unethical or immoral conduct and represents a psychosocial threat to his or her personhood (mɔgɔya) in society. Thus, an allegedly shameless individual (malobali) is often publicly criticized with the epithets mɔgɔ tɛ ("She/he is not a person") and mɔgɔya t'a la ("She/he has no personhood"). Perceptions of shame and accusations of shamelessness are strongly tied to gendered and generational subject positions. As Lucy Durán notes, the term malobaliya "is used far more frequently in conjunction with women and children than with men" (1999, 28). This has much to do with the way gendered personhood relates to Mande social hierarchies. Many scholarly works have emphasized the division of Mande society into three discrete social categories: hɔrɔnw (free-born persons), ɲamakalaw (endogamous artisans), and jɔnw (captives and slaves).[14] Linking social structure to codes of behavior, Durán, following the work of anthropologist Maria Grosz-Ngaté (1989), succinctly captures the gendering of shame in a patriarchal Mande world, writing:

> There is a conceptual link in the ideology between slave status (jonya), lack of shame, extrovert behaviour including song and dance, and the social construct of "female". This is opposed to noble status (horonya), a sense of shame or self-control, and the construct of "male". Thus the male-female gender hierarchy mirrors the noble-slave social hierarchy. Women are required by the ideology to overcome their "nature", and take on the "culture" of nobility and masculine restraint. (1999, 30)

As Grosz-Ngaté observes, "A sense of shame guides the actions of both women and men and orders relations in all domains of social life" (1989, 179). Yet, this sense of shame, she argues, is differently articulated among men and women. Like slaves (jɔnw), women are conceived as being inherently shameless (malobali) and, thus, childlike. Free-born men, however, embody maturity and dignity and must actively avoid conduct that may be perceived as shameful or demeaning. For men, the consequences of such shameful behavior may include social "death," resulting in cultural stigmatization and alienation from their community.[15] By contrast, women (to paraphrase Durán) are primarily concerned with overcoming their shameless nature by taking on the culture of masculine restraint.

Later in the video, Need One shift their critical commentary from youthful impropriety—shamelessly snubbing and scorning filial duty—to parental negligence. As the rappers contend, the failure to properly punish and resist youthful delinquency reveals the culpability and indignity of community elders who, lacking the respect of their children, do not command respect either. In the following verse, Djo Dama draws explicit attention to this perceived gap between discipline and laxity with a message that strongly condemns urban elders.

| | |
|---|---|
| *Ni muso ye a cɛ barika ɲini,* | If a wife seeks the grace of her husband, |
| *si ka t'a la,* | she has no problem, |
| *a denw bɛ barika!* | Her children will be blessed! |
| *Ni den ye bangebaw harika ɲini,* | If a child has the grace of his/her parents, |
| *si ka t'a la ...* | there's no problem ... |
| *Fa ni baw* | [But] fathers and mothers |
| *tɛ denw lamara bilen.* | do not educate their children any more. |
| *Ni kɔrɔ ko,* | If an elder says, |
| *"K'u k'u lamara!"* | "[Parents] must educate [their children]!" |
| *U b'a fɔ, "I yɛrɛ e ma lamara!"* | They say, "You yourself are not educated!" |
| *"I bɛ kila ka mɔgɔ wɛrɛ den lamara?"* | "How can you teach another's child?" |
| *"N'i tɛgɛ sɛra ne ma sisan"* | "If you raise your hand up to me now" |
| *"N bɛ ne bolo su i ɲɛ la!" ...* | "I'll put my fist in your eye!" ... |
| *Daka wuli la,* | The porridge is boiling, |
| *sɔnkala tununna!* | [but] the stirring spoon is lost![16] |
| *Denmusow tɛ se ka lamara bilen.* | Young women are not on the right path. |
| *So man kɛnɛ! Sogtigi man kɛnɛ!* | The horse and her master are not well![17] |
| *I m'a ye?* | Haven't you noticed? |
| *Anw ka génération changéla ...* | Our generation has changed ... |

As Djo Dama verbally represents the conflict (conceptual and physical) between competing authorities over moral (in)discipline in society, a young man dressed in a colorful knit cap, faded jeans, and a patterned Malian dress shirt calls the young boy (described earlier) to come to him. The young man is the boy's older brother. As before, the old man is seated with his hand-held reed fan underneath the veranda. When the boy arrives, the young man, gesturing to their father, proceeds to strike his junior for his earlier misbehavior. The old man quickly intervenes to stop the violence and chases off his elder son by threatening to hit him with his fan. The old man then comforts his younger son, apparently forgetting the boy's prior misdeed. Suddenly, Djo Dama appears in the scene, arms spread, imploring the old man and boy with the proverb, "The horse and his master are not well!"

In this scene, the boy's shameful act (arrogantly refusing to run his father's errand) is met with violence, which, while diffused by the old man's intervention, highlights the anticipated severity of consequences engendered by male shamelessness in Mande society. Djo Dama's proverbial invocation condemns the elder's decision to appease rather than punish the child's impropriety, while at the same time lamenting the ambivalent and degraded social milieu in which the boy's bad behavior is effectively deemed acceptable. "The horse and his master are not well!" Echoing this lament, and pointing toward a "moral" solution to these gendered and generational rifts, a subsequent scene shows Need One and their posse confronting a girl (the errant daughter described earlier) for insulting her mother and brazenly rejecting her moral duties as a young woman. This scene unfolds during the song's refrain:

| | |
|---|---|
| *Den-nin-o,* | Oh-young-child [girl], |
| *i tunka sabali!* | you must chill out![18] |
| *I woloba kumara,* | Your mom has spoken, |
| *i tunka sabali!* | you must chill out! |
| *Cɛ-nin-o,* | Oh-young-man, |
| *i tunka sabali!* | you must chill out! |
| *I wolofa kumara,* | Your dad has spoken, |
| *i tunka sabali!* | you must chill out! |
| *Kumakan lamen . . .* | Listen to these words . . . |
| *K'i kow lamen . . .* | Listen to these concerns . . . |
| *I bangebaw kumara,* | Your parents have spoken, |
| *i tunka sabali!* | you must chill out! |

As featured artist Amen Fis sings "Listen to these concerns," the girl tries to skirt past Need One and their posse. She attempts to dismiss them as she did her mother, gesturing with her hand for them to back off, but they follow her, step for step, singing, "Your parents have spoken," and chanting, "You must chill out!" In contrast to the violence bestowed on the boy, the verbal scolding the girl receives from the male rappers emphasizes the "masculine restraint" she is expected to show to overcome her shameless "nature" and uphold her feminine morality. "Oh, young woman," they sing, "you must chill out!"

The refrain introduces a didactic quality to Need One's critique of the wayward morality of Bamako youth. Their prescription is inherently performative, and, like their critique, strongly gendered. "If a wife has sought the grace of her husband," Djo Dama raps, "she has no problem. Her children will be blessed." Playing the part of a hard-working husband, Djo Dama, wearing a dress shirt and slacks, arrives home. His (onscreen) wife, dressed in a full-length robe and matching headscarf, awaits him in the compound, bows down, and takes his briefcase. As he sits, she brings him water with which to wash his hands. His dinner awaits him on the ground at his feet. Through her dress and gesture, the woman embodies the pious obedience of the Mande wife, whose morality is confirmed by her dutiful submission to her husband. As anthropologist Kassim Kone writes, "It is believed among most Mande that when a mother is well behaved, i.e. listens to her husband, respects and treats him well, her children will escape from the problems of life" (Kone 1996, 10). In short, good wives produce good children, and, by extension, good mothers are good women (see Osborn 2011). In the video, Djo Dama's wife embodies this sense of feminine morality, on which subsequent generations depend to "escape the problems of life" (see also Modic 1996, 185).

As freshman exponents of a global musical genre (hip-hop) that has, since the early 1990s, been considered a source of youthful misconduct and cultural degradation (Schulz 2012), Need One stylistically represents an image of urban youth culture that defies delinquency and actively seeks to reorient itself toward the moral structures of traditional society. In other words, through ethical agency (in this case, mediated hip-hop performance), they seek to represent a revitalized urban morality in Bamako, and among its youth in particular. Throughout the video, the rappers embody a cultural style of vernacular cosmopolitanism (Werbner

2006), alternately wearing sports jerseys and colorful kaftans. Their words, too, lace an informal street language with proverbial speech and esoteric knowledge normally associated with artisanal "masters of the word," the storytelling (male) bards of *jeliya*. This hybrid Afropolitan style, embedding an ethical hip-hop stylistics in the moral structures of Mande society, goes for certain women presented in "Sabali" as well, who, in periodic dance sequences, demonstrate a studied proficiency of hip-hop choreography while sporting the long skirts and blouses associated with modest and dignified feminine couture. And yet, the voices of these women are loudly silent, and their dancing bodies, clothed though they may be in tradition, are more often sexualized as curved torsos, twisting hips, and big butts—gestural figures Need One made sure to catch on camera in each one of these scenes. In the end, the ethical scope of Need One's Afropolitan aesthetics remains narrow, specifically along gendered lines.

## The Ethics of Afropolitan Urbanism

In this chapter, I have presented a variety of case studies, elaborated through close listening and thick description, to elucidate the ways in which urban social space is conceived, lived, and perceived in contemporary Bamako. Moving through these texts and contexts—from Need One's mediated urbanism to Sissako's filmic *mise en espace* and the ethnography inscribed on the built spaces of the city—I have observed a pronounced discursive tension, between a popular ideal of civility, centered symbolically on the family compound *(du)* and its environs, and an increasingly predominant and expansive conception of wildness, conflating notions of the "the city" *(dugu)* and "the bush" *(kungo)*. I have also noted the highly ambivalent perceptions of morality and ethics this sociospatial tension produces. In the creative works considered here, the domestic sphere becomes an object of celebratory and anxious interest, evoking a morality that is both deeply valued and manifestly tenuous. Across multiple media and genres of expression (in popular music videos, art film, and public writing), one encounters ample praise of the solidarity, tradition, and convivial relations particular to Bamako social life. Yet, in all cases, there is a palpable precariousness, whether implicit or explicit, characterized by forms of opportunistic and provisional agency—the tactics of getting by, making do, and mixing it up—that appear increasingly estranged from extant moralities.

As an everyday encounter with urban estrangement, such practice entails significant existential risk, intensified by the abstract space of gross poverty, political disenfranchisement, underemployment, foreign cultural influence, insalubrity, and a generalized sense of abjection. Such is the dystopian African lifeworld portrayed in Sissako's *Bamako* and the deracinated urban youth culture represented in Need One's "Sabali." In both the film and video, urban morality appears significantly constrained and threatened. In both, the family compound is the site of intense contestation, argument, and debate. In both, exogenous influences—over domestic politics, local economies, and cultural style—are condemned for the deleterious effects they are having on local social space. And, in both, prescribed solutions posit a revitalization of traditional lifeways, characterized, in both, by a strong sense of custom and tradition. In *Bamako*, these traditions manifest in acts of socially constitutive ritual and calls to sustain, support, and strengthen communal labor. In "Sabali," the call is for a patient (though no less urgent) return to established gendered and generational subject positions, particularly among the urban youth. In both, the consequences of failing to heed these calls are dire, including ongoing and persistent exploitation, alienation, and ever-greater anomie.

Elsewhere in the city, from a different existential point of view, we hear the celebratory verses of tracks like "Bolibana," played loud over speakers in cybercafés and on stereos at street-side hangouts. And, we see the moralizing poetry written on household walls, on the signs of shops and market stalls, and on taxis, trucks, and public transportation. In both cases, the "perceived space" produced by verbal art and popular poetics resists reduction to mere hearing and seeing. In "Bolibana," the locative poetry of Need One's lyrics conjures image upon image of neighborhood landmarks, reinforced—not supplemented—by the visual scenes presented in the video. Through the urban iconography, we encounter words and images portraying scenes and evoking ideas that draw upon the moral lexicon of everyday life. These are signs that speak, objects that enable as they inscribe the spoken word. The urban public is, in other words, "a space of appearance" (Arendt [1958] 1998, 198) as much as it is a space of audition. In this way, recorded sound and inscribed speech deepen the moral promise made by countless Bamako urbanities as they leave home, moving between the civil and the wild. "They will hear it," they say, entering a public space in which their antiphonal greetings coexist with the calls of icons and lyrics coming from the built space of the city itself, to which *Bamakois* daily respond. If morality is threatened in contemporary Bamako, it remains, nonetheless, vital, variegated, and always vocal.

Here, then, we begin to qualify an Afropolitan ethics in Bamako through the struggles engendered by urban abstraction and the sentiments cultivated through public performance. One encounters the city, thus, as both essentially immoral and potentially moral, as a menace to civility that is simultaneously a wilderness to be cultivated. It is a social space that produces, as it is produced by, a public conflation of celebration and anxiety, possibility and constraint, promise and peril. An ethics of African urbanism appears, as it resounds, through a negotiation of these fields—the civil and the wild—manifest in localized forms of urban African modernity: of hip-hop in a cybercafé, cinema in a compound, and writing on just about every wall. This is an ethics born of being an urbanite, of occupying the social position of a city resident. It is a mode of being that draws on existing moral discourses—of culture and religion, in particular—but engenders a uniquely urban ethics, an existential project of keeping constraints in check and possibilities in play. "If it's not mixed up," *Bamakois* say, "it'll never work out."

That such an ethics is characterized as a principally masculine project, as we observed in Need One's "Sabali," implies that only some people's agency may be considered legitimately ethical and, by extension, Afropolitan. Women, in particular, would seem to be altogether excluded from ethical agency in the city, being, as the Mande cultural prejudice would have it, inherently shameless. It is with this question in mind—of who is (and is not) ethical in the Afropolis—that I turn, in the next chapter, to the social position of the urban artist. (I address the question of a feminine ethics in the Bamako art world in chapter 3.) Through ethnographic observation of performance practice and biographical portraits of particular artists, we observe the fluid (and contested) character of the musical profession in postcolonial Mali. As artists move across genres of expression and modes of identification, they produce a more expansive understanding of ethical agency, even as they confront challenges particular to their musical mode of being in the world.

# CHAPTER 2

# Artistiya

*Artistiya ka gelen. Bɛɛ tɛ se.*
Being an artist is difficult. Not everyone can do it.

Mariam Doumbia, "Artistiya"

## Exile Is Bad

Following the proclamation of the newly independent Republic of Mali on September 22, 1960, a group of young musicians in the capital's Bamako Koura (New Bamako) neighborhood formed an orchestra.[1] Their style was Afro-Cuban, consonant with the popular Caribbean and Congolese sounds that suffused the continent at this time (see Perullo 2008; Shain 2009; White 2002), with players on guitar, timbales, tumbas, horns, and vocals. They took the name Pionnier Jazz to support the work of the neighborhood Pioneers, a national Scouting group. Recruited by municipal officials to "perform the nation" (Askew 2002), members of Pionnier Jazz composed songs to support Mali's nascent nation-building project. One of their first songs was "Tunga Man Ni" ("Exile Is Bad"). As Amadou Traoré, a founding member of the group, explained to me, "[Tunga Man Ni] spoke to [Malians] in other countries . . . to tell them that Mali is independent. . . . We called on them to return to Mali, to work, to build the nation." The refrain of the song went like this:

| | |
|---|---|
| *Tunga man ɲi de!* | Exile is bad! |
| *Jarabi! Na anw ka Mali la.* | Dearest! Come back to our Mali. |
| *Sanu bɛ Mali la.* | There is gold in Mali. |
| *Wari bɛ Mali la.* | There is silver in Mali. |
| *Danbe bɛ Mali la.* | There is dignity in Mali. |
| *Kelenya be faso la.* | There is unity in the homeland. |
| *Aa! Janfa man ɲi de.* | Ah! Betrayal is not good. |
| *Jarabi! N'anw ka Mali la! Aa!* | Dearest! Come back to our Mali! Ah! |

*Tunga man ɲi de! Jarabi!*        Emigration is bad! My love!
*Na anw ka faso la.*              Come back to our homeland.


When French West African territories became independent nations, many Africans suddenly found themselves displaced from their new homelands. Workers from the Soudan Français (now the Republic of Mali) repaired locomotives in the workshops of Senegal (Jones 2002), labored in the cocoa plantations of Ghana (Dougnon 2007), and traded in the cities of Côte d'Ivoire (Gary-Tounkara 2008). Some heeded the call to "return home." Others remained abroad as expatriates. Still others adopted the nationalities of their host countries. Yet, the calls to return home continued. In the late 1960s, Mali's Ensemble Instrumental National (a state-sponsored music group) once again called on Malians abroad to repatriate, using familial terms of place to inspire national solidarity. The piece was called "Yan ka di" ("Here Is Good"):

| | |
|---|---|
| *Yan ka di* | It is good here |
| *Nne wa to m fa bara* | I'm going to my father's home |
| *Wali dugu sigi man di n ye* | To stay abroad doesn't please me |
| *Mali de ang faso ye* | Mali is our homeland |
| *Ni i ke la man[s]a ke* | [Even] if you become king |
| *I ka nyi i fa bara* | You are better off in your father's home |
| *Mali de yaun faso ye* | Mali is your homeland |
| *Ni i ke la banamba ye . . .* | [Even] if you become a great man . . .[2] |

For a country like Mali, there was urgency to the homecoming calls issuing from groups like Pionnier Jazz and the National Ensemble. At independence, Mali was a poor and largely agrarian society with no major industry to speak of. Following the breakup of a federal union with Senegal on August 19, 1960, Mali was left landlocked. Unresolved political disputes with Senegal led to the stoppage of train service to the Dakar port, grossly inhibiting Mali's prospects for economic development. The Malian government's ambitious modernization goals required skills and manpower to overcome these immediate geopolitical deficits. State-sponsored artists were called on to inspire and mobilize a newly independent citizenry to "rise and build the nation!" (*wuli ka fasobaara kɛ!*), words made famous on the radio waves in the mid-1960s by artist Boubacar Traoré in his national hit "Mali Twist" (first released in 1963).

Nearly a half-century later, I sat with Pionnier Jazz founding member Amadou Traoré in his crowded Bamako Koura residence. There, where no less than fourteen people live off his modest earnings and retirement benefits, we reflected on his career as an artist, a career spanning the entirety of Mali's postcolonial history. "Back then," he told me, "during the independence era, there was automatically a sense of patriotism. . . . Everyone was proud. We had patriotism in our hearts." The great burdens of nation building were met, according to him, by an equally great and homegrown nationalist fervor. At a later meeting, he explained to me that "to be an artist at that time was to be more patriotic. I worked voluntarily, without pay. We were proud to be Malian musicians. Patriotism was predominant."

"Times have changed," I remarked. "Yes," he said, "they have." "So, how would you describe Malian artists today?" I asked him. He paused, searching for words, "the artist today, in Mali . . ." He trailed off before looking at me directly, saying, "The artist in Mali, I don't know what to call him. But, he is the most miserable of people." He paused again, "That is, if he stays in Mali." Here, Traoré, who as a member of Pionnier Jazz once made spirited calls on Malians abroad to repatriate, began to explain why artists today are obliged to expatriate. "One must have a group, and contracts, but not in Mali. No! Contracts abroad, official contracts, which allow groups to get out. Then, they will go and play at European festivals, or elsewhere in Africa, or in other countries. . . . But, in Mali, you earn nothing! Even if you do marriages, gigs here and there, it's not easy."

In this chapter, I explore the social and musical lifeworld that informs this narrative of professional crisis in postcolonial Mali. These are stories of a status and identity known locally as *artistiya* (literally "artist-ness") that emerged from a burgeoning urban popular culture in the 1950s, became professionalized through state patronage in the context of post-colonial nation building in the 1960s only to be uncoupled, beginning in the 1970s (a decade of postnational statism) and accelerating through the '80s and '90s (decades of structural adjustment and globalization), from a narrowly nationalist mode of being (see Skinner 2012b). These are stories of being an artist in Mali—of *artistiya*—in what might be called the post-postcolonial era of neoliberalism (Ferguson 2006; Piot 2010). These are also stories of what AbdouMaliq Simone calls "worlding" in urban Africa (2001b): a centrifugal, deterritorialized ethos of exigency and opportunity that manifests not only in a desire to leave the abstract space of the African city but also in opportunities to push the boundaries of the social and

cultural within the Afropolis; a sometimes transgressive and always playful urban ethics manifest, as we shall observe, in new modes of identification and forms of musical expression among Bamako artists.

I begin with the postcolonial ambivalence of the phrase *tunga man ɲi*
("Exile is bad") in order to emphasize the continuities and disjunctures
of artistic personhood in the Malian postcolony. I approach the theme of
exile not as a literal index of patterns of travel to or from a perceived homeland, but as a metaphor for a salient shift in postcolonial being-in-the-
world: from an ideal of repatriation bound to a strong sense of national
citizenship to the necessity of expatriation in the context of diminished
sociopolitical solidarity. In both cases, it is the artist who gives voice to
this ambivalent exilic discourse and the precarious political subjectivity
to which it refers. To encounter exile, then, is to hear the way professional
artists mediate modes of identification in postcolonial Mali, including
their own status and identity, or *artistiya*. From the musical discourse
of exile, I turn to questions of what and how it means to be an artist in
Bamako. I move between historical and ethnographic modes of analysis
to address the identity politics and poetics of *artistiya* in the late and postcolonial Afropolis, through thick description of performance practice and
biographical portraits across five decades of musical lives and works.

## But "People Today" Are Worse

Amadou Traoré's lament about the state of the music economy in contemporary Mali ("The artist today . . . is the most miserable of people")
is not unique. Throughout my research, whether in formal interviews or
informal conversations, artists would tell me about the impossibility of
earning a living as a musician in Bamako, where virtually all of the country's on-again, off-again music industry is concentrated (about which
more in chapter 5). With the exception of a select group of praise-singing
divas (mainly female griots, or *jelimusow*; see Durán 1995a), whose tak-
ings at local life-cycle ceremonies can verge on (and sometimes exceed)
the exorbitant, it is not an exaggeration to say that all artists are, in some
way or another, looking to tour and record abroad, especially in Europe
and the United States. For a new generation of Malian artists, the refrain "Exile is bad" continues to be sung—indeed, it is one of the most
widely represented themes in Malian popular music today—but, unlike
independence-era calls to "return home" and "build the nation," modern-
day songs of exile are cautionary tales, acknowledging the urgency of travel

abroad while at the same time warning of the threats to local lifeworlds such travel poses. Take, for example, this lyrical exchange between singers Nana Soumbounou and Karounga Sacko from the track "Immigration" (Triton Stars 2006), in which a man (Karounga) announces his departure for France and a woman (Nana) pleads with him to not forget her when he leaves.[3]

### Karounga

| | |
|---|---|
| Visa min na na le, | With the visa that arrived, |
| ko ne ka waa tunga taa la. | I am going to travel abroad. |
| Ko ne bɛ n jarabi de fɛ. | I love my darling so much. |
| Aa, ne tunbɛ n diyaɲemɔgɔ fɛ. | Ah, I have cherished my beloved. |
| Wuladiyaɲe kanu man ɲi de. | Love from afar is not good. |
| Ne siran na ɲɛnafin ye. | I am afraid of longing. |
| Ɲɛnafinjugu man ɲi de. | Severe nostalgia is not good. |
| Ko ne siran na ɲɛnafin de n ye. | I am afraid of this nostalgia. |
| . . . Anw bɛ nin kɛ la de? | . . . What can we do about it? |
| Ma chérie, ne dun taatɔ de! | My dearest, I must go! |

### Nana

| | |
|---|---|
| Ko kuma kan kelen bɛ ne bolo, | I have but one voice, |
| Ne b'o fɔ jarabi ye. | I speak it to my dearest. |
| Ko n'i taara Faransi taga la, | If you go on a journey to France, |
| Kana ɲine i jarabi ko. | Do not forget your love. |
| Ko n'i taara Faransi taga la, | If you go on a journey to France, |
| mon amour, | my love, |
| kana ɲine i diyaɲemɔgɔ ko. | don't forget your beloved. |
| Aa! Diyaɲe de gɛlɛman! | Ah! Love is not easy! |

### Chorus

| | |
|---|---|
| Aa n kanu! N tɛ se ka ɲine i ko! | Ah my love! I cannot forget you! |

### Karounga

| | |
|---|---|
| Ne waara tunga taa la. | I have embarked on my exile. |
| Tunga ma diya ne la . . . | Exile has not been good to me . . . |

| | |
|---|---|
| *Ko ne waara bɔ n jarabi ye.* | I went away from my love. |
| *Aa chérie, ne tunbɛ i de fɛ.* | Ah my darling, I have loved you. |
| *Ko ni ne kan tɔ Faransi sigi la,* | If my voice remains in France, |
| *ko ne tunbɛ miiri e de la.* | my thoughts have only been of you. |
| *Ko ni ne kan tɔ Faransi sigi la,* | If my voice remains in France, |
| *anw kanu, ne tunbɛ sugo e de la.* | I have only dreamt of our love. |
| *Chérie! Ne tunbɛ i de fɛ.* | My darling! I love you. |

Later in the song, rumors circulate that the man has married a white woman in France. Distraught, the woman wonders what has become of her husband. He has not called. He has not written. Meanwhile the man tells of his plight from afar. In France, food is hard to come by. Money is even harder. He moves from place to place. Everyday struggles make phone calls and letters impossible pleasures. At the end of the song, rumors of infidelity back home and the strains of exile abroad come together in a condemnation of "people today" *(bimɔgɔw)*, referring specifically to the perceived duplicity of contemporary Malians (who, the singers suggest, take pleasure in spreading lies for personal gain) but also, more generally, to a modern world that enables (and even requires) such conflict and deceit—the dense bush of global modernity that, as we observed in the previous chapter, produces a surfeit of "wild space."

*Chorus*

| | |
|---|---|
| *Bi jamana mɔgɔw man ɲi de.* | People in this country today are not good |
| *Ne tunbɛ n diyaɲemɔgɔ fɛ!* | I once had a loved one! |
| *Ne siranna bimɔgɔw ɲe.* | I am afraid of today's people. |
| *U kana n ka kanu duman sa!* | Don't let them ruin my sweet love! |

"People in this country today" *(Bi jamana mɔgɔw)* represent a populace to be feared, whose apparent predilection to sow the seeds of dissent stands in dramatic contrast to the dignity and unity of the newly minted Malian people Amadou Traoré lyrically praised nearly five decades prior. In Traoré's independence anthem, betrayal *(janfa)* belongs to those who refuse to return home, to those who reject calls to mine the "gold" and "silver" of a potentially prosperous Malian homeland. For Nana and Karounga, betrayal can be found in equal measure at home and abroad. France (and the Global North more generally) becomes, in Karounga's lyrical experience, the "heart of darkness" for migrants struggling to endure their exile *(tunga)*, for whom the promise of prosperity in a European elsewhere ends in a prolonged psychosocial and socioeconomic tragedy (on the inversion of Joseph Conrad's metaphor of African obscurity, see Skinner 2010, 27, 30–33). "If I could do it all over again today," Karounga sings, "I would not have gone away to France." Mali, for its part, is consumed by "cruel speech" *(juguya kan)* and "family animosity" *(balima jugu)* at the heart of civil space, among brothers and sisters, whose words keep Nana's fraught character up at night "counting the grooves in the corrugated roofing."

"Exile knows no dignity" *(tunga tɛ danbe dɔn)*, the saying goes, but, increasingly, neither does home (see Whitehouse 2012a). I addressed this sense of intensified wildness within the social space of the Afropolis in the previous chapter, stressing, however, the agential ethics of those who resist indignity by reinscribing a moral sense of place in the city—varied and fragmented though it may be—through public song, speech, writing, and image. For the remainder of this chapter, I further explore the constraints and possibilities of Afropolitan being-in-the-world through the particular experience of professional musicians in Bamako. I present, first, a brief history of *artistiya* in postcolonial Mali, a history that I have dealt with more extensively elsewhere (Skinner 2009; 2012b) and to which I return in chapter 5. Here, my intent is to provide a sense of the shifting ethos of *artistiya* in postcolonial Mali—across public and private, national and transnational sectors and interests—as well as offer a survey of the relevant literature. I then turn to a particular performance I observed with the nightclub singer Issa Sory Bamba and his group, which I consider both in terms of the socioprofessional concerns it evokes and as the historically layered product of (post)colonial artistic practice and identity in Bamako. Finally, I present the creative and entrepreneurial work of Dialy Mady Cissoko, a self-styled "modern griot" whose professional identity suggests a cautionary counterpoint to Amadou Traoré's representation of the Malian artists as "the most miserable of people." In particular, Cissoko's rooted practice of artistic personhood nuances the claim that African socioeconomic futures are predominantly defined by "extraversion" (Bayart 2000), dependent upon a world to which access remains provisional and precarious.

## The Artist in Postcolonial Mali

The concept of the artist (French, *artiste*; Bamana, *artisti*) emerged in Mali during the years following independence in 1960, initially to refer to actors, dancers, and musicians with formal (or quasi-formal) ties to the state. *Artistiya,* however, has its roots in the pre-independence theater troupes, military fanfares, popular youth associations, and dance bands of the post–World War II era of decolonization (Cutter 1971; Jézéquel 1999; Kaba and Charry 2000; Kanouté 2007; Meillassoux 1968; Skinner 2009). A history of the modern Malian artist thus begins in the late 1940s, when French colonial authorities could no longer contain the demands for labor reform, citizenship rights, social welfare, and cultural autonomy among their African subject populations (for examples of musical performance and politics at this time, see Camara, Charry, and Jansen 2002 and County and Skinner 2008; for a broader regional history of postwar labor politics, see Cooper 1996). Local artists—whether colonial functionaries or not—played a significant role in articulating these demands and would later make important contributions to the cultural policy of nation building in Mali's First Republic (1960–68) through the formation of national troupes, ballets, ensembles, and orchestras (Arnoldi 2006; Bamba and Prévost 1996; Charry 2000a; Counsel 2006; Cutter 1968; Hopkins 1972; Touré 1996; Skinner 2012b).[4]

The social status and identity of Malian artists, defined largely by their relation to the state, would fundamentally change in the years following the military coup in 1968 that put an end to the increasingly authoritarian presidency of Modibo Keita, Mali's first president (Bamba and Prévost 1996; Bagayogo 1992; Mamadou Diawara 2003; Keïta 2009). This was a time of widespread expatriation, with artists fleeing political and economic insecurity at home and relocating to cities with more viable culture industries, especially Abidjan (Côte d'Ivoire). As I have elsewhere argued:

> In the early 1970s, artists who remained in Mali witnessed a new
> statist regime of cultural patronage come into being. If before art-
> ists had worked to sustain a nationalist ideology in the service of
> a highly centralized one-party state, patronage of the arts after the
> coup, while still bound to the state, emphasized individual alle-
> giances to agents of state power over the party or national bureau-
> cracy. (Skinner 2012b, 525)

Under the military junta's rule and the nominally civilian "constitutional" form it took in 1979, political cronyism, environmental crises, regional conflict, budget shortfalls, and neoliberal economic reforms engendered new forms of artistic patronage that were outside of, or parallel to state authority, including, by the mid-1980s new international interests such as the "world music" industry (see, for example, Mamadou Diawara 1996; Eyre 2000; and Maxwell 2003). This time has been referred to as a period of artistic "effervescence" because a large number of private orchestras and ensembles were formed as national, regional, and municipal state-sponsored groups were gradually cut back or eliminated altogether (Touré 1996, 98). The 1991 fall of the military-cum-civilian junta and the democratic reforms that established Mali's Third Republic (1992–present) intensified this transformation of Malian cultural policy, as cultural production moved from principally public interests and media (national cultural festivals, municipal dance halls, and single-channel radio and television broadcast) to private ones (world music festivals, privately owned nightclubs, and multichannel radio and satellite television).[5] Malian artists, largely severed from the state, were henceforth bound to the contested and provisional space of the neoliberal marketplace (see Skinner 2012a), a space that has become even more precarious in the wake of the March 2012 coup (a topic to which I return in chapter 6).

The urban artists with whom I have worked in Bamako over the past decade are the products of this effervescent late-twentieth-century move from public patronage to private enterprise. These artists emerged from a postcolonial African history that set them apart from other sociomusical groups, particularly the clans of musical artisans known as "griots" (or, among the Mande, jeliw; see Hale 1998). As early as the 1960s, artistiya had come to signify a community of urban musicians and related set of musical practices not restricted by lineage or clan-based patron-client relations, as jeliya is. For many observers of the Mande world today, artists and griots remain strictly distinguished, generally in terms of the modernity of the artist and the tradition of the jeli (see Skinner 2004, 149–51). In practice, such distinctions are difficult to circumscribe. More and more, griots embrace artistiya to build commercial credentials as performers of modern ("popular" and "world") music, and artists cultivate jeliya to secure ties to patrons and ground their work in tradition.[6] But, this implies more professional choice than cultural affiliation. In Bamako today, the terms "modernity" and "tradition" and their related musical personifications, artisti and jeli, have become more expressive tropes than generic types (compare Charry 2000a, 24–27). Thus, most "traditional" griots are also "modern" artists, whose professional lives are wrapped up in state and commercial interests that articulate beyond local patron–client relations. And, many artists find an expedient and culturally salient mode of expression in *jeliya*, which, as a commoditized genre of musical expression, is among the most popular in Mali.

Further, the formal and stylistic conventions of *jeliya*—in which declamatory praise song and spartan instrumental accompaniments are juxtaposed with choral refrains and dense instrumental polyphony—have strongly informed the sociomusical structures of *artistiya* in postcolonial Mali. By the mid-1970s *jeliya* had become the preferred genre of the ruling elite and, by extension, the national music industry they managed. Artists, griots and non-griots alike, were called on to sing the praises of their political patrons, becoming "agents of propaganda" enlisted to flatter a nepotistic cadre of officers in high-ranking positions within the government (see Keïta 2009, 37). The status of *jeliya* as a national music would persist into the 1980s, though within an increasingly decentralized and privatized culture economy as the statist regime of Mali's Second Republic (1968–91) declined. The artistic dominance of *jeliya* at this time is evidenced by the commercial rise of prominent female vocalists such as Ami Koita and Kandia Kouyaté, dubbed "the superwomen of Malian music" (Durán 1995a). Their work would inspire the next generation of Malian artists and open up new opportunities for women pursuing artistic careers. Though the 1990s and 2000s would see the status of *jeliya* as Mali's national music challenged by other genres, notably *wasulu* (Durán 1995b; 2000; Maxwell 2002, 2003, 2008) and hip-hop (Schulz 2012), it is still a significant generic resource for Malian artists.

Bamako vocalist and bandleader Issa Sory Bamba's musical work testifies to the enduring influence of *jeliya* in the city's contemporary music culture. Issa is a Bamako artist who makes a living by singing for urban life-cycle ceremonies *(sumuw)* and at nightclubs, largely because of his talent as a praise singer *(fasadala)*. For his patrons, Issa is, for all intents and purposes, a *jeli*, despite not being born into this traditional "caste" of musical artisans. What is important is Issa's ability to perform the part, which, as we shall observe, he does just about every weekend, microphone in hand, backed by a lively group of instrumentalists (drums, keyboards, electric guitar, bass, and *kora*; Figure 10). Further, Issa's music situates the generic hybridity of the Bamako art world within a broader history of popular urbanism and political patronage—a history of (post)colonial *artistiya*. In what follows, I begin with the latter historical resonances evident in Issa's

*Figure 10. Groupe Issa Bamba. Photograph by the author.*

musical worldview, echoing from the word *ambiance*: a pervasive and etymologically rich term of sociomusical style used to describe Issa's principal music venue in Bamako (as of 2007), the Komoguel II nightclub. Then, I present an extended close listening of a particular praise song Issa performed for a prominent patron at this venue, through which the singer channels the art of *jeliya* to make a living, but also affirm his identity as an artist—an act, I assert, of Afropolitan ethics.

## "It's the Ambiance!"

I had been following Groupe Issa Bamba's Saturday night performances at Komoguel II, a respectable downtown nightclub in the Bamako Koura district, for several weeks when I arrived at the *espace culturel* on a hot night in May 2007. My intention was to record a full two-hour show for the group to use as an addendum to their application for Radio France Internationale's Découverte Award, a highly competitive and coveted prize that promises to open the door to international recognition for francophone artists worldwide.[7] Conscious of my presence and eager to give their best possible performance, the group exhibited the full spectrum of their live act that evening, including original Afropop tunes from their debut album, *Siyoroko*;[8] spirited doses of Congolese rumba and Ivoirien *couper-décaler* (a popular club dance rhythm at the time); a smattering of French chanson and American pop; and lengthy excursions into orchestrated Malian "folklore" (as Issa calls it), including swinging, pentatonic "Bambara Blues" pieces from central Mali and, most prominently, electrified urban *jeliya,* the band's generic forte.

Komoguel II lies in the shadows on a busy side street off the bustling Boulevard de l'Indépendence. Outside the club entrance, one finds the usual fare of cigarette, chewing gum, and hard candy vendors crammed between rows of motorbikes and cars lining the sidewalk in front of the venue. A mixture of dust, exhaust, and humidity thickens the air, which, even though the sun set hours ago, is still hot. A few clients linger outside by the curb, sharing a conversation and a smoke, or both, while others, faced with oncoming traffic, hurry inside. The interior is divided into two sections, a dimly lit open-air bar and a larger "bar-restaurant" with a stage area and dance floor. To enter the latter, one pays a doorman 1000 or 1500 CFA francs ($2 or $3), though, if you're a friend of the band or the club management, a brief greeting and handshake may suffice. Seating in the club is in booths and at tables around the venue's perimeter, which sits under an aluminum canopy and, given the "mixed couple" nature of some of the venue's clientele (composed mainly of well-heeled men who bring along dates or seek the company of local escorts), remains dark and anonymous. The band sits on a raised section of the floor at the back of the venue. In front of the band is a large covered dance floor, inside of which hangs a set of speakers, colorful flashing stage lights, and a disco ball. On Saturdays, music starts at 11 P.M. By midnight, the dance floor is packed, and the band is hot. "At Komoguel, *c'est l'ambiance!*," Issa exclaims.

In my field notes I write: "IT'S THE AMBIANCE!" This is not the first time I have heard Bamako music culture described in this way. Indeed, Issa's perfunctory phrase resonates with deep popular cultural significance in francophone African cities. It qualifies a sociomusical ethos in places like Bamako (Dakar, Abidjan, or Kinshasa) that couples an Afropolitan aesthetics with urban *artistiya*. Before delving into the concert at Komoguel II, in which an ethics of *artistiya* emerges in the course of a remarkable vocal performance, it is worth digressing to attend to the historical meaning of the term *ambiance* and its relation to artistic personhood in late and post-colonial Bamako. We may begin with a basic definition. *Ambiance* is a French word implying "mood," "feeling," and "atmosphere," which, in its usage in francophone urban Africa, conveys a specifically musical sense of "vibe" and a general sentiment of conviviality in public spaces of music making and listening.[9] Ambiance is also the historical product of Bamako's particular late-colonial urbanism with resonances throughout the city's postcolonial history, of which I offer a few salient examples later in the chapter. As anthropologist Claude Meillassoux noted during his research in Bamako in the early 1960s:

> *Ambiance* was a fashionable word.... We know that it was also the name of the *jeli-tō*, of a Malian hit tune, and of fashionable native loincloth. Among Bamako youth, to be *ambiant* meant to be gay and lively. In the colloquial French of the teenagers in France, *ambiance* means "in the mood"; *ambiant* is not used. (1968, 136, fn41)

The *jeli-tō* (or *jeli tɔn*) in Meillassoux's note referred to the Association des Artistes du Mali, l'Ambiance, a significant institution of public culture in 1960s Bamako (Meillassoux 1968, 107–12; see also Charry 2000a, 268). Stylistically, the Ambiance Association was indicative of urban trends in 1960s Bamako. Alongside popular foreign styles (from Europe, America, and the Caribbean), urban music at the time was strongly marked by *jeliya*. Most Ambiance musicians identified as griots, and the Ambiance ensemble included instrumentation specific to urban griot performance practice,[10] including the *kora*, but also the *bala* (xylophone), *dundun* (bass drum), and *tama* (pitched pressure drum), as well as the electric guitar, which had been gaining prominence within regional griot ensembles since the 1940s (Charry 2000a, 242–307). That said, the group's name referred not to *jeliya*, or griots, but to an association of Malian *artists* (my emphasis), a discursive move claiming a modern sociomusical identity in the postcolony: *artistiya*.

At Ambiance events, musicians, their friends, families, and neighbors—at its height, the group claimed more than 300 members—would gather in neighborhood streets and perform popular songs from regional repertoires for local residents. Yet, participants had another audience in mind as well. Ambiance artists self-consciously performed vocal and instrumental pieces with nationalist overtones that appealed to the ruling political party, the Union Soudanaise de Rassemblement Démocratique Africaine, or US-RDA (Meillassoux 1968, 110–11). To heighten this rapprochement with the one-party state, these urban griots amplified their performances with large speakers, carrying the group's *ambiant* and ambient sociomusical message throughout the neighborhood and its environs. Significantly, the presence of electric lighting and sound amplification at these and other events in Bamako marked a shift in the visual and aural experience of urban popular culture in the 1960s, in which incandescent illumination and electrified soundscapes were becoming bound up with expressions of *ambiance*, or musical conviviality, at popular cultural events.[11]

Prior to independence, *ambiance* signified still other sociomusical lifeworlds. Throughout the 1950s, Bamako's popular dance bands would perform for formal functions at the bequest of French authorities and new African elites as well as for popular neighborhood soirées. Locals referred to these informal get-togethers with the French term *bals poussières*, or "dust parties," named for the effect of all-night dancing on an earthen floor. "When we didn't have a place to play," bandleader Panka Dembelé told me, "we'd organize a dust party."[12] These events attracted large numbers of urban youth, whose physical proximity in city wards presented new opportunities for sociocultural experimentation across domestic, clan, ethnic, racial, and political lines (Meillassoux 1968, 118; see also Manthia Diawara 1997). "There were a lot of people and a great *ambiance*," Dembelé explained. "It lasted until sunrise. . . . At certain points in the night, there was so much dust all around, on our clothes and in our hair, that we had to water the grounds regularly" (P. Dembelé, cited in Mangin 1998, 168). Dembelé's band called itself, appropriately enough, Ambiance Jazz.

Contemporaneous with the dust parties in the 1950s were neighborhood youth clubs that would organize parties named for popular African dance rhythms with origins from throughout the subregion, including *gunbe, sabar, balanin,* and *bara*.[13] Together with the soirées, these clubs were the basis of a late-colonial Afropolitanism defining urban cultural life in cities throughout the region. While the neighborhood clubs emphasized regional popular culture, the dust parties were more international in scope, but the two were not mutually exclusive. On Saturdays in Bamako in the mid-1950s, Panka Dembelé remembers performing for neighborhood *gunbe* and *sabar* street parties from the morning to the evening, going home for a quick dinner with his family, and then gathering his band, Ambiance Jazz, for an all-night *bal poussière* elsewhere in the city. In the mid-1950s, "Bamako was great, even better than New York!," Dembelé said. "We had everything. There were people from all over— from Nigeria, Ghana, Côte d'Ivoire, and Senegal. All day and all night, there was *ambiance!*"

In Bamako today, *ambiance* is not, generally speaking, applied as a noun to persons, songs, or things, and it isn't nearly as popular as a band name as it was in decades past. Ambiance is still, however, widely present in discourse about music, retaining the strong semiotic connection to urban popular culture highlighted in Meillassoux's earlier description.[14] "At Komoguel," Issa declared, "it's the *ambiance!*" For a musical event to be ambiant it must evoke sociable pleasure (being "gay and lively," in Meillassoux's words); this is achieved as much by the music itself as by the relations between and among performers and audiences. Returning, now, to the Groupe Issa Bamba's 2007 nightclub performance, I consider some of the performative poetics and identity politics involved in establishing sociomusical relations in Bamako's contemporary music culture. This will necessarily move us from questions of aesthetics to ethics, from musical conviviality to musical meaning, from ambiance to *artistiya.*

## A Praise Song for Uncle Sékou

Midway through the band's set, and following a lively Afro-Cuban rendition of the dance band hit "Mami Wata" (a widely interpreted regional pop song named for a serpent-bearing female water deity), singer Issa Bamba called out to the audience, "*Tonton* Sama Sékou, this one is for you!" Naming a patron before a praise song was not surprising—Issa is well regarded by club patrons for his performance of laudatory *jeliya,* which makes up more than a third of his band's sets on Saturday nights— but this particular recipient of Issa's praise was noteworthy. Sama Sékou, to whom Issa referred affectionately as *tonton* (French for "uncle"), was the proprietor of Komoguel II and its larger counterpart, Komoguel I, located across the river, making him the group's primary club patron (a song, "Komoguel," is dedicated to Sama Sékou on the band's second album). He was also a well-known friend and confidant of then-president Touré, himself basking in the success of his 2007 reelection campaign. Sung for a commercial patron of the arts with strong ties to Mali's ruling elite, Issa Bamba's praise song for Sama Sékou struck me as an evocative convergence of politics and economy in contemporary *artistiya,* as well as an eloquent example of how expressions of culture and identity—morality and ethics—come together in the performative production of artistic personhood in Bamako today.

Along with the patron to whom the song was addressed, Issa Bamba himself added layers of political and economic meaning to this performance. His father, Sorry Bamba was among the first generation of professional musicians identified as artists in Malian society. From his late-colonial popular youth association (then dance band), Groupe Goumbé, to his role in creating the renowned state-sponsored Orchestre Régional de Mopti, to his period of exile in Côte d'Ivoire and later migration to France where he developed his solo musical career abroad, Sorry Bamba came of age in and witnessed the passing of an era when artists, as clients of the postcolonial patron-state, were defined and judged by their national status and identity, professionalized as public servants (Bamba and Prévost 1996). His son Issa began his artistic career along similar lines, as a student at Mali's Institut National des Arts (INA) and the principal vocalist of the school's popular orchestra, the INA Stars. But, unlike his father, Issa's state-sponsored education would not lead to a state-sponsored music career; nor, given the decline and neglect of Mali's modern-day artistic institutions, would such a career even be desirable. After three years of study at INA, Issa left the school without a degree to pursue his career as an artist. "I know that I have a future in music," he told me. "I know that one day, if I work hard and make an impression, one day I will be a great musician. That's my ambition. The life cycle ceremonies and the club gigs, they are formalities. I am educating myself. I see the big picture."[15] For Issa, his professional future lay in the private sector music economy, with the access to global markets in the form of world music it promised. In this sense, his band's weekly show at Komoguel II under the patronage of the wealthy and well-connected Sama Sékou was an important first step, a site of (potential) professional mobility (Figure 11).

"Uncle Sama Sékou, this one is for you!," Issa declared, as guitarist Sékou Coulibaly picked out A minor and G Major chords in rising and falling arpeggios. *"Tonton, c'est pour toi!,"* Issa repeated in French, now joined by keyboards, *kora,* drums, and bass in lively polyphony. With the band's instrumental accompaniment, or *kunbɛn* established, Issa intoned the following refrain twice, using a vocal style characterized by the regular melodic and metrical patterns typical of Mande choral song, or *dɔnkili.* (I deepen my discussion of contemporary Mande musical aesthetics in

*Figure 11. Issa Sory Bamba. Photograph by the author.*

chapter 3, though certain features of this performance practice, introduced here, will help clarify the significance of Issa's praise song.)

| | |
|---|---|
| *Muru da ka di!* | The knife blade is sharp! |
| *Issa ka muru da ka di!* | Issa's knife blade is sharp! |
| *A mana da ladiya,* | If its blade is good [well sharpened], |
| *n tc boli,* | I will not flee, |
| *ka ba ni fa lamalo.* | and shame my mother and father, |
| *N t'o kɛ!* | I will not do it! |

When Issa sang that he "will not flee" the "well-sharpened" knife his reference was to male circumcision, which all Mande boys must traditionally endure upon entering adolescence. The fact that Issa sang these words about himself (an initiated adult) metaphorically served to affirm the singer's moral subjectivity, establishing his commitment to the traditions and mores of Mande society (such as gendered life-cycle rituals); that is, to the culture of civil space. In the following verse, sung twice for added emphasis, Issa again affirmed these communitarian morals, addressing the "shame" *(malo)* of betraying and dishonoring one's parents *(masaw)*:

| | |
|---|---|
| *Fa ni ba malo* | In this world, it is wrong |
| *man ɲi duniya!* | to shame one's mother and father! |
| *Mɔgɔw kana masaw malo jira* | People, do not bring shame to your parents |
| *duniya.* | in this world. |

Having grounded himself through song in the social position of Mande culture, Issa then sang a verse, following a brief guitar solo, that served to frame his praise for Sama Sékou and, as I argue, invoke his own ethical subjectivity as an artist.

| | |
|---|---|
| *Anw kana bila numu la!* | We must not offend the blacksmith! |
| *Ko n'i bilala numu la,* | For if you offend the blacksmith, |
| *I ye ko jugu kɛ.* | You have done a bad thing. |

"The blacksmith" *(numu)* to whom Issa referred was Sama Sékou, whose family belongs to this particular caste of Mande artisans (see Conrad and Frank 1995; McNaughton 1988). Issa's vocal invocation, phrased in terms of a warning to highlight the Mande blacksmith's social power and prestige, lyrically identified this song as a *numu fasa,* or praise song for the blacksmith. Though still textually rooted in cultural themes of tradition (that of the *numu*), this sung passage marked a formal and stylistic shift to the recitational expression of laudatory *jeliya,* a move signaled instrumentally by a lively and ornamented guitar solo, musically heightening, or "heating up" the performance (see Waterman 1948). Paralleling Issa's vocal shift from the style and structure of choral song *(dɔnkili)* to the metrically and melodically fluid mode of vocal praise *(fasada)* was a subjective move from the morality of culture to the ethics of identity, that of the artist himself. What would follow was not merely a typical praise song but a unique expression of Issa's competence as a praise singer *(fasadala),* an identity that, for him, as a modern artist practicing the traditional art of *jeliya,* was inherently ambiguous; for Issa is not, by birth, a griot. Entering this sociomusical "wild space" of subjective ambiguity, Issa began his praise song for Uncle Sama Sékou.

| | |
|---|---|
| *Ee! n bɛ ŋana jɔn mawele?* | Eh! which hero am I calling? |
| *Ko n bɛ ŋana jɔn mawele?* | I said, which hero am I calling? |
| *Tonton Sama Seku, i ni su!* | Uncle Sama Sékou, good evening! |

At this point in the piece, the instrumental accompaniment became more spartan, with the keyboards and bass guitar adopting a light staccato double pulse on the downbeat of the triple meter. Arpeggiated chord progressions from the guitar and *kora* dropped in volume while the drums retreated to a quiet syncopated rhythm on bass and snare. In this way, the music became "cooler," creating a "good" ethico-aesthetic space for Issa's praise song (see Thompson 2011), allowing the sung lyrics to take precedence over the backing instrumentation. Referring to Sama Sékou as a "hero" *(ŋana)*, Issa proceeded to describe his patron's accomplishments and character, highlighting the national and international scope of his career and his great financial generosity shown to friends and enemies alike.

| | |
|---|---|
| *Mopti janjon diyara* | The hero who accomplished |
| *ŋana min na!* | great deeds in Mopti! |
| *Bama Nare janjon diyara*[16] | The hero who accomplished |
| *ŋana min na!* | great deeds in Bamako! |
| *Faransi janjon diyara* | The hero who accomplished |
| *ŋana min na!* | great deeds in France! |
| *n bɛ ŋana jɔn mawele?* | which hero am I calling? |
| *Nisɔn ani jugusɔn,* | Friend and enemy, |
| *a bɛ wari di a la!* | he [the hero] gives money to both! |
| *N'i bilala ŋana na* | If you come across this hero |
| *a nisɔnbag'i la!* | you will find him to be kind and generous! |
| *Dɔnbaga ma fili.* | A person of renown does not mislead. |
| *Ne bɛ ŋana jɔn mawele?* | Which hero am I calling? |
| *Tonton, i ni su!* | Uncle, good evening! |
| *Ne bɛ ŋana jɔn wele?* | Which hero am I calling? |
| *Tonton, i ni su!* | Uncle, good evening! |

More recitation than song, Issa's praise narrative began with the preceding litany, articulated unhurriedly with clear line breaks, before moving to more rapid, textually dense and metrically fluid passages whose meaning was grasped by those in attendance more for its dramatic vocal effect than for its word-for-word meaning. Throughout, Issa punctuated his praise with the line "Which hero am I calling?," sung periodically with such intensity and volume that it verged on yelling, without conceding to cacophony. This, combined with the strong reverb on his microphone, made Issa's vocal performance resoundingly strident and impressive.

## Genre Trouble

To hear (as I do) Issa's vocal tribute as an artful commentary on the social value of existential projects in modern-day Mali is to perceive its "performativity," what Judith Butler describes as a "dramatic and contingent construction of meaning" (1990, 139). In this way, the genre of praise song is "troubled" (in Butler's sense of normative disruption) in the course of a performance cast in a scene of artistic role play. As a dramatic expression of contingent meaning, Issa's praise is inherently ambiguous, addressing the ethical agency and politics of identity of both the praise recipient (Sama Sékou) and the praise singer (Issa). On the one hand, following the public affirmation of Sama Sékou's morality as a blacksmith, the praise song highlights the ethics of Sékou's professional and personal life. The sung and spoken words describe a man who, having built his career over time at home and abroad, has only enhanced his magnanimity and munificence. "If you come across this hero," Issa sings, "you will find him to be kind and generous. A person of renown does not mislead." Strongly rooted in his cultural mores and traditions, Sama Sékou has braved the "wilds" of business and politics, cultivating a successful professional identity without succumbing to self-interest or public parsimony (or so we are told).

On the other hand, Issa's vocal abilities testify to his own ethical orientation as an artist, distinguished, but also troubled by his performative competence in the art of praise song *(fasada)*. In the opening refrain above, Issa affirms his commitment to a morally grounded ethics by refusing culturally shameful behavior: "I will not flee and shame my mother and father. I will not do it." Yet, as a musician who does not belong to an artisanal clan of griots, whom some may dismiss as being socially and professionally "fake" (Hale 1998, 211–12), and who practices the art of praise song, which others have condemned as distasteful and exploitative without traditional substance (Keïta 1995b), Issa's chosen professional identity as an artist can appear unethical, and even, for conservative critics, shameful and immoral. Such existential risk is, as I have argued, an essential principle of ethical agency in Mande social thought, which is exacerbated, in Issa's case, by the moral ambiguity of his social position as an artist. Yet, Issa is well aware of the stakes. When confronted with this criticism he tells me, simply, "I am an artist, not a griot." Then, turning the critique on its head, he adds, "It's good that *jeliya* is a part of *artistiya*. When you perform *jeliya*, it works the voice. It makes me a better musician." *Jeliya*, from this perspective, becomes a generic resource, available to all who wish to explore its aesthetic nuances and complexities. Though, as a resource, it is also a source of potential value, both aesthetic and economic. As Issa puts it, "In Mali, when you sing a man's praises, he is happy. He gives you money. We do this to make a living."[17]

For Issa, there is no contradiction between his cultural values and his professional identity. Though perhaps controversial, Issa's performance of laudatory *jeliya* is certainly real enough to be publicly valued. (At the end of the show that night, Issa received warm compliments and a generous monetary gift from Sama Sékou.) Moreover, Issa's *artistiya* is strongly rooted in its own traditions of (post)colonial popular culture in Bamako: of an eclectic urban ambiance and the (now diminished) legacy of state-sponsored music. His work also follows the well-established practice of modern artists who have built careers through their deft mastery of traditional aesthetics: Afropop legend Salif Keita, who is an accomplished praise singer, being the most esteemed example (Keïta 2009), along with Issa's father, Sorry Bamba, who made his career by integrating Dogon melodies and rhythms into nationalist music of the 1960s (Bamba and Prévost 1996); both of whom are major artistic influences for Issa. To call Issa's artistic work "fake" or mere "flattery" (compare Manthia Diawara 1997) is to miss the point, by disregarding the ethical value of his vocal competence, ignoring the historical depth of his profession, and misinterpreting his artistic aspirations. Issa does not, after all, claim to be a griot, though he is interested in advancing his career, making a name for himself as an artist, and, he hopes, earning a sustainable living in the process.

Cultural purists may take issue with the foregoing statements. In the vast literature on Mande expressive culture (in which I include my own work), *jeliya* holds a sort of sacrosanct position of cultural authenticity, becoming the symbol par excellence of musical "Mande-ness" (see Charry 2000a; Hale 1998). Though I am not, in a Barthesian fashion, declaring here that "the *jeli* is dead"—though the phrase *jeliya tiyenna* ("*Jeliya* is spoiled") is often heard among artists and cultural critics in Mali today—

I am claiming that *jeliya* in the postcolonial era has become more of a generic resource from which artists may draw than an exclusive cultural type that limits expressive culture in terms of clan-based heritage. This qualification of *jeliya* as a generic resource is, however, not absolute. Even if practice reveals a loosening of cultural prohibitions on individual performance, discourse remains more intransigent: One does not become but is born a *jeli*. Further, context remains significant. At a life-cycle ritual, such as a baptism or a wedding, *jeliya* is expected and, generally speaking, highly valued (as we shall observe in chapter 4). Who performs the role of the *jeli* is, as Issa's case suggests, more of an open question in Bamako today.

## "The Artist in Mali . . ."

Yet, such performativity, as Judith Butler reminds us, remains intensely precarious for those on the socioeconomic margins (Butler 2004), representing not just a "dramatic and contingent construction of meaning," but also "a strategy of survival within compulsory systems" (Butler 1990, 139). Thus, I return to Amadou Traoré's grave assessment of the Malian musician ("the most miserable of people"), with which I began this chapter, and the caveat that followed it, "that is, if he stays in Mali." From this perspective, and the postcolonial history that informs it, one might interpret Issa's praise song for Uncle Sékou and the urban art world that is its context somewhat differently than the close reading offered earlier. Through the filter of Traoré's socioprofessional lament, Issa's performance resounds not as an ambient ethics of professional and generic play but as an artful act of "extraversion" (Bayart 2000), an expression of (potential) social mobility articulated through a "global imagination" (Erlmann 1999) in a neoliberal era that has reduced Africa to abjection (Chalfin 2010; Ferguson 2006; Piot 2010). "Which hero am I calling?," Issa asks in full song. "The hero who accomplished great deeds in France." Meanwhile, I continue to record the performance for the group's Radio France Internationale Découverte Award application (unsuccessful, again, that year). After the show, Sama Sékou stuffs a wad of bills into Issa's shirt pocket, about forty dollars. "We do this to make a living," Issa explains. In this abstract space of precarious performance, can one speak of an "Afropolitanism"—of an urban African structure of feeling—when the everyday lives of artists appear as a series of tactics to get by in order to get out? Can one affirm an "ethics"—an existential project of self-making—when the moral foundations of society seem to be in ruins? "People in this country," Nana Soumbounou and Karounga Sacko sing, "are not good."

Such interrogations cannot be readily dismissed, nor should they be. By rhetorically invoking these cautionary criticisms here, my intention is to let them linger; for the Afropolitan ethics I purport to represent in this book must, I believe, incorporate them and the socioeconomic tensions they highlight. Yet, too much emphasis on extraversion and abjection in urban Africa risks obscuring the coherent commitments to local lifeworlds and the innovative and industrious sociomusical practices I have observed among Bamako artists over the past fifteen years. If Issa Bamba's praise song suggests a broadly precarious social position within the Bamako art world, it is also a highly cultivated and historically informed expression of musical subjectivity that couples a laudatory vocal aesthetics with a grounded sense of ethical being-in-the-world—what the Mande call *mɔgɔya,* or personhood. To conclude this chapter, I offer one more portrait of an artist, a sketch of a man whose grounded approach to the musical arts in Mali deepens the sense of artistic personhood I seek to elaborate here, and whose personal and professional history serves as a counterpoint to the "misery" of the Malian artist described by Amadou Traoré. I present the life and work of Dialy Mady Cissoko, a *jeli,* artist, and entrepreneur in postcolonial Mali.

## *Jeli* Trouble

Born in Dakar, Senegal, to a family of griots with roots in The Gambia, Dialy Mady came to Bamako as a child in the early 1970s to live with his father's elder brother and namesake, the late Jelimady Sissoko (Figure 12). The Sissokos (also spelled with an initial C), or "Susos" as they call themselves in The Gambia, are an old clan of Mande griots who trace their family lineage back to the earliest *kora* players, to the Kaabu Empire of the sixteenth through nineteenth centuries (located in and around today's border between Senegal and Guinea Bissau) and to Jali Madi Wuleng (another namesake), purported to be the first *kora* player (Charry 2000a, 118–21). In the early 1960s, Dialy Mady's adoptive father helped to establish the Ensemble Instrumental National du Mali (EIN), a state-sponsored music group that gathered artists from Mali's six administrative regions to represent the diversity of indigenous musical expression in the country and

*Figure 12. Dialy Mady Cissoko. Photograph by the author.*

create an "authentic" national music for the *faso*, the newly independent homeland (see Diawara 2003, 183–84). Such was the importance of the elder Sissoko's role in establishing the EIN that he, along with percussionist Séran Kanouté and fellow *kora* player Sidiki Diabaté, received adjoining plots in Bamako's Ntomikorobougou district, at the foot of Koulouba hill and Mali's presidential palace—a gift of President Modibo Keita himself. To this day, the Sissoko, Diabaté, and Kanouté families live side by side in this neighborhood.[18]

In the early 1960s, the EIN developed a repertoire composed of melodies and rhythms from the Malian countryside, extending into the nation's precolonial past with pieces commemorating the legendary Mande empire builder, Sunjata Keita, and the warrior king of Segu, Da Monzon Jara, among others (see, for example, Ensemble Instrumental du Mali 1977a, 1977b, and 1977c). Further, the ensemble performed pieces with explicitly nationalist themes, articulating a didactic cultural policy characteristic of nation-building efforts elsewhere on the continent (Askew 2002; Ivaska 2011; Moorman 2008; Plageman 2013; Turino 2000; White 2008). Popular pieces included "Maliba" ("Great Mali"), comparing the modern nation-state to the precolonial Mali Empire; "Fasobaara" ("Nation Building"), with a refrain that affirmed, "We are nothing, without work of our homeland"; and "Yan ka di" (Here Is Good), which like Amadou Traoré's contemporaneous piece, "Tunga Man Ni," encouraged newly ordained Malian nationals displaced within the former French Empire to return "home" (Skinner 2012b, 513–14). As Charles Cutter, a contemporary observer of Malian cultural policy in the late 1960s, describes:

> The function of the Ensemble is not only to preserve the past but to make it valid, through selection and adaptation, for the exigencies of the present. Thus, it performs those carefully chosen songs associated with great moments in the history of Mali which will produce dedication and pride. (Cutter 1968, 75)

Such were the sentiments of national pride and patriotism that the younger Dialy Mady heard rehearsed and performed by his immediate and extended family during his youth. Yet, as a child of the 1970s, Dialy Mady also came of age in an era of postnational statism, when, in the wake of the 1968 coup d'état and the rise of a military (then civilian) autocracy, "performing the nation" became increasingly conflated with political flattery (Skinner 2012b, 525), though there was a pre-coup precedent for such performance practice. Writing just prior to the 1968 coup, Cutter observed that the EIN "employs traditional tunes to launch the directives of the party, to sing the praises of party leaders, and to glorify the success of party policy" (1968, 75). Reflecting on this period in an interview with Dialy Mady and his friend and colleague Bruno Maiga, the former director of the Théatre National du Mali (and minister of culture as of 2012–13), the two artists recalled a debate surrounding the so-called *dégriotisation* of the EIN in the late 1970s, a politics spearheaded by Alpha Oumar Konaré, the minister of culture (1978–80, and, later, president, 1992–2002).[19] As cultural minister, Konaré advocated for a return to the nationalist agendas of the 1960s and sought to purge the ensemble's repertoire of political praise directed toward individual statesmen and, as his neologism suggests, "de-griotize" the group. Even as the ruling junta (and many ensemble artists) opposed such cultural political intervention, the terms of this debate would themselves change during the 1980s with the growth of a private sector music economy and the prescribed "voluntary early retirement" of state-sponsored functionaries (as part of broader structural adjustment programs), including many national artists (about which more in chapter 5). This, too, was part of Dialy Mady's upbringing in a community of musicians with professional ties to the postcolonial state.

As a child raised in a family steeped in *jeliya*, Dialy Mady's musical apprenticeship began as a young man in the 1980s. At the time, though, he learned more about making the family instrument, the *kora*, than playing it; his younger brother Ballaké and neighbor Toumani were the heirs apparent to the families' shared performance practice (with a young Ballaké replacing his father as the *kora* accompanist with the EIN in 1982). Indeed, before devoting himself to an artistic career, rooted in the family tradition of *jeliya*, Dialy Mady studied agronomy, perhaps given the uncertain economy of the arts he witnessed in the late 1980s and early '90s. When, in the mid-'90s he returned to the family trade (having observed the rugged and difficult life of the agronomist), Dialy Mady turned to formal study at the Institut National des Arts in Bamako, where, after four years, he received a postsecondary diploma in music education. During his time at INA, Dialy Mady began to perform regularly at a local restaurant and *espace culturel*, the San Toro, owned and operated by Malian social advocate, antiglobalization activist, and future minister of culture

(1997–2000) Aminata Drahmane Traoré. He also took on several *kora* students (among them, me). In 1999, Dialy Mady entered the Malian civil service, taking a position as an elementary music teacher in Bandiagara before moving, in 2000, back to Bamako. A year later, he was hired as the head *kora* instructor at INA and had formed his own band, Dialyco.

Much of my time as a participant observer in Mali in 2006 and 2007 was spent with Dialyco, with whom I frequently performed as an accompanist, backing up, or, at times, replacing Dialy Mady on *kora*. Dialyco specializes in the performance of *jeliya*, featuring music from the *jeli* repertoire and instruments commonly associated with contemporary *jeli* ensembles (*kora, ngoni, bala, dundun,* and *jenbe* along with bass and electric guitars). Unlike other purveyors of the griot arts in Bamako, praise song and speech do not normally figure into their performances. The group's principle vocalist, Nana Soumbounou (who also sang with the Triton Stars at the time, as on the track "Immigration" discussed earlier), is particularly valued for her ability to tone down the aggressive performer–audience intimacy typical of *jeliya* today, exemplified by praise song and reciprocal tipping or gifting of "praise money" (*jelison wari*). At the banquets, luncheons, and parties for which they are hired, Dialyco provides "traditional" background music, with intimate, light-hearted vocals for the elite urbanites to whom they typically cater. At life-cycle ceremonies, for which they are less frequently called upon to perform but where praise song and speech are generally the rule, Dialy Mady invites his sister-in-law, Tata Diabaté (a *jeli* by birth), to join the group, precisely because of her talent as a praise vocalist (*fasadala*). Tips collected at weddings for public praise can be quite lucrative. Bands may be hired without any fee on the basis of potential earnings from tipping alone (compare Askew 2002; White 2008).

I discuss one of Dialyco's infrequent forays into Bamako's economy of praise in chapter 4. Here, I draw attention to the band's name, Dialyco, which elicits a noteworthy double entendre. *Dialyco* refers to both the Bamana phrase *jeli ko,* meaning "*jeli* trouble," and the corporate slogan, "Dialy Co.," referring to bandleader Dialy Mady's commercial interest in promoting the group and their cultural products, including live performances and independent recordings, but also marketable material culture, like traditional music instruments. This multivalent name captures, much like Issa Bamba's urban performance practice, the way *jeliya* has become embedded in the struggles and concerns of professional artists in contemporary Bamako. On the one hand, "*jeli* trouble" describes the ontological problems of the modern *jeli* lifeworld; a fraught, lived space in which griots are routinely accused of social parasitism in the form of opportunistic praise for cash and undignified (or unethical) public behavior. Griots are said to have sold out and, in Dialy Mady's words, "sacrificed their dignity" for profit. This criticism has a particular postcolonial pedigree, echoing the sentiments of the late cultural critic and writer Massa Makan Diabaté, who once observed that "the griots of the suns of independence have traded gold for copper. They are but simple entertainers who display their flowery eloquence in order to gain small change" (Diabaté 1984, 119; as cited in Keïta 1995a, 84).

On the other hand, the title "Dialy Co." indexes an artistic tactic to secure one's livelihood in an art world structured and defined by neoliberal capitalism. In this way, Dialy Mady's musical "company" attempts to change the ethical shape of discourse about *jeliya* from the cultural critique of selling out (as simple entertainers in search of small change) to the entrepreneurial virtue of *mise en valeur*, or profitability through ingenuity and development in the private sector (compare Perullo 2011; Shipley 2013). Dialyco does this by representing *jeliya* for the highly competitive Bamako music economy, offering specially tailored live performances ("authentic" Mande music for urban elites) and unique cultural goods ("traditional" musical instruments for local and global clients) as products in the urban marketplace. Once again, as the ambiguous sociomusical work of Dialyco and Groupe Issa Bamba suggest, *artistiya* and *jeliya* may be distinguished from each other in terms of modernity and tradition—signifying discourses that, as anthropologist Molly Roth explains, add material and cultural value to such "modernities" and "traditions" as commoditized practices (2008)—but they are not mutually exclusive. Today, these two categories of sociomusical identity, the artist and the griot, are increasingly intertwined in the lives of Bamako musicians. Urban artists adapt to the structures and strictures of postcolonial neoliberalism and globalization by discursively drawing clear boundaries between modernity and tradition, only to transgress them through hybrid, performative acts of identification. This is the Afropolitan ethics of *artistiya* and *jeliya* in Bamako today.

## Possibilities and Constraints

I began this chapter by drawing attention to a particular history of this tension—of tradition and modernity, culture and economy, at home and in the world—from the perspective of a Malian artist, Amadou Traoré, and I ended with that of another, Dialy Mady Cissoko. The way Traoré tells his life story, cultivating a common cultural ethos was essential to the work of economic development in post-independence Mali. In this sense, "Tunga Man Ni" (and many other songs like it) represented a call to both collective action and being, of Malians coming together "to build the nation" *(ka faso baara ke)*. To highlight the "misery" of the contemporary artist is, then, to lament the loss of such collectivity. Exile *(tunga)* has become one of the principle themes of this breakdown of economy and society in Mali today. Drawing on this theme, Nana Soumbounou's and Karounga Sacko's lyrics to the song "Immigration" invert Traoré's post-independence call for expatriates to return home with an anthem for those who must leave in order to get by, only to witness the social fabric unravel as they move. "People in this country today are not good," Soumbounou and Sacko warn us.

A history of *artistiya* in postcolonial Mali serves to fill in the gap between these bookended stories of exile, extending over half a century from the professionalization of an *ambiant* urban popular culture to a musical politics of postcolonial nation building; and from the autocratic aesthetics of public praise for the powerful to a privatized, structurally adjusted, and largely informal economy of culture. This history further contextualizes the specific generic and aesthetic choices made by artists in the course of performance, as we observed with Issa Bamba's nightclub panegyric. It also serves to locate an existential project of artistic entrepreneurship within a postcolonial politics and economy of culture, illustrated previously through the life and work of Dialy Mady Cissoko, about whom I say a few more words.

Traditional artisan, modern artist, classroom teacher, private instructor, bandleader, and, since 2007, the president of a nonprofit organization (L'Association d'Orée, which organizes and stages didactic music and theater performances for rural audiences), Dialy Mady's career path offers an important counterpoint to the historical portrait of artistic abjection proffered by Amadou Traoré. Born into a community of nation-building artists and raised in an era of statist retrenchment and global neoliberalism, Dialy Mady understands well the feelings of pride and patriotism that echoed from the voices and strings of his family in the 1960s, just as he understands the historical sources of socioeconomic misery that, for Traoré, defines the profession of the modern-day Malian musician. Yet,

Dialy Mady also understands the importance—indeed, the necessity—of inserting oneself in and making claims on an economy and politics of culture in order to fashion a sustainable livelihood and meaningful lifeworld as an artist. In a time of economic fragmentation (of private interest and informal markets), this means being entrepreneurial; and, in the context of cultural contestation (over claims to "authentic" modes of being), this means cultivating an existential project. In the Bamako art world, both economic and social imperatives are crucial to a performative and professional ethics, through which artists like Dialy Mady negotiate the generic and fiscal troubles of musical subjectivity (of *jeli ko* and Dialy Co.) along the contentious boundaries of tradition and modernity.

Yet, if Dialy Mady's story suggests a hopeful contrast to Traoré's narrative of sociomusical hardship, it is not my intention to substitute the latter sentiment with the former. The ethics of *artistiya*, like any existential project, must encompass both the possibilities that inspire hope and the constraints that require struggle. Further, their stories serve to situate such possibilities and constraints within a shifting politics and economy of culture, which everyday artistic practices and performances must negotiate. Theirs are the stories, in other words, of the artist in postcolonial Mali, of *artistiya* in Bamako, and of a particular socioprofessional mode of Afropolitan ethics. In the next chapter, I deepen this inquiry into the ethics of *artistiya* by listening in to the aesthetics—or what I call, following Henri Lefebvre, the "perceived space"—of instrumental and vocal performance. I am particularly interested in the specifically musical means by which artists assert, defend, and define their social and professional status and identity. Through the refined art of a concert performance and the creative labor of a group rehearsal, I consider the musical strategies and tactics (compare de Certeau 1988, 37) through which moralities and ethics are claimed, negotiated, contested, and, as we shall observe, embodied and engendered.

# Ethics and Aesthetics

*Music, like identity, is both performance and story, describes the social in the individual and the individual in the social, the mind in the body and the body in the mind; identity, like music, is a matter of both ethics and aesthetics.*

Simon Frith, "Music and Identity"

## Warming Up

Applause from the audience fades. The artist bows his head; his eyes closed. He is alone on the stage. His hands return to his instrument and his thumbs strike a pair of strings. A low drone swells in the darkened theater space, an annex to the French Cultural Center along the Boulevard de l'Indépendence in downtown Bamako. The crowd is silent. Raising his head, illuminated by the soft hues of convergent spotlights, the player explores the low register of his *kora*, executing rapid runs as his thumbs strike alternately up and down the instrument's two planes of strings. Without pause, he pulls his thumbs away from the thick-gauged nylon strings and continues his improvisation with staccato strikes from the long and thick nails of his index fingers. Reaching outward, he glances a few of the thin treble strings before descending, in haste, again with his thumbs, to the lower tones and the thick, deep, and resonant tonal center. Then, in a stepwise ascent spanning three octaves, he strikes the instrument's highest pitch. It produces a piercing dissonance. Moving his hands from the strings to the tuning rings on the neck above, he presses downward on the woven leather band at the bottom of the neck, flattening the pitch ever so slightly and tuning the string. Returning his hands to the strings, he plays with the instrument's higher register for a moment, summoning a shrill consonance in a cascade of notes. The final descent is more methodical, slower and purposeful, emphasizing the perfectly executed technique of his intervallic play. His thumbs repeat an ascending cadential phrase, elaborated a third time to bring this prefatory performance to a close.

It is a cool evening in February 2001, and I am recording a rare solo performance with the world-renowned *kora* virtuoso, Toumani Diabaté. We
are midway through the concert and have just heard the opening section of
the maestro's fourth piece. A highly stylized prelude to instrumental performance, this improvisatory and loosely structured sequence serves to
introduce the audience to a fixed set of pitches, in this case a diatonic scale
corresponding to the Western Lydian mode known in the Mande world
as *Sawuta* (likely derived from the Arabic *sawt,* meaning "voice"). *Kora*
players refer to this introductory segment as *jininkali* to signify a musical
"question." Before beginning a new piece, a player "asks" for the instrument's consent to play further by tuning it (Smith 2011). It is also a time
for a player to warm up (*chauffer,* in French; *ka wuli,* or "rise" in Bamana),
literally in terms of running through rhythmic and melodic patterns with
the thumbs and forefingers and figuratively as a time during which a piece
slowly heats up, like a kettle of cool water placed on hot coals. At this time,
a player may even decide which piece to play next. We are one minute into
this interrogative warm-up and the audience listens intently for the opening gestures of the new piece, as yet unidentified. The theater seats about
three hundred people, and it is a full house this evening. All eyes are on
the lone performer who has enchanted us for half an hour with spells cast
of twenty-one resounding strings. Before the show, Toumani explained
to me that he would perform pieces arranged for a new solo recording.
This would be his first single-handed effort since his breakthrough debut,
*Kaira* (1988),[1] an album named for a piece popularized by his father, the
late Sidiki Diabaté, known throughout West Africa as "the king of the
*kora.*" On stage, Toumani looks upon his audience and intones the telltale
patterns of the new piece's bass line, signaling to all present his family's
signature song, a sonic emblem of Diabaté's *fasiya,* his cultural patrimony
(literally, in Bamana, "father's lineage"): *Kayira* (a Mande term meaning
"Peace" and "Joy").

In this chapter, I observe expressions of collective identity and individual subjectivity in musical performance and perception among Bamako
artists and their audiences. I am interested in the ways in which morality and ethics are heard and felt through the "humanly organized sound"
(Blacking 1973) of instrument and voice in the music culture of contemporary Bamako. In a pair of musical settings—a concert hall and rehearsal
space—I listen in to the sonic architecture and effects of staged and informal music making, acoustically manifest, in both cases, in "hot" and "cool"

exchanges of textural density and minimalism and shifts between dynamic intensity and moderation in instrument and voice. This culturally modeled and locally salient sound structure audibly signifies, I argue, a dialectic social structure of collectively oriented morality and individually motivated ethics. There is, in other words, an iconic relationship between an instrumental and vocal aesthetics and ethico-moral personhood (mɔgɔya) in the Bamako art world (see Feld 1984; 1994b; Turino 1999). I approach this sociomusical space as a "perceived space," in which performance of, attention to, and discourse about music produce a common and coherent aesthetic of sound and sentiment. Moving back and forth between modes of perception and personhood, my argument is that acts of making, feeling, listening to, and talking about music constitute a privileged site of aesthetic mediation between the prescribed social positions and intentional self-aspirations of Afropolitans in Bamako today.

In my analysis, perceived space refers to an embodied and expository, intersensorial and interpretive experience of being-in-the-world. Rendered in Lefebvrian terms as "spatial practices," perceived space is the active engagement of culturally honed senses with the disciplinary structures and dispositional practices of human social life, structures and practices that Henri Lefebvre describes as "conceived" and "lived" space respectively (Lefebvre 1991, 38–40). As a phenomenology of perception, perceived space encompasses the visible, tactile, olfactory, aural, and semiotic dimensions of the cultural world in which bodies encounter, engage with, and comprehend their conceived and lived surroundings (see also Merleau-Ponty [1962] 2002). Further, as the active modality of sociospatial experience—Lefebvre's spatial practices—perceived space describes the emergent sights, forms, scents, sounds, and symbols that continually reproduce the human artifice—Lefebvre's social space. With an emphasis on musical expression, the perceived spaces (re)produced among Bamako artists and their audiences find expression in metaphors of bodily form and shared feeling. Through everyday speech about music—whether prescriptive, descriptive, or interpretive—the perceived space of the Bamako art world manifests in a cultivated and coherent aesthetics (Feld 1994a) that renders musical form, vocal expression, compositional texture, and acoustic intensity in terms of bodily function and physical sensation.

I begin with a close listening of Toumani Diabaté's February 2001 performance. As his rendition of the piece "Kayira" unfolds, I describe some general principles in the structuring of Mande music—and kora music in particular—expressed through metaphors of embodied form and agency. Reflecting on "the body" of Diabaté's music making, I consider the extra-musical associations that invest this structure and practice with moral and ethical significance. I then turn to the question of sociomusical experience, observing the way social practices of musical expression, audition, and interpretation produce a perceived space of value-inflected affective states; that is, I reflect on what it feels like to embody a moral and ethical aesthetics in the course of musical performance. My analysis emerges from a band rehearsal in which palpable group tensions, devolving into open argument, threaten not only the practice session but also the popular dance band's professional integrity. An improvised intervention from the group's principal female vocalist exhorts the moral coherence of her fellow members, revealing the iconicity of sounds and sociability that are "good," from which a discussion of the affective dimensions of musical performance practice develops. I conclude by considering the ways in which musical structure, practice, and affect shape—and are shaped by—the multiple moralities and existential projects of artistic personhood (artistiya), contributing to an ethical sense of Afropolitan being-in-the-world among men and women in the Bamako art world. My contention is that an Afropolitan ethics manifests in the playful resonance of a musical aesthetics, grounded in a strong sense of tradition and employed, through instrument and voice, to address a variable matrix of social positions and existential projects in the social space of a modern African city.

## The Morality of "Meeting at the Head"

On stage at the French Cultural Center, Toumani's "Kayira" begins simply, with two thumbs playing on seven strings in the bass register of the kora (Figure 13). On the right hand, a pendular pulse, moving evenly between the third and fifth intervals of an F Lydian mode. There is a metronomic feel to this bass pattern. It runs continuously, like clockwork, throughout the piece. On the left hand, a swinging four-note sequence, beginning a fourth below the tonal center, rising up a fifth, back down, up a third, and back down again. The two thumb patterns individually maintain distinctive rhythms, individual "musical feet" (folisenw) that, together, produce a complementary, polyrhythmic whole. This whole forms a continuous underlying pattern, or ostinato, that serves as a temporal and tonal reference

*Figure 13. Toumani Diabaté. Copyright Hannah Koenker, 2000.*

for the piece's subsequent musical (melodic, harmonic, and rhythmic) elaboration.[2] In Mande musical thought, this is the *kunbɛn* of a piece, meaning, literally, a "meeting" *(bɛn)* at the "head" *(kun)*. *Kunbɛn* is a term rich in sociomusical significance (see Charry 2000a, 313–28). In warfare, it signifies the gathering of forces on the battlefield prior to an assault.[3] In music, it refers to both a periodic accompaniment (as with the poly-rhythmic ostinato described above) and a particular tuning, used to de-scribe the scale or mode in which a given piece is played (in this case, the *kunbɛn* is F Lydian, or *Sawuta*). On the battlefield, it is soldiers and their arms that are assembled in anticipation of attack; in musical performance, it is the convergence of rhythms and tones that fortifies a piece.

This patterned sonic fortification is the musical embodiment of mo-rality in Mande aesthetics. The *kun* (head) is a focal point and a point of orientation, the seat of authority and reason. It is the leader who extols his soldiers to commit their lives to a common cause, and it is the principle of order and concordance that makes that cause (whether it be a battle or a performance) seem right. There is historical depth to this sense of the common good. The head is the locus of tradition and heritage, the em-bodiment of what the Mande call *fasiya*, the lineage of one's father, who is also the head of one's family. The conjoined term *bɛn* (meeting) adds senses of intimacy and harmony to the concordant reason of the *kun*. *Bɛn* is the active expression of co-presence, of coming together in the spirit of conviviality that the Mande call *badenya*. As a sign of togetherness, *bɛn* signifies comfort and familiarity. It is the feeling of returning home, being among one's kith and kin, hearing the songs that everyone knows, and singing along. In tandem, and in the context of musical performance, *kunbɛn* evokes the convergent and consonant sounds of familiar and tra-ditional rhythmic and melodic patterns; it is the "musical morality" of being in sync and in tune, of periodicity and consonance (see Skinner 2008, 294).

As Toumani introduces the polyrhythmic and contrapuntal *kunbɛn* of "Kayira," anticipation turns to attention among the audience. This is an assembly of intimates, a group of friends, family, and fans gathered in Diabaté's hometown at one of Bamako's premier music venues. Having witnessed Toumani's career develop over the years, we feel a sense of deep familiarity with this piece and Toumani's performance of it. At the time of the concert, Diabaté had recently released two versions of "Kayira," draw-ing attention to the varied sociomusical roots and routes that inform his ongoing interpretation of the piece, in and out of the Black Atlantic (Gilroy 1993). One of them, called "Atlanta Kaira," pairs Toumani Diabaté with blues master Taj Mahal, exploring Mande resonances in African American blues (Diabaté and Mahal 1999). The other, "Kita Kaira," performed with Toumani's longtime neighbor and fellow *kora* virtuoso, Ballaké Sissoko (Diabaté and Sissoko 1998), references a place where the concept of *kayira*—social and musical—took on new significance: Kita. This railway town, 110 miles west of Bamako, is where Ballaké's musical mentor and Toumani's father, Sidiki Diabaté, sojourned after departing his native Gambia in the mid-1940s (Durán 1998); it is also where the elder Diabaté brought his *kora*, an instrument with origins along the Senegambian coast, and helped establish the twenty-one-string harp in the Mande heartland of south-central Mali.[4] In mid-century Kita, Sidiki Diabaté helped found a popular youth association known as the *Kayiratɔn*, a club *(tɔn)* dedicated to *kayira* (joy and peace). To understand the embedded morality and emergent ethics of Toumani Diabaté's performance of "Kayira" a half-century later, it is worth reflecting on this facet of his *fasiya*, or paternal heritage.

Formed in the waning years of World War II, the Kayiratɔn captured the spirit of a particular time and place. Those who experienced the Kayiratɔn's brief florescence remember clearly the joie de vivre it inspired through musical performance. Many spoke of the group's ability to bring community members together for collective work and public celebration. One participant described the Kayiratɔn as nothing short of a cultural revolution! The group's music—performed at weddings, baptisms, in the fields, and at informal gatherings—came to prominence as reforms in the French Empire offered new civic freedoms to African communities and gave rise to new language of political claims making (see Cooper 1996). As a local forum for social criticism, the Kayiratɔn called into question the exigencies of Mande traditional society, especially forced marriage, and drew attention to the excesses of French colonial rule, such as forced labor.[5] Thus, in many versions of the song "Kayira," the lyric, "Rooster, don't cry / The early morning sunrise is hard on me," referred to the onerous reality of *forosɛ baara* (forced labor), involving construction and maintenance work to serve the French colonial economy. Such labor, performed from sun-up to sundown, was popularly known as *diyagoyabaara*, or "whether-you-like-it-or-not-work." Another interpretation of this line echoed the self-determined conjugal relationships promoted by Kayiratɔn members.

Waking up at dawn meant, in this case, furtively and reluctantly leaving one's lover after an evening's tryst.[6]

A musical modernist of his time, Sidiki Diabaté came of age within and helped define this postwar zeitgeist of peaceful celebration, political protest, and cultural revolution (*kayira*). Still, most Malians today remember Sidiki Diabaté, whose death in 1996 marked a moment of national mourning, as a great traditionalist. "One of the last authentic griots," Bakary Soumano, the former *chef de griots* in Bamako (who passed away in 2004), told me during my first stay with the Diabaté family in 1998.[7] Diabaté helped to establish Mali's Ensemble Instrumental National in the early 1960s, arranging pieces from the *jeli* repertoire that praised and celebrated his adopted nation-state (as described in chapter 2). Sidiki is also remembered as a masterful virtuoso, a reputation he established as a member of the Kayiraton in Kita, where he and fellow *kora* player Batourou Sékou Kouyaté, a lifelong friend and rival *kora* player, dazzled local audiences with their rapid and intricate improvisations.[8] (I discuss the importance of such musical "rivalry" to Mande aesthetics later in the chapter.) This instrumental virtuosity can be heard on the Diabaté's and Kouyaté's recording of "Kayra" on an album titled *Cordes Anciennes* (French, *Ancient Strings*) (Diabaté et al. 1970). It was in honor of and response to this classic recording, "the first album ever released of instrumental kora music" (Durán 1998), that Toumani Diabaté and Ballaké Sissoko (whose friendship and musical rivalry parallels that of their elders in many ways) recorded *New Ancient Strings,* featuring the track "Kita Kaira," three decades later.

When Toumani is referred to, as he often is in the company of elders, as *Sidikiden,* or "son of Sidiki," it is to invoke this heritage of musical tradition, civic service, and instrumental virtuosity. In this sense, Toumani is less an individual, an autonomous subject possessed of a distinct identity, than he is a member of a notable clan of griots: the Diabaté family, his *jamu,* the surname of a lineage of *kora* players going back (as the family claims) to the first *kora* players in the late eighteenth century (Charry 2000a, 115–21). When Toumani performs or records the piece "Kayira," he represents a tune for which his family is well known, re-sounding an oeuvre established by his father in Kita in the late 1940s. For those who know this history, much of it part of the collective memory of contemporary Malians, all one needs to hear is the simple, contrapuntal, and polyrhythmic bass line—the *kunben* of "Kayira"—to perceive this patrimony.

This is the sonic expression of a social position; the musical embodiment of a mode of being; the "meeting at the head" of a cultural morality. "A good musical arrangement begins with the head," Toumani once told me. "It is from the head that all else follows, melody, harmony, improvisation."

When playing the *kora*, musical exposition requires a strong foundation, or, in Mande terms, "a good head." Yet, as Toumani reminded me, the head on one's shoulders is not divorced from the appendages below; it stimulates and orients them. Thus, when Toumani intones a classic *kunbɛn*, like the rocking rhythm of "Kayira," one hears the stimulus of a deep sense of tradition and, with the particular history of this piece in mind, an orientation toward musical virtuosity and innovation coupled with social change and renewal. As ethnomusicologist Lucy Durán writes in the liner notes to Diabaté's and Sissoko's *New Ancient Strings*:

> Their music is rooted in the timeless classical tradition of Mali that was once, during the pre-colonial era, played at the courts of kings and emperors; but it is reworked to the contemporary styles that are currently in favour in Bamako—the hot-house of many of West Africa's finest musicians. (1998)

A similar line could be written of Sidiki Diabaté's reworking of tradition within the Kayiraton in 1940s Kita. Social and musical innovation is, in this sense, a family affair. Yet, there is much in Toumani's performance that stresses the distinctiveness of his music and his individuality as a performer. To address these modes of distinction, I turn from the moral wellsprings of the form of his instrumental music to its ethical manifestation in performance, actively embodied in the voice, feet, and hands.

## The Ethics of Embodied Performance

Toumani begins with the unadorned *kunbɛn* of "Kayira," lingering on the swinging bass line to let it sink in. Then, on top of this pattern, we hear a lilting antiphonal melody, rising and falling through two pairs of calls and responses, followed by a cadential phrase that lands on the tonal center in the upper register. This he plays twice, drawing attention to the polyphony created by the bass ostinato, played with the thumbs, and the melodic counterpoint, played with the forefingers. In quiet dialogue with the low *kunbɛn*, Toumani "sings" with his *kora* through these paired treble phrases.

This is what Mande musicians call *fɔlikan,* the voice *(kan)* of musical performance *(fɔli);* in this case, an instrumental melody that resembles vocal
song *(dɔnkili).* The idea of voicing nonvocal music is an important feature
of instrumental aesthetics in the Mande world. To play an instrument,
such as the *kora,* is "to speak it" *(k'a fɔ),* as in the phrase *ka kora fɔ* ("to
play/speak the *kora*"). One plays an instrument as one speaks a language.
As an aesthetic concept, the word *fɔli* encodes this close relationship between music and language. *Fɔli* literally signifies "the act of speaking," with
the verbal suffix *-li* ("the act of") modifying the verb *ka fɔ* ("to speak").
In language, *fɔli* bears the specific meaning of "heightened speech" in the
form of a public greeting or declamation. As a general term for "music," *fɔli*
describes the "musical speech" of instrumental performance (see Maxwell
2008, 29).

The word *kan* refers to the throat and the voice, from which speech
and song resound. It also means, more abstractly, "language," of which
speech and song are composed. The voice of the *kora* lies in its twenty-
one strings, from which its particular language resounds through the
patterned movements of thumbs and forefingers. In this way, the *kora*
publicly speaks through its corded voice to create a singing melody—an
instrumental "song" that is, however, distinct from vocal song, or *dɔnkili*
(figuratively "the essence of knowledge and the dance," a musical concept
I elaborate later). The musical voice is active and expressive, with the term
*fɔlikan* also defined as a musical transmission *(fɔlici)* to communicate
meaning *(kɔrɔfɔ)* (Konè 1995). Some of this meaning is generic. On stage,
as Toumani speaks with his *kora,* one hears his performance of "Kayira"
within the broader musical language of *jeliya.* Some of this meaning is
stylistic. The melodies Toumani pairs with the piece's *kunbɛn* may reference phrases from other players and musical traditions, or develop his
own compositions of melodic themes. As a generic and stylistic gestalt of
musical communication, *fɔlikan* remains susceptible to multiple variations
and creative interpretations, formally modeled as improvisation, similar to
the elaboration of melodic themes in jazz.

At the concert, we have settled into Toumani's delicate polyphonic play
when the piece suddenly "heats up" *(bɛ kalanya)* in a flurry of rapid and
punctuated off-beat phrasing, short staccato phrases that fill the gaps of
the pendular rhythm established by the right thumb, periodically displac-
ing or suspending the regular pulse by half a beat. Heard as a quickening
of musical time, by doubling the tempo, and a thickening of musical tex-

ture, through bursts of noncoincident accents, off-beat phrasing represents a key feature of what the late ethnomusicologist Richard Waterman calls "hot music" in Africa and its diasporas (1948, 25) in which "melodic tones, and particularly accented ones, occur between the sounded or implied beats of the measure with great frequency" ([1952] 1973, 88). In Bamako, when "music is hot" (fɔli ka kalan), it resounds a sonic ideal of textural density—an abundance of notes played in a rich polyphony— and rhythmic syncopation—a variously accented and accelerating metrical pulse—that engenders movement. This is, as Waterman says, "music for the dance" (87). As such, hot sounds in Mande music draw attention to the rhythm, or, in Mande terms, fɔlisenw—literally, "musical feet"—of performance. Like water brought to a boil in a kettle, hot music makes bodies "rise up" and move; it brings you to your musical feet. (The Bamana verb wuli can refer variously to the boiling of water, the rising of bodies, and the warming up of musical performance, among other related meanings; see Bailleul 2000 and Konè 1995.) Constrained to the seats of the theater space, the audience at Toumani's performance is no less mobile. Feet tap, fingers snap, torsos sway, and heads bob. At a certain point, halfway through the piece, the heat of the musical moment raises our hands and voices in claps and cheers, adding the public's own percussive and dynamic heat to the already hot performance.

It is these three embodied musical elements—the "head" of the bass ostinato, the "voice" of the contrapuntal melody, and the "feet" of the hot rhythms—that Toumani uses, alternately and in tandem, to structure the first two-thirds of his performance of "Kayira." In the final third, roughly six minutes into the piece, one final corporeal feature comes forward in the mix: the "running by hand" (bolomanboli) of improvised solos up and down the two planes of strings on the kora. Temporally, these ascending and (most frequently) descending melodic runs interrupt the metrical flow of a piece, creating new (poly)rhythmic currents in concert with the established meter or, at times, abandoning the meter altogether as notes swell and swirl in bursts of virtuosity (the image, here, is of a kettle of water boiling over). Melodically, bolomanboli can act as a vehicle for composition, allowing the performer to adapt and embellish the principal melody or "musical voice" of a piece (fɔlikan) to create an endless variety of new melodic phrases. Here, as well, the player may interpolate melodies from other pieces into his performance. As a lead-in to a passage of improvisation in the final minutes of Toumani's "Kayira," we hear one of his favorite

musical citations, usually employed as an introduction to one of his many
versions of the piece "Jarabi" ("Beloved"): Ennio Morricone's ricocheting
signature phrase from the film *The Good, The Bad, and The Ugly.*

In *kora* performance, running hands, musical feet, and instrumental
voices produce an ethical aesthetics of sociomusical distinction. Such
an ethics may be contrasted with what I described as the moral art of the
*kunbɛn.* This patterned musical foundation—or meeting at the head—
resounds a sense of collectivity, of a cultural heritage passed on from one
generation to another, a patrimony nominally represented by one's surname, or *jamu.* To perform on top of this foundation, to mobilize the
body beneath the head of a musical arrangement is to claim an identity
beyond—though not divorced from—the moral structures of art and society. The artist who improvises a running solo, incites the dance with a
syncopated rhythm, and makes his instrument sing with a novel melody
asserts his dynamic and creative agency as a performer. He claims his individuality, a distinctive subjectivity symbolized by his first name, or *tɔgɔ,*
and the status and identity of being a *tɔgɔtigi*: the achieved state of making a name for oneself, of being an owner *(tigi)* of one's name *(tɔgɔ)*; as
when Diabaté, son of Sidiki, becomes Toumani. There is an existential risk
in such acts of musical distinction and innovation. It involves strategic—
though not permanent—breaks with patterns of patrimonial performance,
with structures of social and musical morality. A spirit of competition mo-
tivates such risk, a sense of deep cultural rivalry the Mande call *fadenya.*

*Fadenya,* or "father-child-ness," refers to domestic tensions between
children of the same father but different mothers in polygamous families
and, most literally, to an assumed rivalry between father and son. More
generally it is a sign of social friction, conflict, nonconformity, and creativity in Mande society (see Bird and Kendall 1980; Jansen and Zobel
1995; Keïta 1995a). As such, *fadenya* represents a highly ambivalent mode
of being, with both positive and negative connotations (Keïta 1990;
Skinner 2010, 24). Positive *fadenya* describes forms of competition that inspire innovation. It can be heard in the intergenerational play of Toumani
Diabaté's and Ballaké Sissoko's *New Ancient Strings,* reworking the "timeless
classical tradition" of their elders to the "contemporary styles" of Bamako's
music culture that they themselves help produce. This positive sense of
*fadenya* is central to the way Diabaté and Sissoko characterize their music
as new, contemporary, innovative, even revolutionary. Positive *fadenya*
also operates between Diabaté and Sissoko. Regarded by many as the best

*kora* players of their generation, these two musical "brothers" (unrelated, though lifelong neighbors) have cultivated a friendly, fraternal competition in crafting the respective careers, much as their elders Sidiki Diabaté and Batourou Sékou Kouyaté did a generation prior.

Yet, in order to retain a sense of moral legitimacy, the innovatory practice of positive *fadenya* must be balanced with an acknowledged respect for one's cultural patrimony, or *fasiya*. Thus, Diabaté's and Sissoko's strings are both new and ancient. Writing on the way the person *(mɔgɔ)* in Mande society conceives of this dialectic of heritage and novelty, Chérif Keïta writes:

> Progress should be conceived not as an evasive move ahead [*une fuite en avant*] but, rather, as a realization [*prise de conscience*] that remains acutely aware of its sources and origins. . . . The lesson that [one] may draw is clearly a message of both rootedness in culture and of a willingness to be open to and advance toward new existential horizons. (1995a, 34)

Such acts of self-conscious rooting and routing strongly characterize Toumani Diabaté's existential project of "progressive" music making, an ethico-moral performance practice audibly embodied—through the musical head, voice, feet, and hands of the *kora*—in his interpretation of "Kayira" at the French Cultural Center in February 2001. Toumani's art is the sonic embodiment of positive *fadenya*, of a socially positioned existential project, of an ethical aesthetics "acutely aware of its sources and origins."

The negative definition of *fadenya* refers to the dissociative nature of competition and conflict that threatens to break down sociability and civility. Toumani's musical oeuvre actively and consistently resists such enmity. A pioneer in the genre of world music, his career has been broadly defined by intergenerational, intercultural, and interethnic dialogue. There is no question of this modern griot's strong respect for tradition and the rooted authenticity of his contemporary performance practice. Yet, musical practice does not always rest on such solid moral ground. As I described in chapter 1, Bamako's urban culture encodes an ethos of profound socioeconomic precarity and provisionality. Further, this unsettled and risky lifeworld is manifest, as discussed in chapter 2, in the shifting and, at times, contentious, subjectivity of the professional artist in Mali's postcolonial music culture. This art world is rife with competition (*fadenya*), personal and professional; positive and, as we shall observe, negative. In the following story, I move from a musical context of sympathetic intimacy to one of open animosity, from a convivial concert hall to a hostile rehearsal studio. This shifts my discussion of perceived space in the Bamako art world from the embodiment of sonic structure and practice to the visceral effects of musical performance on uncertain moral terrain. In an outburst of negative *fadenya*, we observe the ethical urgency to rectify immoral behavior, the risks involved in such acts of social redress, and the specifically musical potential to intervene in social crisis.

## "Quiet Your Strings, I'm Going to Sing a Little"

Nana Soumbounou is the lead female singer of an aspiring Bamako dance band, the Triton Stars (whose song "Immigration" we considered in the previous chapter). This band, like many contemporary pop groups in Bamako, calls itself an "orchestra" (French, *orchestre*), composed of Western instrumentation (electric guitar, bass, drum kit, electric keyboards, and occasionally horns and violin), a few choice traditional elements (in their case, an *ngoni* lute and a *jenbe* hand drum), and lead and choral vocals. Their musical arrangements—which favor Afro-Cuban, reggae, and Afropop renditions of local musical themes and styles, such as *jeliya*—are strongly reminiscent of the modern state-sponsored orchestras of the late 1960s and '70s (see Counsel 2006; Skinner 2012b). This stylistic resonance with the past reflects the influence of their artistic director, Aliou Traoré, a former member of the Orchestre National du Mali and music instructor at the Institut National des Arts, Mali's postsecondary arts academy of which all the band members are recent graduates.

I had been following Triton Stars' rehearsals, concerts, and studio sessions for several weeks when mounting conflicts within the group forced a month-long hiatus. Their work, in anticipation of a new record release, was put on indefinite hold. Prospects for the recording did not look good. In addition to the endemic problem of music piracy, with little promise for returns on record sales (see chapter 5), internal arguments over creative rights and remuneration (for concert performances, rehearsal time, studio work, and eventual royalty allocation) festered among the band members and their management. When, after nearly four weeks, the band regrouped, having replaced a third of their members with new personnel, rehearsals resumed but tensions remained high. It was during their second full rehearsal following the hiatus that I witnessed firsthand the troubles that were afflicting this urban orchestra—a manifestation of personal and professional *fadenya*, in its negative guise, causing friction within their group and threatening its permanent breakup.

A few days prior to the rehearsal, I spoke with the band's former bass player, Fassiriman Dembelé. He told me that the group fell apart because of unreasonable expectations from the band's management. The artists were asked to sign a contract stating that they would not accept recording and tour contracts from other groups. Some signed. Others did not. Fassiriman, who rehearsed and performed with at least two other groups on a regular basis and did not sign, scoffed at the management's arrogance. "They're not serious!," he exclaimed, adding that he had still not been paid for arrangement work at the last recording session. For him, the band was one gig among many, and certainly not worth an absolute commitment. For Nana, who did sign the contract, things were different. She spoke of her band mates as brothers and sisters, her *balimamɔgɔw*, implying bonds of affinity that go beyond the contractual disputes that Fassiriman decried. Racine Dia, the band's principal patron, gave Nana her first break while she was a student at INA, asking her to join his artistic troupe on a tour to northern Europe. Nana was also romantically involved with Karounga, the band's talented lead male vocalist (they are now married). From her point of view, the band was not just another gig; it was family.

As night descended on the band practice, Aliou, the artistic director, brought the rehearsal to an abrupt halt. He was irate. "It's awful! It's really awful!," he screamed. The source of his scorn was his son, Adama, who had recently moved from violin to electric bass following Abdoulaye's departure. A fine violinist, Adama was, at best, a satisfactory bassist, playing the right notes but hesitantly, often riding slightly behind the beat as he struggled to learn his part. Aliou's temper was tremendous. For several minutes, he lambasted his son's performance. The director's commitment to the group was genuine, but so were his frustrations. Stories of his work with the band almost always began with his studies in Cuba in the early 1960s and the great promise and bitter failure of his stint with the national orchestra in the 1970s (see Skinner 2012b). In his son and in the present group, he clearly saw a chance at redemption, to secure his deserved reputation as one of Mali's pioneering artists. But, he was a tough artistic director and a demanding father. At a time when the band was attempting to rebuild and move forward, this outburst of pent-up frustration—a literal incarnation of the paternal rivalry that is *fadenya*—was clearly frustrating. The group erupted into argument. Speaking into her microphone, Nana encouraged the musicians to start again, *"Ne ko, anw ka taa ka morceau wɛrɛ ta!"* ("Come on, let's do another song!"). Following her lead, the keyboardist called out *"Anw bɛ 'Kɛmɛ Buruma' ta!"* ("Let's do 'Kɛmɛ Buruma'!"), a standard griot praise song. What came next was a remarkable example of ethical *artistiya* (Figure 14).

The song began slowly, tentatively. At first, only the keyboardist and Nana performed, with others noodling on their instruments or arguing among themselves as Aliou continued to hurl criticisms. Then, the group's new guitarist joined in. He searched for the right notes with assistance from the keyboardist, who played and sung the melody to him, until he found the piece's accompaniment pattern: an arching phrase, up and down a minor third, followed by an ascending phrase, leaping to the seventh before falling once more on the fifth. Within a few measures, the band had fallen into a steady groove, with the music loud enough to quiet truculent voices. At this point, Nana, who had been seated, stood up to "call the horses" *(ka sow wele)*. This loud and melismatic vocalization, intended to draw attention to her and what she was about to say in her Maninka-inflected song,[9] descended melodically and dynamically as she called on the group to "quiet their strings," or lower their volume.

| | |
|---|---|
| *Aaaaaaaaa! iiii-eeee!* | [Nana "calls the horses"] |
| *Alu jurulu lasumaya sa!* | Quiet your strings [the music]! |
| *Ko ne bɛ dɔɔnin fɔ to le,* | I'm going to speak a little, |
| *balima ɲumanw ye!* | of good family relations! |
| *Ko ne bɛ dɔɔnin fɔ to le,* | I'm going to speak a little, |
| *sinji ɲumanw ye!* | of good personal relations! |
| *Juruw bɛnnen.* | Strings are together [in the groove]. |
| *Bolow bɛnnen.* | Hands are in the groove. |
| *Adamadenw jama bɛnnen* | Solidarity among all people |
| *ka di nin bɛɛ ye!* | is better than all of this! |
| *Triton Stari jama sigilen bɛ yan!* | Triton Stars members are gathered here! |
| | |
| *Ala ni balimaya ani sinjiya,* | God and fellowship and empathy, |
| *olu bɛ anw se yan!* | they are among us! |

*Figure 14. Nana Soumbounou. Photograph by the author.*

With "strings quieted," Nana's voice paused before rising in a dramatic crescendo on the line "I'm going to speak a little," before quieting again, with graceful glissando, through the phrase, "good family relations"— rising and falling vocal dynamics that she repeated in the next two lines, pausing before and after them to let the meaning of the words sink in. With an intake of breath, Nana's voice gained strength and volume as she remarked, enunciating her words carefully, on the musical groove established by strings and hands, and then added, with a stroke of proverbial wisdom that the solidarity among group members—all human beings, *adamadenw*, or children of the biblical Adam—"is better than all of this." Invoking the moral pillars of God (Ala), fellowship *(balimaya)*, and empathy *(sinjiya)*, she addressed her band mates in a rapid, improvised, and nonmetrical recitation that hovered between song and speech.[10] This gave her words a stylistic sense of urgency and emotional weight as she vocally drew attention to the familial nature of the group.

| | |
|---|---|
| *[Ne] ko, dundun bɛnnen!* | [I] said, the dundun [music] is in the groove! |
| *Baara fɛn o fɛn de,* | Regardless of the work we do, |
| *adamdenya ka di nin bɛɛ ye!* | our humanity is better than all of this! |
| *Triton Stari jama nana yan* | Triton Stars members have come here |
| *k'alu fɔ, aw ni balimaya!* | to tell you of good fellowship! |
| *Alu nana yan!* | You have come here! |
| *Alu ko sinjiya!* | You speak of empathy! |
| *Balima bɛnbalilu,* | Family members who do not get along, |
| *aw bɛ ta anw na?* | do you see us? |
| *Aw nana jigi de la,* | You have come because of hope, |
| *ani balimaya.* | and fellowship. |

Pausing between lyrical segments to let her accompanists "speak," or respond instrumentally, Nana rhythmically established a give-and-take of instrument and voice to highlight the group's musical groove and convivial ethos. The band's accompaniment served as the sonic foundation on which Nana's lyrical invocation of the themes of empathy and fellowship, that moral space of humanity that is "better than all of this," could build and accrue sociomusical meaning. Moreover, the accompaniment seemed to sonically embody such ideals, through tempered patterns of interlocking rhythms and polyphony. By this time, Aliou, the once-truculent band director, was seated, frowning, but listening.

| | |
|---|---|
| *N'a diyara mɔgɔ min ye,* | If it does a person good, |
| *balimaya ka di!* | fellowship is good! |
| *N'a goyara mɔgɔ min ye,* | If it offends a person, |
| *Balimaya ka di!* | fellowship is good! |
| *Balimajugu bɛ cogo mina.* | This is how family discord happens. |
| *ni balimayakun bɛ cɛn,* | If there is no camaraderie, |
| *balimayakun tɛ kɛ!* | then fellowship is ruined! |
| *Triton Stari jamalu,* | Triton Stars members |
| *alu nana le, ɛ Ala!* | you have come, oh God! |

As tempers calmed, Nana continued her vocal plea for moral community and group reconciliation, moving in a gradual descent through swells and drops in pitch and volume to the phrase "oh God," sung softly with a deep, throaty vibrato. Then, bringing her musical oratory to a close, Nana spoke and sang directly to the conflict confronting the group that night, vocally alternating, as before, between rapid lyricism and crescendo and subdued spoken and sung phrases and diminuendo. Her words acknowledged the family discord between Aliou and Adama that was "tossed" among the group, exacerbating tensions within the band management and artists. Returning to the ideal of conviviality, she concluded her commentary on the measured and melodic phrase, "If you have nothing, and you come to the Triton Stars, you will be good."

| | |
|---|---|
| *Balimayajugu tunbɛ seri* | Family discord was tossed |
| *anw ka jama de la yan!* | here among this group! |
| *Ni balimaya tunkɛra* | If fellowship took on |
| *balimajugu ɲe na,* | the manner of discord, |
| *balimaya tuntɛ kɛ!* | fellowship would not come about! |
| *Triton Stari jama nana* | Triton Stars members have come |
| *k'alu ka bɛn de.* | to bring you together. |
| *Ni fen tɛ mɔgɔ min fɛ,* | If [you] have nothing, |
| *n'alu nana Triton Stari la,* | and you come to the Triton Stars |
| *alu bɛ diya!* | you will be good! |

While addressed to her bandmates, Nana's convivial message, articulated on top of a grooving musical accompaniment (to which Adama, Aliou's son, now contributed intently on bass), seemed to speak (and sing) of a broader purpose: that those who encounter this group of musicians will "come together" and "be good"; that the discord that threatened conviviality at their rehearsal went beyond that space; that artists have an important role to play in confronting such discord in society: to reinforce social solidarity, bring people together, and promote social welfare. To socially achieve such goals requires a self-conscious sensitivity to the expectations and exigencies of moral community, especially when that community falters. To musically address them demands an attuned sense of sonic form, style, and sentiment. To understand this sociomusical habitus we must reflect further on the phenomenology of musical perception in the expressive culture of Bamako artists. In Toumani Diabaté's concert performance, we observed the gradual and methodical "heating up" of perceived space, elaborated through an embodied aesthetics of instrumental expression. What Nana's vocal intervention demonstrates is a complementary and no less ethical "aesthetic of the cool" in Bamako popular music, what Robert Farris Thompson (2011) describes, more broadly, as the refined art of moral accomplishment in Afro-diasporic societies.

## An Aesthetic of the Cool

There has been a great deal of recent scholarship describing the embodied reception of sound and its impact on social space and cultural practice (see, for example, Feld 2012; Gray 2013; Novak 2013; and Sakakeeny 2013; for a recent review, see Samuels et al. 2010). Inherent to much of this work is the way auditory perception invokes "a complex of culturally and historically honed sensory modalities" (Hirschkind 2001, 638; see also Porcello et al. 2010). As Steven Connor explains, "To understand the working of any of the senses, it is necessary to remain aware of the fertility of the relations between them" (2004, 154). In Bamako, musical perception is intersensorial, articulating the full palette of the senses in practices of listening. Intersensoriality produces particular aesthetic experiences through the psychosocial ebb and flow of the senses, expressed through interpretive "patterns of attending, disattending, foregrounding, or backgrounding" (Feld 1994a, 83). As Feld explains:

Lived experience involves constant shifts in sensory figures and grounds, constant potentials for multi- or cross-sensory interactions of correspondences. Figure-ground interplays, in which one sense surfaces in the midst of another that recedes, in which positions of dominance and subordination switch or commingle, blur into synesthesia. (1996a, 93)

In this way, patterns of perception may exhibit sociocultural specificity, articulating a locally distinct and variegated perceived space, as certain senses are privileged (foregrounded, attended to) over others. In this penultimate section, my interest is in the multisensory experience of musical sound in Bamako popular culture.

In Bamako, when sensitive listeners cite the well-known Mande proverb, "It is the meaning, not the drumming or singing, that is good" ("*dundun ma ɲi, dɔnkili ma ɲi, a kɔrɔ de ka ɲi*"), they suggest that it is not the music itself that carries meaning, but what lies beneath musical sound (with the word *kɔrɔ* literally meaning "underneath"). Such sound is, as John Blacking famously noted, "humanly organized" (1973). Grounded in human social action, musical meaning can be referential, communicating as language (in the metaphoric sense of *fɔlikan* or literally through heightened speech and song), and affective, stimulating the body through prosody, dynamics, rhythm, texture, tempo, and timbre. In the aesthetics of Mande music, in other words, there is meaning in the symbolic and the sensual (compare Feld 1982). Previously I discussed the communicative organization and transmission of such meaning through metaphors of the body, giving formal and expressive shape to a moral and ethical aesthetics. Here, I shift my analysis from these meaningful embodiments of form and practice to the equally significant expressions of sensation and sentiment as observed earlier in Nana's dramatic vocal performance and a broader popular discourse about music. Specifically, I am interested in the interplay between hearing and feeling "hot" and "cool" sounds in Bamako popular music, audible and interpretive manifestations of an intersensorial perceived space that incorporates the gestural, sartorial, and aromatic arts as well.

For performers and audiences of popular music in Bamako, musical sound is most often related to the sense of touch and the sensation of temperature. Thus, good music "touches" a person's soul (*a bɛ se mɔgɔ niyɔrɔ ma)* and "deeply penetrates" peoples' bodies *(a bɛ don mɔgɔw la kojugu).* When strings are in tune, they meet each other *(juruw bɛnnen don).* The same expression may also refer to musicians who are "in the groove" *(fɔlifɔlaw bɛnnen don).* A good musical arrangement is well seated *(fɔli sigilen don)* and grooves when its disparate parts come together *(a bɛnnen don).* Further, a groove that is loud, fast paced, intense, and exciting is "on fire" *(fɔli ɲagalen don)* and must be balanced with complementary sections that are cool, quiet, slowed-down, and subdued *(fɔli sumalen don).* As such, a theory of aesthetic meaning in Bamako's music culture would necessarily emphasize these expressions of embodiment and feeling, articulating between hot (loud, fast, intense) and cool (quiet, slow, subdued) sounds and tempos whose melodies and rhythms come together in a well-seated arrangement to produce music that is both touching and penetrating.

When a performer wants to begin or return to a sung refrain or verse, or interject an improvised praise narrative into an extended jam, she may call on the band to cool down *(a'ye lasuma)* by playing slower and more quietly, as Nana did at the band rehearsal. Instrumental coolness is the sonic basis of verbal expression in Bamako popular music—and Mande music more generally—because the singing and speaking voice is meant to be heard and interpreted without being lost or misunderstood in the cacophony of ambient noise (see Durán 1995a, 202). From an instrumental space of relative calm, "song" *(dɔnkili)* is heard along a continuum of chorus—"a fixed melody and text which recurs at different intervals of a performance," often performed as a refrain with standardized thematic content—and recitation—defined in Mande verbal art as an "improvised text, without any metrical scheme, either spoken, or recited to a syllabically set musical line" and typically performed solo with an emphasis on social commentary, evaluation, and praise (Durán 1978, 736; as cited in Hale 1998, 164).[11] In Bamako, one may hear the choral "fixed melody" described as *kunbɛn,* the vocal equivalent of an instrumental accompaniment, and the recitational "improvisation" as *tɛrɛmɛli* (Durán 2007, 589), a term that implies verbal negotiation and bartering (Bailleul 2000). Here, I note that Nana concluded her impassioned and hot recitation by returning to the cool chorus and text associated with the piece "Kɛmɛ Buruma," accompanied thereafter by an overall rise in volume and increased polyphonic density of the instrumental accompaniment until the cadenced conclusion of the piece.

It is the tension between the patterned collectivity of the chorus and the improvised individuality of recitation that characterizes verbal art in Mande music. Like the value-inflected aesthetics described in Toumani Diabaté's *kora* performance—balancing instrumental music's well-balanced head with its agile and experimental appendages—the singing-speaking voice is suffused with moral and ethical meaning. Among music aficionados in Bamako, a popular definition of "song" *(dɔnkili)* is either the "essence" *(kili)* of the "dance" or "knowledge" *(dɔn)*.[12] In the latter sense, song communicates musical meaning through the poetry of language. In the former, it is the source of embodied musical practice. As the proverb goes, "It is the meaning," symbolic and sensual, "not the drumming or the singing, that is good." To vocally negotiate the tension between sung themes and spoken commentaries while motivating and encouraging a good instrumental groove are two sides of the same musical coin (heads, epistemology; tails, corporeality). This is the ethico-moral genius of Nana's vocal intervention at the rehearsal—the essence of her vocal knowledge and dance. Through lyrical eloquence and prosodic passion, Nana artfully and ethically addressed the angry sentiments that divided her band and effected (for a time) a socially and musically good balance of sound and sentiment. Such ethico-aesthetic practice speaks highly of her status and identity as an artist—her artistic personhood *(artistiya)*—in the contemporary Bamako art world (about which more later in the chapter).

Yet, vocal expression is only a part of the ethics of Bamako artists' musical aesthetics. The song of the vocalist is incomplete, like a sentence without punctuation, if it lacks a strident instrumental response from the backing musicians. This is when the music heats up *(foli kalaya)*— gets louder, faster, and more energetic—often described by metaphors of "boiling" *(foli wulila)* and "raging fires" *(foli nagalen don)*. As we observed of Toumani Diabaté's *kora* performance, this instrumental excess often takes the form of *bolomanboli*, the "running by hand" of an improvised solo. Before boiling over, this instrumental hotness is necessarily countered by vocal injunctions to cool down and return to an accompaniment pattern, or *kunben*, figured around an underlying ostinato. "Quiet your strings," Nana vocally implores, "I'm going to sing a little." Thereafter, the song itself heats up, most frequently in the recitational form of vocal praise *(fasada)*. As Nicholas Hopkins has observed, praise song can have a "swelling" effect on audiences, filling them with pride, but also engendering an excess of affect. Praise, he writes, "causes the individual targeted to swell up ('to swell with pride' as we say in English), in extreme cases to explode" (1997, 52). Such vocal excess requires a return to a cool aesthetic, as the elder Sidiki Diabaté once noted: "There must be a balance between the *kumben* [the fixed melody of song] and the *tèrèmeli* [vocal improvisation in the mode of recitation]. Too much *tèrèmeli* takes the power out of the music. . . . This is music without any foundations" (as cited in Durán 2007, 589).

Such play between hot and cool voices and instruments embodies the artful and deliberate ethics of aesthetics in live musical performance. This is exemplified in a recent article written by ethnomusicologist Lucy Durán on the subject of *ŋaaraya*, a term denoting musical excellence and performative prowess in the Mande world (2007). Durán writes that "the power of the instrumentalist over singers is acknowledged in the often-sung phrase 'Slow/cool down the instruments, or you'll push me into *ngaraya*'" (574). Here, *ŋaaraya* implies not only musical excellence and prowess, but also excess and power. As instrumental performance gets hotter, it may provoke impassioned speech and song from the vocalist and engender an abundance of potentially dangerous "vital energy" *(ɲama)* emanating from the spoken and sung word (see Hoffman 1995).[13] The implication here is that musical excess may have socially disruptive—that is, unethical—effects. To resist such sociomusical excess, Durán observes that the ethics of musical excellence *(ŋaaraya)* "combines simplicity with force" (590) emphasizing expressive "elegance and economy" (from McNaughton 1988, 109) and subordinating expression and technique to "respect for formal relationships" and "communicative clarity" (from Chernoff 1979, 122).

Similar ethically inflected antiphonal patterns emerge within other structures of musical performance, such as choral call and response (Maxwell 2002, 155–56) and the formal and stylized affirmations of "responsive listeners" *(namunamunaw)* whose periodic utterances (*"Namu!"* "Yes!" *"Tiɲe don!"* "That's true!") dialogically delimit and sometimes narratively direct Mande verbal art (see Johnson and Sisòkò 2003). Dance is also structured by musical (often percussive) movements between hotness and coolness, moving bodies on and off dance floors and to and from each other as musical sounds and sentiments heat up and cool down. Beyond the strictly musical, social relationships, too, find expression in this ethico-aesthetic dialectic intersensory discourse. In an article on the mediated reception of popular music in Bamako, Dorothea Schulz discusses the vocal quality of "*kuul*-ness" among radio show hosts who, in their candid on-air discussion with listeners on intimate topics of marital relations and sexuality, are able to "convey the full complexity of a problem without naming it in too explicit a manner" (2002, 816). This, she writes, "adds a further layer of meaning to the semantics of 'cool' . . . which describes a man or a woman who is laid back, careful and deliberate in her or his actions and thus represents the opposite of someone 'hot' . . . who 'heats up' quickly and, at worst, is temperamental, impatient, and overly ready to engage in (fistful) arguments" (816fn49).

Indeed, though the focus of popular musical aesthetics is generally on the sounds of musical performance, a whole host of social activities contribute to its perceived space, operating through the full range of the senses. When Bamako residents attend a live musical event—whether at a nightclub, a courtyard baptism, or a posh wedding ceremony—they are typically dressed to the nines. Young people may be outfitted with sneakers, tight shirts, and fashionable (if imitation) designer jeans and skirts. Adults may opt for a sport coat or an evening dress. More traditional men might wear a brightly colored and elaborately embroidered *dulɔkiba* (kaftan, literally "long shirt"). Women may sport skillfully folded headscarves in variety of colors and patterns. Mingling among the clientele at a Bamako club, or walking down the street during a marriage ceremony, one is struck by the wide variety of perfumes and incensed fragrances emanating from peoples' bodies and clothing, becoming stronger ("hotter") with proximity and weaker ("cooler") with distance. As Adame Ba Konaré has described in her recent novel, *Quand l'ail se frotte à l'encens* (2006), crafting bodily fragrance is treated as an art form in Bamako. Then, there is the flavor of savory sauces, fried fish, and grilled meat, together with the sweetness of bottled soft drinks, hot tea, and the cold bitterness of a local beer. As a result, popular music is seen, smelled, and tasted as much as it is heard in Bamako.

In sum, in the perceived space of Bamako's music culture, good musicality is also about good sociability. Aesthetics and ethics go hand in hand with intersensuality and intersubjectivity. In Bamako, when people say, "This sounds good," they are also saying, "This is good" (see Frith 1996, 275). Likewise, when someone says, "This sounds bad," there is the implication that good sociability has been upset by a breach of assumed ethical behavior. "It's awful! It's really awful!," Aliou screamed at his struggling band. At stake in these judgments of sound and sociability is the status and identity of the artist as an ethico-moral person *(mɔgɔ)* in Mali today. As observed in the foregoing ethnographic analysis, a locally modeled musical aesthetics—embodied and expressed through instrument and voice—constitutes a privileged means by which urban artists actively cultivate and confirm their artistic personhood, their *artistiya*. This artful ethics can be heard and felt in the formalism and virtuosity of Toumani's traditional-yet-modern musicianship and the poetics and effects of Nana's verbal art. To conclude this chapter, I reflect further on the way music in Bamako creates a locally salient context of values, a social space of multiple moral interest and investment, a structure of feeling that may be described as "Afropolitan."

## Afropolitan Music and Afropolitan Sensibility

In the Bamako art world described in this chapter, good sound—music that stirs bodies, triggers thoughts, and incites emotions—affirms good subjectivity, audibly expressing the persistence of cultural mores and social imperatives in counterpoint with the interests, desires, and aspirations of individuals. Good music, in other words, thoughtfully and feelingfully— that is, meaningfully—resounds moral and ethical personhood *(mɔgɔya)*, coupling custom, tradition, and collectivity with creativity, self-mastery, and intentionality in a common and coherent, embodied and affective perceived space. At the Triton Stars band rehearsal, this musical personhood manifests in a dramatic performance of vocal praise. For Nana, her band mates are her *balimamɔgɔw*, her (musical) family members. Faced with antagonism boiling over among this artistic kin, Nana steps forward to dispel social tensions, performing a cool vocal aesthetic to confront animosity and promote conviviality. While intended to rebuild and strengthen moral community within the group, this performance is ethical insofar as it exhibits Nana's social and musical talents as an artist, distinguishing herself among her peers. By calling on her band to "quiet their strings" so that she can "sing a little," Nana ventures into that uncertain and risky terrain of an individual ethics, where she alone is accountable for the actions she initiates.

For Toumani Diabaté, an artful personhood emerges through a refined and embodied approach to technique, form, and style (of the head, feet, voice, and hands), a deep respect for tradition, especially that of his family, and, perhaps most important, a progressive spirit of rivalry and innovation.

This combination of musical method, patrimonial deference, and positive *fadenya* can be found throughout his professional oeuvre, whether he is performing solo at a formal venue, as in the concert at the French Cultural Center, or with his popular dance band, the Symmetric Orchestra, at a local Bamako nightclub. Echoing the ethico-moral "new ancient strings" aesthetic of his duet with Ballaké Sissoko, Diabaté describes the music of the Symmetric Orchestra (which I discuss further in chapter 4) as a "new sound" for a "new generation." In Toumani's words:

> The Symmetric Orchestra reflects the spirit of Mali's new democracy since 1992—a spirit of equality, and creativity. There's a public in Mali today that loves traditional music—griot music—but not the griot milieu. With the Symmetric, they feel free to enjoy this music without the obligations of tradition. And this gives us the freedom to present the tradition in new ways. (Diabaté and Durán 2006)

To paraphrase, this egalitarian and creative practice of freeing oneself to present tradition in new ways frames innovative and potentially contentious musical agency—beyond the obligations of tradition—as an ethics of artistic personhood, of *artistiya*. Such innovatory artistic activity must be balanced, however, with an acknowledged respect for one's cultural patrimony in order to retain a sense of moral legitimacy. As John Miller Chernoff notes, describing a comparable ethico-aesthetic environment, "The formal relationships are vitalized and enhanced in good music, but the musical form is open rather than rigid, set up so that it affords a focus for the expression of individuality that subtly distinguishes an occasion within the context of tradition" (1979, 126). On his *kora* and with his band—in Bamako, on the continent, and throughout the world— Toumani Diabaté seeks to push boundaries, not abandon foundations.

Yet, though Diabaté represents his music beyond (though not divorced from) tradition, he also locates his artistry beyond (though not to the exclusion of) culture. The new generation of which he speaks reflects "the spirit of Mali's new democracy since 1992." He describes a new politics and new modes of leisure and habits of consumption. He represents, in other words, a new economy and society of which his music is an important part. Similarly, Nana's vocal performance cannot be reduced to an exercise in cultural affirmation and valuation, rooted in a commitment to moral community and routed through an ethics of artistic excellence. No less important is the pragmatic work she accomplishes in bolstering group morale so that her band can carry on with their rehearsal and imagine the possibility of realizing their professional goals. That Nana does this as a woman further casts her call for group solidarity and professional integrity in a broader history of and struggle for women's socioeconomic mobility in contemporary Mali.

As described in chapter 1, proper subjectivity for women is conceived through expressions of moral fortitude, where womanhood is tied to marriage and childbirth and a lifelong commitment to cultivating conviviality (or *badenya*, in the literal sense of "mother-child-ness") in the household (Grosz-Ngaté 1989). As such, a female ethics maintains a tight orbit around the moral world of civil space and may include activities such as selling homegrown produce at the neighborhood marketplace or performing in community life-cycle rituals (see Modic 1996). Men, by contrast, are judged both by their submission to tradition (or *fasiya*, in the literal sense of paternal heritage) and their ethical agency in the "wild spaces" outside the home or community, symbolically described in Mande cosmology as the wilderness *(kungo)*. Ethical agency for men may include formal or informal work abroad, such as the frequent touring required of professional artists. This poses a problem for young female artists, like Nana, whose profession necessarily takes them out of the household and into the ethical wilds of the local and global music industry, spaces considered by many to be unethical and essentially immoral for women.

Forming a mounting critique of conservative notions of female personhood in the Malian art world, recent studies by Lucy Durán (1995a; 1995b; 2000), Heather Maxwell (2002), and Dorothea Schulz (2002) have emphasized the important role women have played in interrogating normative gender roles through popular music in Mali. The songs of artists like Kandia Kouyaté, Ami Koita, Nahawa Doumbia, Oumou Sangaré, and Rokia Traoré, among many others, critically address issues of cultural subordination, social stigma, and domestic abuse, and include celebrations of women's lives and works that extend domestic feminine morality to the male-dominated public sphere of ethical distinction. Such forms of what may be called "feminist *artistiya*," expressed through the genres of *jeliya* and *wasulu* in particular, have been increasingly prominent since the 1980s, when the Malian music industry experienced what has been called a widespread "feminization" (Mamadou Diawara 2003, 197), characterized by the rapid rise and public prominence of female "stars" (French, *étoiles*). Much like Toumani Diabaté's sociomusical appeal to new publics, in and out of Africa, these female artists insist on new opportunities to critically and creatively engage and intervene in this emergent African world. While not (yet) a diva (French, *vedette*), Nana's performance practice belongs, I believe, to this broader existential project of a progressive musical ethics in contemporary Bamako, creating a "context of values," in Chernoff's terms, "where criticism is translated into social action" (1979, 143).

In this book, the name I have given to this urban African context of values is "Afropolitan." In this chapter, I have elaborated this Afropolitanism from within a particular African art world to represent aesthetics and social action in an Afropolitan music idiom: Mande popular music. Through situated observation and critical inquiry, I have thickly described the sonic and social means by which Bamako artists and audiences "achieve an integration of music and community" (Chernoff 1979, 37), in which community is itself an integrative product of "the various patterns of social, economic, and political life" (35). These Afropolitan sounds and sentiments speak and sing, through instrument and voice, in an African vernacular firmly embedded in the world (compare Feld 2013; Kelley 2012; Muller and Benjamin 2011). Just as *kora* players make their instruments speak in a musical language as ancient as it is new, Afropolitans give voice to the world through traditions and innovations they claim as their own, "relativizing roots" and "domesticating the unfamiliar," as Achille Mbembe observes, to produce "an aesthetic and a certain poetics of the world" (2010, 229, 232). John Miller Chernoff, whose sociomusical insights are embedded throughout this chapter, began to elucidate such an Afropolitan sensibility in the 1970s, observing Africa's "astounding diversity of musical situations and musical activity" across a range of social positions: "nationalistic and tribalistic, Animist and Christian or Muslim, traditional and Westernized" (1979, 35, 156).[14]

In the following chapters, I extend my inquiry into popular music's integration into the various patterns of social, economic, and political life in Bamako by inhabiting social spaces in which religion, intellectual property, and national identity are most salient. To the urban lifeworld, artistic personhood, and embodied and affective musical aesthetics elaborated thus far I add the pious voice of Islamic interpellation, the (non)governmental culture of musical ownership, valuation, circulation, and citation, and the performative politics of postcolonial and post-national modes of identification. Together, these social positions of urbanism, profession, aesthetics, piety, economy, and politics create a context of values of a varied and vital Afropolitanism. In the next chapter, I examine how this Afropolitanism dynamically and ethically translates into social action through a locally salient mode of religious identification in urban Africa. Specifically, I consider how the pious voice of Islam resounds as a privileged discursive resource in Bamako popular music. Through poetic invocations of a common faith, artists and audiences repeatedly call their Muslim community in being, reaffirming a moral sense of place in what they perceive to be an increasingly immoral world.

# CHAPTER 4

# A Pious Poetics of Place

## Three Scenes

"I take refuge in God from the accursed Devil," Tata Diabaté declares, enunciating her words clearly in the sacred verse of classical Arabic. She stands, clothed in shimmering green robes, accented in gold, before a bride and groom in a capacious hall at the Hotel de l'Amitié, the prominent five-star high-rise in downtown Bamako. Seated behind Tata, accompanying musicians dutifully follow her moralizing invocation, anticipating the praise song to follow. Anticipation mixes with anxiety, however, as the musicians recall party organizers' earlier injunction to refrain from vocal praise, a plebian and vernacular practice they believe to be out of place at this upscale, cosmopolitan event. Undeterred, Tata raises her voice, microphone in hand, and proclaims her premeditated panegyric.

Elsewhere in the city, a boom box resounds under the shade of a streetside veranda. A small crowd of young men, sheltered from the afternoon sun, listens as they huddle over a boiling pot of tea. "Every soul shall taste death / What the Almighty has said, the Almighty will do," raps Dixon, a member of the hip-hop trio Tata Pound, juxtaposing phrases in Arabic, the language of the holy Qur'an, and Bamana, the urban lingua franca. In response to these words, one of the men cups his hands together and passes them in front of his face, whispering the Arabic *busmula* ("In the name of God, the compassionate, the merciful") as the next round of tea is served. They sip the sugary infusion slowly, loudly, bobbing their heads as the next track kicks off. "Hey, policeman! Tata Pound's in the area!"

Still elsewhere, in a global city far away from the riverine bustle of Bamako, a video game player listens to a recorded version of "Mali Sajo," a staple of traditional Mande music and the "fetish" piece of Toumani Diabaté's urban dance band, the Symmetric Orchestra. The track, titled "Tapha Niang" on the album *Boulevard de l'Indépendence,* is featured on *LittleBigPlanet,* a new game for the Sony PlayStation 3 console. What this gamer hears are not the Friday night crowds that gather at Le Hogon, the Symmetric Orchestra's nightclub home in Bamako; not the pride of place the original piece inspires among Malian listeners, as an informal anthem, playing on the multiple meanings of the word *Mali* (Hippopotamus, Nation-State, Empire); and not the lyrical lament of singer Moussa Niang, who mourns the death of his younger brother, a young Senegalese soldier killed in combat. "Tapha is gone / That is why we are crying." What this listener hears is the Qur'anic verse that opens the track, the same Sura heard back in Bamako from the rap group Tata Pound, to which Niang adds another Qur'anic verse, "All that is on Earth will perish" (Surat al-Rahman, v. 26), a reminder that his brother's fate is one that we all share.

## Three Concerns

From the three scenes just sketched, this chapter addresses three lines of inquiry that present Afropolitan ethics as a religiously motivated project. First, this chapter tells stories and makes claims about the way urban artists and their audiences in Bamako invoke Islam across diverse genres of popular music. My interest is the sense in which one "is" a Muslim in this West African city. Second, the chapter describes the principally vocal means by which such popular piety is ideologically achieved. My analysis focuses on what I call "a poetics of recognition" in which singers interpolate Qur'anic verse into vocal performances to interpellate moral subjectivity (in the Althusserian sense, of which more later) within Bamako's Islamic public sphere. Finally, third, this chapter considers the territorial politics of this pious poetics, as moral subjects are called on—and at times contested—across multiple scales of place. My concern, here, is for a sense of locality, expressed through popular appeals to Islam, within the increasingly deterritorialized urban culture of contemporary Bamako.

I begin by situating these three concerns—for a religion, a vocal aesthetics, and a sense of place—within the social space of popular culture in urban West Africa. My argument is that part of what makes "culture" popular in contemporary Bamako is an audibly shared sense of Islamic subjectivity. My claim is that this common experience of Islamic *inter-est* manifests in the recursive appeal to Muslim morality through a vocal poetics of recognition in popular music lyricism. My understanding of this Islamic call-and-response in Bamako popular culture draws on Hannah Arendt's notion of the "subjective in-between" forged in dialogue about common concerns that "constitute . . . something which inter-est, which lies between people and therefore can relate and bind them together" ([1958] 1998, 182–83). Islam is, as we shall observe, is one such shared interest (born of mutual existence, or inter-est) in the popular culture of contemporary Bamako, giving rise to a "web of human relationships" that crosses—as it connects—multiple genres of expression and cultural styles through modes of speaking and singing about public piety.

I then return to the three scenes presented at the start of the chapter, developing them through ethnographic and textual analysis. In each case, I elaborate the vocal practice of Islamic interpellation, by which subjects are positioned within an ideological system (Islam) through the performance and perception of popular song, across several genres of musical expression (jeliya, hip-hop, and Afropop). My final example, however, diverges from this interpellative coherence to follow the circulatory path of a song ("Tapha Niang") through the social media of the global culture industry. In particular, I observe how the song's recent remediation (as video game soundtrack) has engendered a politics of misrecognition in popular media and blog reports (compare Novak 2010). This case emphasizes the precarious particularity of a what may be called "popular Islam" in Bamako, exemplifying a process AbdouMaliq Simone calls "worlding" (2001b), or a "state of being 'cast out' into the world" in a struggle over the possibility of local meaning and being (17).

## Islam, Music, and Popular Culture in an African City

For nearly a millennium, Islam has been part of the rich and varied mix of cultural forms that shape the social worlds of West African societies. In contemporary West Africa, Islam's deep regional history manifests in a modern-day continuum of belief systems and social practices, ranging from the more orthodox and conservative to the more heterodox and liberal (see Levtzion and Pouwels 2000). Echoing along this continuum are Islam's many West African voices—voices that inspire piety, silence dissent, engage dialogue, and reveal new paths of spiritual growth and religious identity. That these Islamic voices are strikingly musical is readily apparent to visitors to the region, particularly in its expansive cities where Islam finds its most diverse and dynamic expression (see Charry 2000b). To walk through a city like Bamako (or Dakar, or Conakry, or Niamey) is to move through a dense soundscape of social sound and urban noise.

Much of the former echoes the edifying verbal arts of local Islamic practice (compare Hirschkind 2006). Against the bustle of car horns, marketplace haggling, and local industry, one may hear the muezzen call the
Muslim faithful to prayer (Arabic, *adhan*), a mellifluous Qur'anic recitation from a respected spiritual leader (French, *marabout*) played on a taxi-
cab tape deck, the cyclical chants of an itinerant Sufi brotherhood (Arabic,
*tariqa*), or the public benedictions (Arabic, *baraka*) of praise singers (French,
*griots*) amplified by oversized speakers at outdoor marriage and name-giving
ceremonies. These are all part of the "multigeneric lifeworld" (Warner 2002,
63) of Islam in urban West Africa.[1]

In this chapter, I attend to the generically varied contributions of
popular music to the Islamic soundscape of a West African city, Bamako.
My emphasis is on what Fiona McLaughlin calls "Islamic popular music,"
which she distinguishes from "popular Islamic music" in West African
urban cultures (1997). With regard to the latter category, McLaughlin
describes a range of essentially Islamic musical forms cultivated within
the sectarian milieu of contemporary Senegal, where multiple Sufi orders (Arabic, *turuq*) coexist within a broader Islamic community. In Mali,
such music from varied communities of faith is often described as *zigiri*
(from Arabic, *dhikr*), encompassing a wide range of musical expressions
of Islamic praise. Performed on occasions of ritual gathering and pilgrim-
age, and consumed through a variety of media (digital, analog, broadcast,
and streaming) as an everyday sign of public piety, popular Islamic music
is typically characterized by chanting to the glory of God, accompanied
by electrified and acoustic instruments and dance. This popular Islamic
music is consonant with a broader Sufi tradition of Islamic mysticism,
which, dating back to the twelfth century, and predominant throughout
much of West Africa, emphasizes religious music as a means of heightening the righteousness of the pious listener by bringing him or her closer to
the spiritual world of God.

McLaughlin's article also observes the more recent emergence of an
Islamic popular music in West Africa, in which sacred themes are integrated
into the secular popular music of urban dance bands. In the Senegalese
context McLaughlin describes, the traditional form of praise song for respected patrons, common to many genres of West African popular music,
has been transposed to the relationship between disciple (Wolof, *taalibe*;
from Arabic, *talib*) and spiritual leader *(marabout)* that defines the social
and religious order of Sufism. This creates a distinctly Islamic form of mu-

sical praise that marks a singer's and his or her audience's allegiance to a particular Sufi order or Way *(tariqa)*, such as the prevailing Tijaniyya and Qadiriyya orders in the subregion. Popular among urban audiences, for whom religious identity and popular culture are not perceived as discrepant, Islamic popular music has opened up new forms of spiritual and religious expression, which local and global popular music industries make widely available on recordings, radio and television broadcasts, and in the secular spaces of concert halls and nightclubs. Following McLaughlin, I consider, here, what qualifies popular music as "Islamic" in the Malian context. Yet, I also argue that a broad and coherent appeal to (or call upon) Islam is part of what makes music "popular" in Bamako.

## Voicing Afropolitan Piety

In chapter 3, I described how moral and ethical behavior and forms of vocal and instrumental expression mutually constitute an aesthetics of artistic personhood *(artistiya)* in Bamako today. Bamako artists and their audiences share a number of social and musical predilections, among which is the ideological hegemony of Mande social thought in musical discourse, articulating a common musical value system of embodied expression. Here, I consider a significant musical element of this ethico-moral aesthetics, the discursive and expressive logics of which are more socioreligious than ethnocultural, more Islamic than Mande. Specifically, I consider the poetic insertion of Qur'anic verse into popular music song texts as means of interpellating moral subjectivity among urban artists and audiences. Yet, my intent is not to draw a stark analytic line between the cultural and the religious as modes of being. Rather, by drawing attention to popular music in Bamako as such, I propose that the popular accrues its musical— and, more broadly defined, cultural—coherence through a common set of locally salient dispositions, including artists' urban and professional identities (chapters 1 and 2), and expressive resources, such as Mande music (chapter 3) and, as we shall observe, the Islamic voice. All are modes of a variegated and vital Afropolitan ethics in the audible art world of contemporary Bamako.

In the stories and texts that follow, my analysis focuses on spoken and sung references to Islamic thought and practice in three genres of popular vocal performance: Mande praise song, Malian rap, and Afropop lyricism. Within these genres of verbal art, I observe how Bamako vocalists invoke Islam as a sign of religious ideology to interpellate listeners as moral subjects. By "ideology," I mean those paradigmatic systems of social and cultural hegemony (such as religion) that prescribe (without wholly determining) modes of identification in society. In Stuart Hall's reading of Althusser, whose notion of "interpellation" I draw on here (Althusser 1971), ideologies represent "the frameworks of thinking and calculation about the world" in which subjectivity emerges as *"the recognition of the self within ideological discourse"* (my emphasis). In other words, ideology is "what it is that allows subjects to recognize themselves in the discourse and to speak it spontaneously as its author" (Hall 1985, 99, 107). It is precisely this interpellated form of self-recognition, expressed through popular culture and within the ideological context of Islam in contemporary Bamako that interests me here. My attention is thus drawn to the specifically (though not exclusively) Islamic morality of subjects called forth—or interpellated—in live and mediated musical expression.

In this way, I follow McLaughlin's analysis of an "Islamic popular music" (1997) as part of a broader Islamic popular culture. Religiously marked, the popular signifies as "unofficial" vis-à-vis the "official" culture of a nation-state (Mali), defined, at least nominally, by a politics of *laïcité*, the ideological sign of secular society in this former French colony. While discrepant with the *laïc* discourse of the state, Islamic popular culture nonetheless appeals to a national audience of people who identify themselves both as Malian and Muslim.[2] In this unofficial-yet-national public sphere, the popular becomes Islamic in the voices of praise singers, rappers, and dance band vocalists. Islam is, in turn, popularized through these artists' multigeneric and interpellative verbal art. Rendered, thus, as a popular mode of expression and identification, Islam represents what anthropologist Benjamin Soares calls a "supralocal" signifier that can "promote unity between Muslims in Mali" and connect them to a broader Islamic world (2005, 238, 239).[3] Yet, this global sense of Islamic "unity" is not always consonant with the local "unity" of Islamic popular culture, as my third case study will show, in which anonymous criticism from ecumenical orthodoxies abroad calls the very culture of popular Islam in Mali into question.

Still, at the local level, on which my first two case studies focus, Islam is a unifying means by which moral subjects are called into being within the heterogeneous public of popular culture in Bamako. By "moral subjectivity" I mean, once again, a mode of being through which individuals and groups make claims on customs, conventions, and norms—both as acts of personal volition and collective subjection—to socially position themselves within a larger community. In Bamako popular music, Islamic interpellation produces moral subjects through a poetics of recognition, characterized by vocal citation of Qur'anic verse in lyrical song and speech within a self-identified Muslim community. Such citations are marked (or recognized) as interpellating signifiers (constituting a poetics) in terms of language use, vocal quality and style, intertextual reference to surrounding lyrics, and lyrical placement in the overall performance—categories on which I elaborate further later in the chapter. As public acts of interpellation, there exists, however, the possibility of misrecognition, in which locally and globally circulating sounds "call on" listening subjects who misconstrue the ideological signifier and critically recontextualize its meaning. In other words, there is a politics to the poetics of moral subjectivity in Mali's Islamic popular culture, at home and in the world.

## A Call to Praise

We return, now, to the wedding party gathered at the Hotel de l'Amitié in downtown Bamako. There, the band is in the middle of a set of light instrumental music, featuring the sounds of the twenty-one-stringed *kora* performed by bandleader Dialy Mady Cissoko. The group goes by the name Dialyco, which, as I described in chapter 2, refers both to the Bamana *jeliko* ("griot trouble"), indexing the problems and struggles faced by traditional musicians (or griots) in contemporary Mali, and the title Dialy Co., describing the modern and market-driven work of such musicians. (Both senses of the name—the troubled tradition and the capitalizing modernity—resonate in the scene I describe here.) As guests filter in and converse amid the ambient sounds, Marie, the evening's itinerant organizer,[4] informs the group that the bride and groom are about to make their entrance. The music abruptly ends. Tata Diabaté, the evening's principle vocalist, leans back to Dialy Mady to signal the song for the *intronisation*—the public presentation of the newlyweds. A moment later, the band kicks off with the piece, "Jeliyaba," meaning "The Great Art of the Griot."

A staple of the Mande repertoire in Mali, "Jeliyaba" celebrates the virtues of the identity and work of griots (*jeliw*) in Mande society. The song highlights griots' status and identity as clan-based artisans (*ɲamakalaw*)

who practice a centuries-old tradition of musical performance, historical panegyric, and social mediation (Hoffman 1995). In performance, the
piece features the four principal elements of musical expression employed
by these traditional bards and storytellers: instrumental performance
(fɔli), dance (dɔn), song (dɔnkili), and speech (kuma). In particular, the
value and virtue of vocal praise, or fasada, is valorized as a means of binding communities together through laudatory performance. Fasada describes the vocal act of establishing one's cultural heritage (fasiya, meaning "father's lineage" or, more generally, "patrimony"), by "putting it in
place" (from the verb, da, "to place"). In "Jeliyaba," the cultural heritage in
question is that of the griots themselves. The piece is, thus, a praise song
for praise singers whose "great art" is celebrated as an icon of conviviality
in the Mande world.

As a marital exordium, the choice of "Jeliyaba" was certainly striking at
an event in which vocal praise had been excluded by a prior agreement—
insisted upon by the groom, one of Dialyco's principle patrons—to sup-
plement public gifting with a nominal performance fee. Typically, when a
singer performs fasada, she expects the person to whom the praise is addressed to offer a gift, normally cash, referred to as jelisɔn wari (a "gift of
money for the griot"). But, with so many international guests in attendance
(from Spain, Italy, and the United States), a traditional wedding with extended praise performances would not suit the cosmopolitan ethos of this
modern celebration, or so the groom reasoned. He told Marie, the party
planner, to ask Dialyco to limit their praise songs solely to the bride and
groom. With this in mind, Tata's song choice appeared deliberate. "One
person's gift is not a gift" (Mɔgɔ kelen ka sɔnni tɛ sɔnni yɛ), she told me later.
"One person's offering to a griot is not a lot" (Mɔgɔ kelen ka jelisɔn wari, a
man ca). Because praise song and speech represent an important source
of income for professional musicians at such events, in the form of gifts of
cash for personalized extolling performances (jelisɔn wari), and because
the reciprocity of praising and gifting is an important means by which a
cultural sense of personhood (mɔgɔya) is established in the Mande world,
Tata took it upon herself to moralize, through an invocation of praise,
what she perceived to be a potentially immoral public.

Through the lens of my video camera, I watch and listen intently as
Tata performatively invokes jeliya, the art of the griot, using a standard
prefatory genre of vocal praise described, functionally, as ka kɛnɛ ɲama
fifa, meaning "to sweep away the dangerous energy of a place"[5] (Figure 15).

*Figure 15. Tata Diabaté and Dialyco. Photograph by the author.*

Still seated, Tata intones the first theme of this verbal incantation by praising the gathered celebrants, whom she addresses as *jama*, a Bamana term derived from the Arabic *jama'a* meaning "assembly," "congregation," "audience," or "public" (see Bailleul 2000).

| | |
|---|---|
| *Ɛ iyo! A jama!* | Eh yeah! This public! |
| *Nin jama ye hereba ye.* | There is great happiness among this group. |
| *Ɛ iyo! A jama!* | Eh yeah! This public! |
| *Bi n'u ke herebu ye.* | This will be a time of great peace. |
| *Bi n'a ke sewa don fana ye.* | This is also a time of joy. |
| *Ɛ iyo! A jama!* | Eh yeah! This public! |
| *Bi n'a ke here duman ba.* | This time will bring wonderful happiness. |

At this point Tata comes to her feet, though she does not leave the stage. Her voice and the music rise along with her. The effect of her standing gives a subtle edge of intensity to the group's performance. All eyes are now on her as she continues her song.

| | |
|---|---|
| *Bi n'a kɛ hɛrɛba ye, ɛɛ, aa!* | This is a time of great happiness, eh, ah! |
| *Bi n'a kɛ ye ɲagari don fana ye.* | This is also a day of celebration. |
| *Ɛ iyo! A jama!* | Eh yeah! This public! |
| *Bi n'a kɛ hɛrɛba ye.* | This is a time of great happiness. |

After a short pause, Tata introduces the second theme of the vocal performance, a praise song to God and His terrestrial and celestial works.

| | |
|---|---|
| *A-u zu Billahi mina Syɛtan a rajim,* | I take refuge in God from the accursed Devil, |
| *Ala-hu!* | God! |
| *A-u zu Billahi mina Syɛtan a rajim,* | I take refuge in God from the accursed Devil |
| *Ala!* | God! |
| *Ala! min ka sankolo da,* | God! who created the heavens, |
| *Ala-hu!* | God! |
| *Ala! min ka dugumakolo da,* | God! who created the earth, |
| *sebagaya ma.* | the almighty. |
| *N bɛ mansa min fɔ fɔlɔ-fɔlɔ,* | First, I greet the king |
| *min ye n da!* | who created me! |
| *Ni nɛ ye Ala walɛ nyuman dɔn.* | I have recognized the righteous acts of God. |
| | |
| *Fɔlikɛlalu, n'i Ala sɔnn'a ma,* | Musicians, if God wills it, |
| *n'aw ye juruw da,* | if you calm (quiet) your music |
| *o bɛ diya n ye!* | that would please me! |

This passage begins with a citation of the *Ta'awwudh* (Arabic, "I take refuge in God from the accursed Devil"), sung twice through parallel melodic
descents with successive resolutions to the tonal center to emphasize its
lyrical significance. This phrase is often invoked before Qur'anic recitation, or before embarking on a sacred task, which, in this case, symbolically
heightens the morality of Tata's invocation of public praise. Throughout,
she treats the word *Ala* with aesthetic emphasis by accenting the final
vowel sound either as a punctuated abbreviation (in the fourth line) or
with a sustained vibrato to which she adds the cadential phoneme *hu*
(in the second and sixth lines) as a descending melisma, indexing classical Arabic and echoing the vocal stylistics of the *adhan*, or Muslim call

to prayer. Reserving her first praises for God—creator of heaven, earth, and of Tata herself—she concludes the passage by asking the musicians to "calm" or "quiet" their music. "This would please me," she sings as the musicians lower their volume, employing a common vocal device in Mande music intended to draw attention to her spirited song and the vocal praise that is to follow (as described in chapter 3).

This leads Tata to the third and penultimate theme of the song, an assertion of the "moral purity" of the gathered celebrants. With instruments quieted, she begins this theme with a strident griot vocal genre known as "calling the horses" (*ka sow wele*), which in bygone times was used to extol gathered soldiers in preparation for battle.

| | |
|---|---|
| *So-ooow!...Iiiii-Eee!...* | [Tata "calls the horses"] |
| *Sukelemansadenw, ɔ ɲɛna ne ma!* | Great warrior princes, it is pleasing to me! |
| *Nin jama, i ni su tugunni.* | This group, I greet you once again. |
| *Ni nɛ ko jama.* | If I said "group." |
| *Ni nɛ ko jama, jama, jama, jama!* | If I said "group, group, group, group!" |
| *Nin jama ka sana, ɛ Ala!* | This group is pure, oh God! |
| *Silamɛ jamalu.* | Islamic groups. |
| *Misilimu jamalu.* | Groups of Muslims. |
| *Fɛn o fɛn, n b'a fɔ la,* | Above all else, I will say it, |
| *layi ilayi ila Ala* | There is no God but God |
| *ni Mohamed rasulu Lahi!* | and Muhammad is the Prophet of God! |

The arch of her swelling song descends to the phrase, "'This group is pure, oh God," followed by an affirmation of the religious conviction of her audience, whom she calls "a group of Muslims." The effect is to symbolically join her public to the broader Muslim *umma*, or "community of faith." Following the universal Muslim declaration of faith, the *shahada* (Arabic, "There is no god but God, and Muhammad is His Prophet"), Tata culminates her performance with the fourth and final theme of this opening movement, captured in a single line: "You will all find respect in the art of the griot" (*Aw bɛɛ bonya bɛ jeliya la*).

Tata's vocal introduction of the piece, "Jeliyaba," is composed of four principle elements: (1) a celebration of shared joy, (2) a supplication and

praise to God, (3) an acknowledgment of collective belonging to a common community of faith, and (4) an affirmation of the reciprocal virtue of
*jeliya*. The social effects of this performance are both critical and productive. Tata voices a public response to the official interdiction of vocal praise
while at the same time affirming the intersubjective value of the laudatory
performance. She does this by performatively recontextualizing her apparently "cosmopolitan" audience, interpellating them through a poetics of
recognition in which both audience and performer are oriented toward
what Tata deems the morally appropriate tradition of *jeliya*. This mutual
orientation manifests in the reciprocal gestures of vocal praise and public
gifting, with wedding celebrants called upon by the griot to demonstrate
their dignity and generosity by rising up to present cash gifts for personalized panegyric. Islam is the ideological vehicle of this poetic interpellation, invoking a locally salient moral community in which the socially and
economically valuable practice of *jeliya* can take place.

Before turning to my second scene, I use Tata's performance as a model
to make some preliminary claims about Islamic interpellation in Malian
popular music, elaborating on the vocal poetics of recognition I sketched
out earlier. We then observe how this poetics applies to hip-hop and dance
band lyricism in (and out of) Bamako. First, sung/spoken texts are vocalized in classical Arabic, often with lexical and/or syntactic inflections
of, or code switching with African languages. In Tata's performance, she
juxtaposes sacred verse with public praise, through a call-and-response of
classical and colloquial language, Arabic and Bamana. Second, Qur'anic
references are clearly enunciated and often repeated, as Tata's text exemplifies, to draw attention to the words' sacred and, thus, moral significance.
The vocalization may also reflect canonical modes of Islamic verbal art.
Tata's song, thus, evokes the Muslim call to prayer, to which we might
add, in the broader field of Malian popular music, Qur'anic recitation and
sermonic speech. Third, references to the Qur'an are chosen to speak to
the broader themes of the spoken/sung narrative, whether in the form
of public praise, as at the wedding party, or through lyrical criticism and
sentimental verse, as the following case studies will show. Finally, fourth,
Islamic interpellation typically introduces a lyrical passage, founding the
vocal expressions that follow on an ideological edifice of sacred morality.
In this way, Tata invokes Islam as a key prefatory feature of her praise song,
"sweeping away the dangerous energy" at the cosmopolitan wedding party
before the laudatory *jeliya* begins.

*Figure 16. Tata Pound's* Revolution. *Courtesy of Soumaoro Sidy.*

## Bamako Hip-Hop as an Islamic Counterpublic

I turn now to the artful and ethical crafting of one of the previous decade's most anticipated albums in Mali, the hip-hop group Tata Pound's *Revolution* (2006) (Figure 16). As presented on this album, "dangerous energy" (*jnama*) is not confined to a particular venue or event (like a cosmopolitan wedding), but is perceived to permeate Malian society as a whole in the form of police abuse, political corruption, endemic poverty, and a pervasive sense of moral decline (see chapter 1). Since their "underground" beginnings in the mid-1990s, Tata Pound members have been outspoken spokespeople for such socioeconomic concerns, to popular acclaim, but their subcultural criticism is also didactic—a topical vehicle of what they call *conscientisation*. As Tata Pound member Djo Dama Diarra explains, "A rapper is someone who is there to debate the real problems in society, to raise awareness and awaken people's sensibilities. That is our way of contributing to the edification of Malian society."[6] As such, Tata Pound represents what might be called "a hip-hop counter-public" in Mali, using their words and beats to "provide a sense of active belonging that masks or compensates for the real powerlessness of human agents in capitalist society" (Warner 2002, 81; see also Schulz 2012).

Most poignantly, Tata Pound has frequently pointed fingers at and named names among the country's political and financial elites, accusing this dominant "public" of perpetuating a culture of corruption. Theirs is a brazenly critical counter-publicity, in which "it is hoped that the poesis of scene making will be transformative, not replicative merely" (Warner 2002, 88). In this way, Tata Pound's previous album, *Cikan* (*The Message,* a reference to Grandmaster Flash and the Furious Five's classic 1982 hip-hop track), released in the wake of the 2002 presidential elections, signaled the emergence of hip-hop as a powerful medium of political critique in Mali. More generally, it established the group's national renown, further legitimizing hip-hop as a popular art form in the country. In the title song, Tata Pound directs their "message" of popular politics to the presidency itself:

If politicians claim elections are to be transparent, / the people must demand improved conditions, / which means real and unmistakable legitimacy, / These are inalienable rights. / Tata Pound is sending its message to the president, / who came to make change, / who came for equality, justice, and well-being at all times. / But, we demand social progress not only in speeches, / but made real, / felt even by the birds in the countryside. (Tata Pound 2002)[7]

In a public gesture still widely recounted in discussions over afternoon tea, the newly elected (and now deposed) president Amadou Toumani Touré addressed the "young people of the country" on national television and said, "I have heard the message." Tata Pound's follow-up album, *Revolution*, with its angry denunciations of corruption in the police force, among Bamako's borough mayors, and in the presidency itself, is an indication that hip-hop's political "message" remains vital and significant.[8] What the following analysis demonstrates is how this subcultural politics resounds from a pronounced moral center in Malian society. Specifically, I observe how Islamic interpellation enables Tata Pound's edifying social criticism, qualifying their subversive status and identity in religious terms, as an Islamic counter-public.[9] I then relate hip-hop's critical lyricism to the praise singer's moralizing poetics of recognition, drawing these disparate genres of expression together within the broader public of Islamic popular culture in Mali today.

Tata Pound's *Revolution,* which saturated the sociable streetside sound-scape during my year of doctoral fieldwork in Bamako (2006–7), begins with an aural rendering of urban sociability: a brief passage of densely layered, dialogic, and playful conversation, or *baro.* Dorothea Schulz describes such conversational sociability as "the central medium and expression of commensality" in urban Mali. Describing *baro* as "talk-as-action," she emphasizes its capacity "to create sociality . . . that is crucial to a person's being-in-the-world" (2002, 811). As exemplified by the oft-repeated phrase, *baro ka di,* or "Talk is good," everyday banter, stimulated and paced by three rounds of sweetened green tea, is the quintessential sign of urban conviviality in Mali today.[10] It is also a vital site of ethico-moral discourse, in which the everyday back-and-forth of speech about culture and society voices the ethical and moral promise and perils of politics, economy, and sociality in urban Mali. Popular music, as it critically engages with a broader range of topics through a greater diversity of generic forms, filters into these tea-infused streetside conversations with greater and greater frequency, among larger and larger segments of the population.

Among urban, and predominantly male youths, hip-hop has, since the late 1990s, become an especially privileged locus of social, economic, and political discourse (Schulz 2012). It is from this popular center of gravity that Tata Pound introduces their album, talking among themselves about themselves, in a self-aggrandizing mimetic performance of their conversational urban audience.

"Hey guys, how's it going?" one of them asks. "Fine, just fine." Another responds. "Isn't your tea ready yet?" inquires the former. "I'm demoralized," another interjects. "I listen to the radio, and all I hear is Senegalese and Burkinabé rap [and Tata Pound] has been silent for three years." "And you know why?" yet another inquires. "I heard that they've been corrupted by those in power. They have nothing more to say!" "Eh! You don't know anything!" one of them retorts. "Rumors! What crazy rumors!" "Don't get mixed up in things you don't understand," says another. "Tata Pound is coming!" (Tata Pound 2006)

Though the content of this staged conversation sets up a canonical expression of hip-hop counterculture and braggadocio (see Smitherman 1997, 12–13), signifying the diasporic authenticity of this emcee trio, the intersubjective character of the exchange is firmly rooted in a local moral praxis, foregrounding the edifying space of vocal sociability *(baro)* in contemporary Bamako.

This dialogic "intro" is followed by the dark and ethically cautionary track, "Allahou Akbar" ("God Is Great"), in which listeners are warned of the existential perils of an individualistic and unethical life that spurns the blessings of God. In the refrain, Tata Pound members sing, and occasionally scream, the following lines:

| | |
|---|---|
| *Ɛ Ala!* | Oh God! |
| *Alahu akbar!* | God is great! |
| *Ɛ Ala!* | Oh God! |
| *Jabar!* | The Irresistible! |
| *[Ɛ Ala! . . .] Fo bɛɛ ka don* | [Oh God . . .] Everyone must know |
| *ko se tɛ jɔn ye* | that we are powerless |
| *Fo bɛɛ ka dɔn* | Everyone must know |
| *[Ɛ Ala! . . .] ko saya tɛ mɔgɔ tɔ* | [Oh God . . .] that no one is exempt |
| | from death |
| *Abada! Abada! Abada!* | Never! Never! Never! |

It is the word *Ala* that the group sings throughout, alternating between a gently rising and an even melisma on the final *a,* reminiscent of singer Tata Diabaté's *adhan*-inflected "call to praise." In between these sung invocations of the Almighty, rapper Djo Dama cries out to his listeners, "God is great!" and "The Irresistible!" With the latter cry, he cites one of God's ninety-nine names *(al-Jabbar)* from Surat al-Hashr (verse 23). "Everyone must know," he then warns, "that no one is exempt from death," echoing one of the track's signature Islamic themes.

In the third verse, Dixon—the Tata Pound member known for his deep, melodic, and measured verbal art, reminiscent of Dub poetics— pronounces, in Bamana, that "we must fear tomorrow / We must fear God" *("Anw ka siran sini ɲɛ / ka siran Ala ɲɛ")* before citing, in Qur'anic Arabic (as phonetically spoken in Bamana), verse 185 of Surat al-'Umran, "Every soul shall taste death" *("Kulu nafsin zayekatu mawata")*—the latter line vocalized with a slow and eloquent prosody, suggestive of the diction and delivery of Qur'anic recitation. In this passage, and in the previous refrain, the rappers' juxtaposition of colloquial and classical language (Bamana and Arabic), clear articulation of Qur'anic text, and intertextual treatment of scripture on an Islamically themed track resonates strongly with the poetics of recognition articulated earlier by Tata Diabaté. The praise song and rap also share a critical poetics centered on an existential defense of locality. Both call upon moral subjects within the ideological framework of Islam, while at the same time calling out social forces—capitalist cosmopolitanism and unmoored modernity, on the one hand, and political corruption and socioeconomic struggle, on the other—that are perceived to threaten moral community in Mali today.

Both the praise song and rap also call up and qualify their publics before interpellating them under the sign of Islam. Tata's performance begins by celebrating the marriage that brings her public (*juma*) together. Tata Pound invokes its audience through a representation of intimate urban talk (*baro*), the most common social space of hip-hop audition in Bamako. Just as Tata Diabaté primed her public for praise through collective recognition and Islamic interpellation, it is the two opening tracks on Tata Pound's *Revolution*—juxtaposing conversational sociability and an appeal to a common faith—that provide the moral prologue for the remaining eight tracks of scathing social, political, and economic critique of Mali's ruling elite. These critiques constitute the "revolutionary" message for which the album is named, and that have inspired both great enthusiasm from fans and public censure from the Bamako oligarchy. As such, Tata Pound lyrically interpellates both a moral listening public and the immoral subjectivity of those in positions of power. Respect is joined with criticism, much like Tata Diabaté's affirmation of her audience's virtue and implicit critique of her patrons for objecting to laudatory *jeliya* at the wedding. Yet, this Janus-faced co-presence of the moral and immoral in Islamic interpellation is not always so clearly demarcated or stable. It is, thus, to the poetics and politics of misrecognition that I now turn.

## Urban Afropop in the Islamic Ecumene

In this third and final case, I track a locally popular song destined for the world music market through its various mediations and remediations. The song is "Tapha Niang," the penultimate track on two-time Grammy Award–winner Toumani Diabaté's debut—and highly acclaimed—album with his Bamako dance band, the Symmetric Orchestra, *Boulevard de l'Indépendence* (2006). "Tapha Niang" is one of the band's many versions of the piece "Mali Sajo" (two are featured on the album), a staple of the contemporary griot repertoire in the Mande heartland. Senegalese vocalist Moussa Niang sings the song in his native Wolof, though he opens with a short citation of Qur'anic verse, from the same Surat (al-'Umran) cited earlier by Tata Pound: "Every soul shall taste death" *("Kulu nafsin dha'ikat al-mawti")* to which he adds, "All that is on Earth will perish" *("Kulu man 'alayha fanin")* from Surat al-Rahman, verse 26.

I first met Niang in 2000, when he was one of several singers who performed with the Symmetric Orchestra every Friday night at a downtown nightclub called Le Hogon. At this time, the group had been together for nearly ten years and developed an extensive and well-established repertoire of electrified Afropop, mixing modern Western instrumentation (including electric guitars, drum kits, and synthesizers) with traditional instruments of the Malian countryside (such as *kora, jenbe, bala,* and *ngoni*). Over the next few years, the band would refine its translocal, traditional-yet-modern sound (see chapter 3) in preparation for the 2005 recording sessions in Bamako that would result in *Boulevard de l'Indépendence*. Yet, the commitment and rigor of the band's work ethic was, at first glance (or listening), tempered (or, rather untempered) by what could often be unruly and always raucous performances at Le Hogon. Indeed, "loud" does not begin to describe the Symmetric Orchestra's sound, heard late at night (around one or two in the morning), with all members assembled, playing at full volume—amplified by a fair amount of on-stage socioacoustic rivalry *(fadenya)*. Though, according to bandleader Toumani Diabaté, there was musical method to this occasionally ear-splitting madness:

> Anyway, the atmosphere's basically like a jam session, it's like one big village fête. The group really brings the house down, but in fact the gigs are actually work sessions for me. They're really rehearsals in front of a live audience that give the Symmetric Orchestra the chance to try out certain tracks on stage, playing them live several times to mixed audiences. (Diabaté 2006)

And, audiences did come, from near and far, and by the hundreds, to hear the Symmetric Orchestra's hot and lively sound every Friday night; that is, until Le Hogon was shut down in the summer of 2008. At that time, the nightclub's landlord decided to evict the club manager and rent the property to a private Islamic group that wanted to turn the space into a *zawiya*, an Islamic prayer lodge tied to the Tijaniyya Sufi order. The decision to close Le Hogon was apparently financially motivated, with weekend concerts unable to sustain the popular venue. Though, from an aural vantage, replacing the nightclub with a *zawiya* has produced a dramatic remixing of the neighborhood soundscape, with Friday night jam sessions replaced by Friday afternoon prayers and chants of the Muslim faithful. Still, the show goes on. The Symmetric Orchestra now plays, as ever on Friday nights, at Le Diplomate, an addition to the Bamako club scene (as of 2007) located north of the city, along the road to Koulikoro.

"Mali Sajo" remains one of the group's signature pieces—a crowd pleaser, to be sure, but also a frequent vehicle of Islamic interpellation, as we shall observe. Traditionally, the song is a lament, mourning the loss of loved ones. In all variants (of which there are many), the symbol of such loss is the hippopotamus with white dappled feet (a *mali cajo*, in the Khassonké vernacular from which the name derives), an animal that lived peacefully with the people of Bafoulabé ("the town where two rivers meet," in western Mali) but was killed at the hands of a foreign hunter. In many versions, this hunter is a French colonial officer who bears the surname Sauvage.[11] Rendered, thus, as an act of "savage" colonial violence, the death of the hippopotamus—whose Mande name, "Mali," is also that of a postcolonial nation and a precolonial empire—represents a profound loss of sovereignty within an imperial hegemony.

In the chorus, vocalists sing:

| | |
|---|---|
| *Bafilaben mali sa!* | The hippopotamus from Bafoulabé is dead! |
| *Sa, Mali Sajo!* | The hippo with white dappled feet is dead! |
| *Oo! mali sa!* | Oh! The hippopotamus is dead! |
| *Sa, Mali Sajo!* | The hippo with white dappled feet is dead! |

In one of Toumani Diabaté's earlier versions of the song, titled "Mali Sajio" and recorded for the album *Songhai 2* (Diabaté, Ketama, and Soto 1994), griot vocalist and renowned traditionalist Kassé Mady Diabaté sings the following passage:

*Aa! Jili jalali wa likirami*        Ah! The possessor of majesty and honor
*Mansa kelen tile te duniya ban*  One king's reign is not eternal
*Juru Kara Nani, wo tile*            Even Alexander the Great's reign has
    *banna le*                            ended[12]

Beginning with a phrase, sung phonetically with a heavy Mande accent (heard especially in the line's characteristic voweling), from verse 78 of Surat al-Rahman, (in Arabic, *Dhi-l-jalali wa-l-ikrami*), Kassé Mady reflects on the transience of life that spares no one, not even great kings. (The Mande term for Alexander the Great, *Juru Kara Nani,* is derived from his Arabic name *Dhu-l-Qarnayn,* meaning "the two-horned one.") Here, again, Islam interpellates the morality (and mortality) of its listening subjects through the spirited voice of Qur'anic verse.

In Moussa Niang's version, he sings of the passing of his younger brother, Mustapha, a soldier in the Senegalese Army who died in the contested southern region of Casamance (Figure 17). At the song's outset, Niang calls on Islam and bonds of family to confront his grief. "Tapha is gone," he sings. "That is why we are crying." Through the same poetics of recognition that preceded Tata's praise song at the wedding party, the social criticism on Tata Pound's *Revolution,* and the traditional lament in "Mali Sajo," Niang invokes Qur'anic verse to morally ground his vocal dirge, situating himself and his listeners in a pious sociomusical space. Following this sacred incantation, Niang publicly addresses his sadness, a sadness shared, moreover, by all those who have experienced loss. "This is what Tapha Niang shares with Mali Sajo," he tells me, describing the setting of his lyrics to this Mande classic. "When the hippopotamus is killed by the French soldier, it represents a loss for everyone."[13] Like Tata Diabaté's vernacular apologia and Tata Pound's popular call to arms, Niang's lyrical lament suggests, once again, a defense of local sense and sentiment, articulating the universal mortality of all living things ("All roads lead to Rome," Niang likes to say) with the personal experience of mourning in the wake of loss. Niang's reference to internecine conflict in Senegal echoes Mali Sajo's (post)colonial critique of imperial militarism; both are contexts of war that transcend as they envelop the local and both are expressed in deeply personal terms. "I am crying, [and] I am crying again," Niang sings. "I am alone."[14]

Yet, Niang's lyrical piety and personal grief resonate beyond this local

*Figure 17. Moussa Niang. Courtesy of Moussa Niang.*

elegy. On an album destined for global audiences, the invocation of scripture is also, as bandleader Toumani Diabaté explains, "a way to attract and
inspire people toward Islam" (as cited in Totilo 2008). Such public affirmation of faith is an integral part of Diabaté's musical persona, and serves
as a reminder that songs like "Tapha Niang" are multivalent, with multiple
claims made on their musical content.[15] For Niang, the song's meaning is
profoundly intimate, and he employs Islamic interpellation to moralize
and publicize this intimacy, through a poetics of recognition (the vocal
interpolation of Qur'anic verse). To this, Diabaté adds a touch of Islamic
evangelism, representing the religion in positive terms to an international
audience largely outside this community of faith. As Diabaté's record
label, World Circuit, states, "Toumani never performs without speaking
about God, either before, during or after the performance" (Totilo 2008).
Of course, for many world music fans, reference to Islam signifies no more
than an appeal to the exotic (Said 1978), an allure that sustains the international careers of groups like the Symmetric Orchestra. For such audiences, this version of "Mali Sajo" is attractive and inspiring not for its
personal and positive invocation of Islam but for the "African-ness" of its
global pop groove: its upbeat tempo, catchy horn riffs, dense texture, and
complex syncopated rhythms.[16]

It is precisely this musical alterity that made "Tapha Niang" a featured
track on the PlayStation 3 video game *LittleBigPlanet,*[17] providing the soundtrack to the "Swinging Safari" level on the game, an auditory and visual
fantasy of primitive Africa. Here, the game's scruffy protagonist, an an-
thropomorphic puppet named Sackboy, runs, jumps, and swings through
a cartoonish African wilderness filled with safari animals, tribal iconography, and percussive instruments aplenty. "Tapha Niang" plays in the
background, turned down slightly in the mix to let the game play resound.
With a well-timed jump or smash of a gong, Niang's poetics of recognition might easily be lost to the gaming world's "invention of Africa" (see
Mudimbe 1988). The vocalized Qur'anic verse became, however, more than
just an exotic sound bite when, on October 16, 2008, it was heard anew.
An anonymous Muslim gamer revealed the Islamic reference in an open
letter to Sony and game designer Media Molecule after noticing "some
very familiar Arabic words from the Quran." Citing the concern of "certain
Arabic hardcore gaming forums," the gamer states, "We Muslims consider
the mixing of music and words from our Holy Quran deeply offending.

We hope you would remove that track from the game immediately via an online patch, and make sure that all future shipments of the game disk do not contain it" (Luke K 2010). Within days, Sony had recalled the game from retailers and delayed its release. This triggered lengthy debates about political correctness, artistic censorship, and the practice of religious piety in the public sphere on popular gaming blogs (see, for example, Graft 2008). It also drew critical attention to Toumani Diabaté's particular blend of faith and music. "In my family there are two things we know, the Koran and the *kora*," he told the BBC, referring to the Muslim holy book and the Mande harp (cited in Michaels 2008). Describing this musico-religious sentiment to me two years later, Diabaté raised his left hand, forming an O-shape with his index finger and thumb with the remaining three fingers raised. "You see?" he asked, indicating the correct hand position to hold and play the *kora*. "It says, *Allahu*," suggesting that musical performance and religious piety go, literally, hand in hand.[18] Yet, the event had taken its toll. "I don't want anybody to joke with . . . and [disrespect] Islam," Diabaté told the BBC, acknowledging that the controversy had left him "sad" and "disappointed" (Michaels 2008).

## At Home in the World?

What this incident reveals is the real possibility of interpellative mis-recognition in the mediated space of global culture, in which decontextualized voices "call on" consumer publics who (mis)apprehend the vocal sign—in this case, an apparently "unorthodox" expression of Islam—and (re)assess its value and virtue. It also brings the vital though increasingly precarious experience of locality in urban Africa (addressed in chapter 1) into greater relief. In Bamako, Diabaté's musico-religious fusion is part of a broader Islamic popular culture, in which moral subjects are interpellated through a multigeneric poetics of recognition. As the case studies presented have shown, this poetics is defined by the juxtaposition of classical and colloquial language registers, stylized vocal expression with resonances of Islamic verbal art, lyrical intertextuality of scriptural and poetic themes, and a prefatory function in performance, live or mediated. When Tata Diabaté invokes this poetics, she refuses a salaried, cosmopolitan art world by interpellating her public as moral participants in laudatory *jeliya*. When Tata Pound calls on Islam, they do so as a cautionary prelude to a revolutionary critique of postcolonial statism. And, when Toumani Diabaté defends Moussa Niang's religiously inflected lament against conservative critics, he also demands that the poetic voice of Islam in his music be recognized for what it is—a rooted expression of faith—and not denied, as an ecumenical aberration. In all cases, Islamic interpellation through Qur'anic interpolation testifies to the ethical and aesthetic vitality of popular culture in Bamako today, becoming a vocal icon of locality—a pious poetics of place—against the social, political, and religious orthodoxies of globalization and the myriad forms it takes in everyday life.

In the following two chapters, I interrogate such global orthodoxies further, moving from questions of cultural aesthetics and public piety to those of cultural policy and political subjectivity. In chapter 5, I examine the historically emergent category of intellectual property, rendered as *le droit d'auteur* in French copyright law and interpreted within the shifting politics of culture in postcolonial Mali. Beginning with widespread anxieties about the social and economic value of the arts in an era of private markets and decentralized politics, I present a genealogy of music copyright and its criminalized corollary, piracy, from the late colonial period to the present. Emphasizing the production, circulation, and performance of music, this history reveals the long-standing and steadily deepening economic precarity that has shaped the subjectivity of most contemporary Malian artists. In the final chapter, I consider the extent to which one may consider such artists and their music to be "Malian"—political subjects of a postcolonial nation-state—in a time of regional crisis, internecine conflict, and ongoing statist abuses.

# Money Trouble

## *Wariko*

In November 2006, the Triton Stars, an aspiring Malian dance band (whose work we encountered in chapters 2 and 3), finished up a four-day run at Studio Bogolan in Bamako (Figure 18). The recordings were for the band's second album, a follow-up to their first release, *Immigration*, which had been on the market since January of the same year without any sales to speak of. In an effort to rejuvenate the band's prospects, producer Racine Dia decided to re-release the first album in January 2007, to be followed soon thereafter by the second (as yet untitled) album, building on the anticipated success of the first. The problem, Dia told me, was that nobody in Mali knew the Triton Stars. They didn't have "a name" (or *togo*, meaning "a reputation") in the city. To rectify this, the group would play a series of weekly concerts free of charge.

*Figure 18. Triton Stars. Photograph by the author.*

On a Friday evening in early December, audience members—including friends of the band, shoppers from the nearby Sogoniko market, and a large contingent of neighborhood youth—sat noisily on plastic chairs laid out on a small grassy field in front of the concrete stage. Others stood behind them, or along the wall marking the perimeter of the Centre de Recherche Culturelle et Artistique, a privately funded cultural center. At 9:30 P.M., the Triton Stars took the stage, right on schedule, kicking off with a track from their new album, a piece called "Wariko" ("Money Trouble"), a hard-edged and fast-paced Afropop arrangement. Lyrically, the song addressed a theme to which everyone present could relate: the socioeconomic precarity inherent to a loosely regulated and generally inequitable cash economy. In the opening verse, lead singer Karounga Sacko belted out the following lines:

| | |
|---|---|
| *I ma dɔn tile min ye* | Don't you know that the sun today |
| *tile farin farin?* | is a very hot sun? |
| *Kow bɛɛ dalen wariko de la.* | Everything is tied to money trouble. |
| *Aaaa! Wari man ɲi de.* | Ahhh! Money is not good. |
| *Balima dama ye ɲɔgɔn na bila,* | Family members are beset by dispute, |
| *ko nin kun ye wariko!* | because of money trouble! |
| *Furuɲɔgɔn dama ye ɲɔgɔn* | Married couples are beset by dispute, |
| *na bila,* | |
| *ko nin kun ye wariko!* | because of money trouble! |
| *Sigiɲɔgɔn dama ye ɲɔgɔn na bila,* | Neighbors are beset by dispute, |
| *ko nin kun ye wariko!* | because of money trouble! |
| *Jɛɲɔgɔnmɔgɔw ye ɲɔgɔn janfa la.* | Close friends have betrayed each other. |
| *Aaaa! Wari man ɲi de.* | Ahhh! Money is not good. |
| *Ne dun siranna.* | As for me, I am afraid. |
| *Ne bɛ siran wari ɲɛ.* | I am afraid of money. |
| *A ye furu sa.* | It kills marriage. |

During my fieldwork in Bamako, the phrase *wariko,* much like the incessant heat of the afternoon sun (as Sacko poetically notes), was ubiquitous. When a roving hawker entered into a family compound in hopes of selling his wares, he was almost always greeted with a polite *"Wariko,"* meaning, "Sorry, we don't have money to spend today." When a friend or a relation approached her companion, brother, or sister for some extra cash to get through the week, she often heard *"Wariko"* in response, implying: "I'd like to help, but I have the same problem right now." In the market, the phrase echoed in the mouths of peddlers and hagglers with such redundant frequency that it became a sort of vocal leitmotif in Bamako's urban soundscape. Echoing this refrain, Sacko probed its psychosocial dangers. Because of money trouble, extended families, neighbors, siblings, and close friends are embroiled in argument and betrayal. Money inspires fear and kills marriage. It threatens both self and society.

Later in the show, the subject of money trouble returned, this time in the words of two emcees (French, *animateurs*), whose stage patter between songs playfully referenced the precarious livelihoods of professional artists in Mali. "Everyone will get together to buy this cassette," one of the emcees announced. "So, what's the problem? You only need to listen to the first track on the A side. Honestly, you will hear people making noise! When that track is playing, you will be pleased." What, then, was the problem? As the second emcee explained, it was not simply social and aesthetic; it was also, and perhaps more urgently, political and economic:

> This cassette, it's good from start to finish [*kun f'a kun*, literally "head to head"]. If you know it, you know what's in it. What do we want from you? You can tell others about it. I know it. [The Triton Stars] are young musicians, who are on the rise. The problem these artists face, though, is cassette piracy. If you haven't bought this cassette, if you want these musicians to advance. . . . If you buy this cassette, make your best effort [to buy the one] with the sticker on it and the BuMDA [Bureau Malien du Droit d'Auteur] label. That's the only way artists can make a living.

In this chapter, I historicize this complex "problem" by interrogating the salient and oppositional forms *wariko* takes within the Malian culture industry: copyright (French, *le droit d'auteur*) and piracy.[1] I also consider, like Sacko in his song, the socioeconomic repercussions of this "money trouble" in the working lives of professional artists. Yet, as the Triton Stars' concert made clear, such troubles are not just about money; rather, they index a pervasive sense of precarity that triangulates social, political, and economic uncertainty for which money, and its widespread lack, is the privileged sign.[2] As sociologist Franco Barchiesi describes, in a poignant critique of (neo)liberal economic rationality,

"Precarity" transcends the problematics of employment insecurity [glossed here as "money trouble"] in conventional policy and sociological debates, emphasizing instead the crisis of work and of an entire normative and symbolic universe that, during the decades of global neoliberal hegemony, has heavily come to rely on the employment imperative. (2012)

For many artists, the professional precarity signified by *wariko* has a clear source: music piracy. "The problem these artists face," the emcee said. It is this qualification of piracy as an objective and strongly negative truth— what Barchiesi calls a "normative and symbolic universe" and what I have described in the present text as a moralizing "social position"—that this chapter seeks to historically contextualize and, in doing so, problematize.

As the scene described indicates, appeals to confront the problem of piracy and affirm the status and identity of local artists as rights-bearing subjects resound within the Malian public sphere. Such arguments echo anxieties about the social and economic value of music in an era of privatized markets and decentralized politics, a sentiment expressed when the emcee spoke, from the stage of a private cultural center, of "*the only way* artists can make a living" (my emphasis). Through such claims on sociomusical justice, a contemporary discourse of neoliberal governance takes shape around the concept of culture, defined as an expedient object of curatorial and commoditized expression (Yudicé 2004). Copyright and its ubiquitous infringement, piracy, represent the normative and aberrant forms through which culture is produced and policed in Mali, as elsewhere (see Karaganis 2011); that is, they are the categorical means by which governmentality—the regulatory and disciplinary politics of population management and control in modern states (Foucault 2007)—operates as cultural policy under the global sign of neoliberalism (see Guilbault 2007).

In practice, however, the politics of culture in Mali has succeeded neither in securing the legal and pecuniary interests of musicians nor in stemming the unauthorized reproduction of musical works. This perceived failure of neoliberal governance manifests in what I have elsewhere called an artistic "crisis of political subjectivity" (Skinner 2012a), in which musicians, caught between a dysfunctional state and an informal economy that flourishes in its midst, struggle to sustain a viable professional status and identity. In what follows, I put these artistic struggles into historical relief by tracing a genealogy of copyright and its criminalized corollary, piracy, through an emergent politics of culture in Mali. This history reveals the long-standing, though steadily deepening social, political, and economic precarity that has shaped the subjectivity of the postcolonial Malian musician. This chapter is, thus, a particular history of *wariko* as experienced by musicians in the Malian art world from the era of independence to the present. It is a critical inquiry, in other words, into the cultural-economic social position of the Malian artist. I begin by bringing the past to bear on this current era of neoliberalism and the pervasive "money trouble" it produces. I then interrogate the governmentalization of culture as a regime of rights and discipline in postcolonial Mali. As a cadential counterpoint, I conclude with a short reflection on what I will call "nongovernmental culture," or the forms of expression that articulate outside—and often in violation—of the disciplinary institutions of neoliberal governmentality. Yet, as we observe in this chapter, Bamako's nongovernmental culture can only be fully understood in relation to the history of cultural governmentalization in postcolonial Mali. The problem of governance as a crucial existential concern for contemporary Malians, artists or otherwise, is further explored in the next chapter.

## Artistic Rights and Labor in Post Independence Mali

In 1957, artists working in the French Soudan (now Mali) and other French colonies were allowed to join the Société des Auteurs, Compositeurs et Editeurs de Musique (SACEM), a French agency that managed the licensing of artistic works and the collection and distribution of royalties for affiliated artists (Diakité 2006, 54; see also Laing 2004, 71–72). This imperial affiliation did not last long. Following independence three years later, all music produced in Mali, in line with the new nation's policy of cutting institutional ties with its former colonizer, fell under the purview of the state. Up until 1977, Mali did not have any codified copyright law or bureaucratic mechanism for distributing royalties. This meant, in practice, that the postcolonial state could act as the sole arbiter of domestic cultural production, distribution, and exploitation. In 1962, Mali did, however, ratify the Berne Convention in nominal deference to international intellectual property law, and, the same year, the government signed the continental accord creating the Organisation Africaine de la Propriété Intellectuelle (Cissé and Traoré 2001, 7). In 1963, Mali reaffirmed its commitment to "the harmonization of copyright law in Africa" at a UNESCO-sponsored meeting of the International Bureau for the Protection of Intellectual Property in Brazzaville but argued that such legislation should "take local context and popular opinion into account" (Ntahokaja 1963, 252–53),[3] thereby affirming the authority of individual African states to legislate intellectual property as they saw fit. Despite the official public rhetoric of international and continental agreement, copyright in Mali remained uncodified and subject to arbitrary state interpretation for nearly two decades.

As copyright goes, so go the artists. In the 1960s, musicians in Mali were beholden to the state as clients of a nationalist politics of culture (Skinner 2012b), although until 1966 they were not employed by the state. For the most part, artists worked informally, living off a share of ticket sales from concert performances, without any formal employment contract.[4] Their musical labor (performed and recorded) was considered property of the state, part of the socialist government's reliance on citizens' patriotic *fasobaara* or "work for the nation." In the early 1960s, this could sometimes mean unpaid labor, described in terms normally associated with colonial rule: *forosɛbaara* and *diyagoyabaara*, or "forced labor" and "whether-you-like-it-or-not work." "They couldn't pay us," recalls Nfa Diabaté, a retired member of the Ensemble Instrumental National, "so they called it *fasobaara*"— a postcolonial expression of *wariko* in the 1960s Malian art world.[5]

And, as artists go, so goes their work. In the post-independence era, musical recordings were made and archived at Radio Mali, the single, state-owned media outlet that housed the country's only recording studio (see Mamadou Diawara 1997). These recordings were, for the most part, propagandistic in terms of content, with themes that emphasized nationalist use value, including comparisons of the modern nation-state to the precolonial Mali Empire ("Maliba," Great Mali); calls for newly ordained Malian nationals displaced within the former French Empire to return home (*Yan Ka Di*, "Here Is Good"); and appeals to work for the homeland (*Fasobaara*, "Nation Building").[6] Exchange value was a lesser concern. Recordings of such "nationalist" music were made principally for radio broadcast. Long-play pressings of state-sponsored Malian groups did not appear until the late 1960s and were not widely distributed until the early 1970s.[7] By contrast, foreign-produced LPs had long been in circulation (since at least the 1940s), especially in the capital, Bamako, where such regional and global sounds were coveted commodities within an urban popular culture that thrived throughout the 1950s, '60s, and '70s (Manthia Diawara 1997).

A disjuncture thus emerged between the circulation and consumption of national and foreign music that, under the increasingly authoritarian rule of the single-party state in the late 1960s, also marked the fault lines of official and unofficial culture. As a young activist of the ruling party asked in December 1967, "Does the Malian revolution need James Brown [or] Johnny [Hallyday] . . . to fill the catalog of its National radio?"[8] Perhaps not; yet, despite efforts to inhibit foreign (which usually meant Western and neocolonialist) cultural influence (see, for example, Arnoldi 2006, 60), such recordings continued to resonate within Bamako's urban soundscape.[9] For Malian artists, this cleavage between the national and the popular, the official and the unofficial, became a source of great frustration. With their domestic labor beholden to a single venue of broadcast distribution at the national radio, and without any legal right to their recorded work in Mali, cultural labor's subordinate status became patent. Internationally renowned musician Sorry Bamba's autobiography (Bamba and Prévost 1996) recounts his attempt to procure copies of an album released on the occasion of Mali's tenth anniversary of independence for his state-sponsored band, the Orchestre Régional de Mopti (1970). His narrative captures the perceived injustice of Mali's centralist policy toward cultural production and ownership (Bamba and Prévost 1996, 134):

Each of the musicians was looking forward to receiving a copy of the disc. But, when they saw the Youth Director giving one disc to the authorities in Mopti and only one for the entire Orchestra, they were shocked by the deception! This meant that just one disc was to be shared, like a wafer, among all of the musicians in the Orchestra!

Such pettiness nauseated me to such a degree that I lost interest, given the circumstances, in this recording. And yet, this disc represented my own research and adaptation, backed up, of course, by the competence of the musicians. If copyright is respected in other countries, here, it does not exist. I know this well, because I have been a member of SACEM since 1968 and released a number of albums in Côte d'Ivoire.

In Mali [in the 1960s and 1970s], all albums were the property of the state. It was not even possible for a composer [auteur-compositeur] to reclaim the studio tapes of his own works if the Youth Ministry decided to keep them for a recording. Radio Mali was not permitted to give out a copy to these artists [auteurs].

In the face of this injustice, a friend of mine managed to acquire

some of my recordings that were being broadcast on the Radio
Mali airwaves. It was only because of this effort, that I had the immense joy of being able to possess just a few of my own works!

As Bamba describes, Malian artists' access to their recorded works through
the 1960s and into the 1970s was restricted by a highly centralized culture
economy and subject to the arbitrary decisions of local and national authorities, subverted only by the surreptitious pirating—to complicate the
shades of illegality the contemporary term *piracy* implies—of the artists'
own music broadcast on the national airwaves.

These frustrations about cultural ownership, production, and circulation coincided with a coup d'état in November 1968, the immediate
aftermath of which (following a brief period of hopeful jubilation; see
Sanankoua 1990, 55) exacerbated artists' woes. After the coup, all cultural
troupes, orchestras, and ensembles were disbanded by the ruling military
junta, the Comité Militaire de Libération Nationale, and remained so for
more than a year.[10] Without salaried contracts and with their status as unofficial agents of national culture under the previous regime, Malian artists faced a stark choice: leave the country and embark on an indefinite
exile, or stay and weather the storm of military rule, hoping for the best.
Many left. Abidjan, the booming capital of Côte d'Ivoire, Mali's richer and
more liberal (if not entirely democratic) southern neighbor, became the
destination of choice. Sorry Bamba described sentiments shared by many
Malian artists in the post-coup years:

> Suddenly, I understood the scope of a Coup d'Etat. All regime
> changes shake people's spirits. Everyone must learn to observe the
> new methods of those who claim power. . . . What's more, I must
> fight vigorously against the despair that surrounds me, faced with
> so much aggression, so uncommon in the artistic community.
> Why so much hostility toward the pioneering musicians of Malian
> music? Our music, born with our country's Independence, does it
> not belong to everyone? If, in my own country, creativity no longer
> has a place, so much the reason to get back on the difficult path of
> exile. (Bamba and Prévost 1996, 112)

The 1970s Ivoirian economy, bolstered by lucrative cocoa and coffee ex-
ports and President Houphouët Boigny's clientelist politics, provided

for a strong patron class in Abidjan. Some of these wealthy and well-placed entrepreneurs had personal ties to Mali and favored the arts, like Souleymane Koli, who recruited expatriate Malian artists into the famed Ballets Koteba (see Skinner 2004, 144–45). Flush with cash and a fondness for popular culture, Abidjan quickly emerged as the capital of the regional music industry. "Musicians came from the four corners of francophone Africa to try their luck in Côte d'Ivoire," writes Chérif Keïta, in his biography of Malian singer Salif Keita, one of Abidjan's seminal figures in the late 1970s and early 1980s. "This situation imposed a new kind of rationality on the African artist, who could no longer hope to survive by courting local audiences or counting on the patronage of the State" (2009, 76). In Abidjan's highly competitive, market capitalist music scene, "artistic rationality" meant seeking out patrons, cutting records, and embarking on tours in the regional, continental, and increasingly international African culture industry. Back in Bamako, the state oligarchy (now in civilian guise as the Union Démocratique du Peuple Malien) maintained its grip on cultural production, patronizing select groups that practiced the art of political flattery (2009, 37); however, by the end of the 1970s, political and economic changes were underway that, within a decade, would herald the end of the centralized and authoritarian regime itself (compare Pauthier 2012).

## The Neoliberal Turn

In 1977, Mali enacted its first copyright law (77–46/CMLN), providing for the protection of the "literary and artistic property" of culture producers, or "authors." This was followed in 1978 by the creation of the Bureau Malien du Droit d'Auteur (BuMDA), whose mission was to "defend the intellectual, moral, and pecuniary interests of authors and their rights therein" (Cissé and Traoré 2001, 5). However, without a clear mandate to enforce intellectual property rights, and given the persistence of statist sponsorship of the arts through the mid-1980s (despite increasingly austere socioeconomic conditions), real changes in artists' professional status and identity (though not necessarily those envisaged by the laws) would not come until the mid-1980s. In July 1984, in a brochure commemorating the closing of the 8th Biennale Artistique et Culturelle, a state-sponsored biannual cultural festival, the director of arts and culture, an adjunct to the minister of culture, prepared a series of responses to questions concerning

the event's successes and failures.[11] His response to the fourth, penultimate question was revealing and prescient given the changes occurring
not only in the Malian culture economy but in the political economy of
the postcolony more broadly.

4. *Monsieur le Directeur,* you know better than anyone else that
broadcast and circulation are the best ways to encourage cultural
creation, yet the works from the last Biennale were not widely
broadcast or circulated. Why?

*RESPONSE: 4th QUESTION*

I am obliged to say what many people would not like to hear. Nonetheless, it's the sad reality. In fact, the reason these works have not
been broadcast and circulated is due to a lack of means. And as you
have so well put it, the broadcast and circulation of these works
is our objective. But it is necessary for us to recognize that we do
not possess for the moment the national structure allowing [us]
to broadcast and circulate works not only from the biennales, but
those of our different artists in a general manner. . . .
     You see, as our proverb says so well, "when you sweat in the
rain, no one notices" *[quand on sue sous la pluie, les gens ne peuvent
pas s'en rendre compte].*[12] But I have to say, to conclude with this
question, that the solution to the problem of broadcast and circulation of our artists' works in general and of those from the Biennales
in particular, can only be found in the creation of a production
facility for cassettes and [long play] discs in Mali. Thus, we call on
our businessmen both in and out of the country to help us to de-
finitively resolve this thorny problem that dangerously hinders artistic creation in our country, not to mention the danger of seeing
our artists emigrate to find a record company in the best of cases,
and, in the worst of cases, to find themselves estranged from the
fruits of their labor by the illicit production of discs and cassettes.

This question-and-answer passage effectively captures the shifting sociopolitical position of Malian artists and the changing perceptions of their
work in the mid-1980s. The question succinctly makes the point that pro-
ponents of "free culture" (Lessig 2004) have long advocated: that cultural

creativity benefits from greater public access to cultural products, in this case through increased broadcast and circulation of recorded works on the airwaves and in the marketplace. The response, however, signals the new orientation of Malian cultural policy—toward an emergent neoliberal governmentality—in a time of socioeconomic austerity: the state, no longer possessing the means to manage the production and distribution of cultural works, must privatize public culture. Written in July, in the midst of the rainy season, the director describes the state's anxiety—"sweating in the rain"—about producing and promoting new cultural works and calls on "our businessmen both in and out of the country" to invest in the development of a private culture industry. This call to liberalize Mali's stagnant culture economy responds to two problems that "dangerously hinder artistic creation": (1) emigration of national artists (discussed previously), and (2) "the illicit production of discs and cassettes" (or what would later be called, simply, "piracy"), the latter being the worst of cases, suggesting the emergent state of the counterfeit market at the time.

As this statement was written, major changes in the social, economic, and political character of the arts in Mali were already underway and would accelerate by decade's end. In June 1984 (a month before the biennial), the Malian parliament passed a law (84-26/AN-RM) to replace the 1977 ordinance defining artistic and literary property. The updated document more specifically elaborated the notion of copyright and included a statement outlining what constitutes illicit reproduction of copyrighted material (articles 31–36) and a list of sanctions for various infractions (articles 135–48)—making media piracy an object of governmental intervention. Two years later, largely in response to the exigencies of International Monetary Fund–sponsored Structural Adjustments Programs (SAPs), the government passed legislation (86-13/AN-RM) to reform the code of commerce, effecting a radical liberalization of the national economy that privatized and liquidated many state-owned businesses—making public sector retrenchment an object of governmental intervention. Enter the private sphere. In 1988, French entrepreneur Philippe Berthier, disillusioned with the punk rock scene in Lyon, shuttered his record store and moved to Bamako, where he established Mali's first private multitrack recording studio. In 1989, Berthier opened the country's first cassette duplication factory, which, along with his studio, formed the base of his new company, Ou Bien Productions (Maillot 2002). A private music industry was thus born in Mali, founded on the codification of copyright, the criminalization of media piracy, investment in private infrastructure, and a radical divestment in public institutions, including state-sponsored artistic groups and festivals.

Yet, expectations of a rationalized culture economy soon encountered the limits of neoliberal governmentality within the fragile Malian political economy. On March 26, 1991, following months of protests in the capital city, the dictatorial regime of Moussa Traoré fell to a coup d'état whose leaders quickly earned popular support by announcing their commitment to democratic reforms. As an interim government stepped into power, civil society expanded, signaled by the mushrooming of private radio stations in Malian towns and cities (Couloubaly 2004, 24; see also Tower 2008). Often cited as evidence of a new democratic spirit surging throughout the continent in the early 1990s, cultural authorities perceived the proliferation of these new media outlets with trepidation. The BuMDA, which was given further autonomy and greater authority to represent and defend the pecuniary interests of artists in a 1990 ordinance (90–55/P-RM), witnessed what it viewed as an unprecedented affront to artistic copyright with the sudden increase in private radio broadcasts. Recorded music of all kinds filled the airwaves as new stations vied for listening publics (see Tower 2005). However, no royalty payments were made for the broadcast of these recorded works, setting an unlawful precedent for private radio broadcast in Mali that continues to this day.[13] Since 1984, in accordance with article 29 of the intellectual property law 84–26/AN-RM, the Office de Radiodiffusion et de Télévision du Mali (Mali's national broadcaster) has paid a fixed annual sum of 5 million CFA francs ($10,000) to the BuMDA, a fee recently (2002) complemented with a further 100 million CFA francs ($200,000) annual government subsidy (Couloubaly 2004, 169). A 1994 amendment (94–043) to the 1984 copyright legislation (84–26/AN-RM) requires private radio stations to pay a similar flat annual fee for the use of musical works, although such payments remain disputed and, thus, commercial radio broadcasts in the private sphere remain, officially, unlawful.

Where media goes, the musicians follow. From the late 1980s, many state-sponsored artists were offered severance benefits, including early pensions for those who qualified, in an effort to reduce civil servant expenses in line with SAP protocols. As a matter of policy, the process of cultural privatization had been underway since the late 1970s, spearheaded by Minister of Culture (and later President) Alpha Oumar Konaré. Artists departing the state-sponsored orchestras and ensembles at this time (including popular divas Kandia Kouyaté, Ami Koita, Tata Bambo, and Nahawa Doumbia from the Ensemble Instrumental National) formed new groups and introduced the notion of the solo artist to regional audiences.[14] Bolstered by the presence of a domestic and private (if limited) record industry (that is, Ou Bien Productions), the decline of Abidjan as a regional center of music production, an influx of foreign capital in the form of world music (then, a new concept; see Feld 2000, 146–51), and the subsequent proliferation of private radio following the 1991 coup (which did much to promote the work of Malian artists, despite official accusations of copyright infringement), many musicians' careers did, in fact, take off. This has been described as a period of "effervescence" in Malian music (Touré 1996, 98). No longer bound to the state, artists were now free to explore private enterprise in an unfettered capitalist terrain. But, just as conditions were ripe for the rise of prominent solo artists in the early 1990s, so too were circumstances ideal for the further "criminalization" of the Malian culture economy (see Bayart et al. 1999) and a parallel effervescence of neoliberal *wariko* ("money trouble") in the artistic community.

When musicians go, the state turns its back. In many ways, this criminalization begins, not with piracy, but with the state's Voluntary Early Retirement (VER) programs, first authorized in August 1986.[15] Between 1987 and 1989, the United States Agency for International Development (USAID) sponsored a pilot program to offer civil servants (*fonctionnaires*) a single lump-sum pension before their anticipated retirement. Six hundred forty-four people left the civil service during this first wave of VER. A second wave, which transpired sporadically between 1991 and 1995,[16] saw 5,023 state employees leave, including *subventionnaires,* a category of subaltern civil servants that included many state-sponsored artists. The lump sum offered to *fonctionnaires* was 2,500,000 CFA francs ($5,000). *Subventionnaires* received 1,500,000 CFA francs ($3,000).[17] In the early 1990s, under the leadership of then-President Alpha Oumar Konaré, the state encouraged artists in particular to opt for the VER, using their pensions as start-up capital to form new orchestras and ensembles.[18] Although many private music groups did form during the 1980s and 1990s, I found no evidence that VER funds contributed to the formation of any orchestra or ensemble. Those groups that did emerge and succeed outside the aegis of the state benefited from the renown of already established artists, as with the solo divas of the Ensemble Instrumental National mentioned earlier (see Durán 1995a). Most artists who opted for VER saw their capital disappear into extant debt, family obligations, and everyday expenses. If private sector aspirations ever were envisioned, they soon became the source of bitterness and despair.[19]

## Anarchy and Control

As state authorities pushed artists into a growing private sector, they did little to monitor or regulate the emergent culture economy that sector fostered. Even so, state discipline, the punitive corollary to privatization, was not entirely absent and, in hindsight, seems merely to have been deferred. In June 1993, the BuMDA conducted a police seizure operation in media markets throughout Bamako and collected 39,500 cassettes, of which 12,274 were determined to be pirated. (It is not clear what happened to the remaining 27,226 "legitimate" cassettes.) As Mandé Diakité reports, "This action was condemned by the authorities, and 'the fight against piracy,' judged inopportune, was suspended until September 1994 due to the insecurity that reigned over punitive actions of any kind in Mali" (2006, 4). In an effort to secure the legitimacy of the new democratic Republic and distance themselves from the recently ousted junta, government authorities under the leadership of President Alpha Oumar Konaré strategically refrained from any overt acts of state intervention. Indeed, after two decades of political misrule (Diarrah 1991) the state had become a conspicuous target of popular animosity. As Diakité describes:

> After the coup d'état [of 1991], there was a period when the authorities could not collect taxes. Why? Because, at the time, there was a sense of overwhelming freedom *[la grande libérté]*. People would say, "I don't respect the State. I don't respect the actions of the State. . . ." Well, each time that we [at the BuMDA] attempted to conduct seizures [of pirated media], we were told "no, all such operations are prohibited." Thus, when [democracy and economic liberalization] came, they manifest themselves as a rejection of authority, [and] this rejection spread to all sectors [of society].[20]

"Henceforth," Diakité writes elsewhere, "piracy would take root with impunity and become habitual among merchants," adding, more polemically, that "over the course of three years, the pillaging of artists and producers would occur everywhere and at all times without risk to the offenders" (Diakité 2006, 4).

Though Diakité's passionate and unambiguously critical take on this history of piracy is clearly driven by his longtime work with the Malian Copyright Office, his observation of the increasingly "habitual" nature of economic informality within an unregulated media marketplace is important. This is because habit engenders assumptions of "natural conditions" and a certain acceptance of things as they are, however disquieting, dangerous, or destructive those things might be. In the context of laissez-faire capitalism, media piracy did, as Diakité argues, become an entrenched fixture of the Malian culture economy. Yet, as described earlier, this cultural economic condition—of the counterfeit reproduction and sale of commercial media—was preceded by the habit of public divestment in the arts, in line with prescribed SAPs, combined with the similarly structured habit of governmental deregulation—to say nothing of the habits of (re)production and circulation that the media themselves produced (see Larkin 2008). Later, a habit of periodic police discipline would develop to confront the counterfeit culture economy; thus, criminalizing piracy, too, became a habit. In other words, the habitual problem of piracy is rooted in the paradigmatic and hegemonic habits of neoliberalism: divestment, deregulation, and discipline. The result is a postcolonial culture economy that is torn between perceptions of anarchy and prescriptions of control (Comaroff and Comaroff 2006), a position that serves only to further entrench neoliberal habits, not redress them.

These habits would gain steam through the 1990s. In March 1994, the legal mandate of the BuMDA was once again strengthened by an amendment (94–043/AN-RM) to the 1984 copyright law (84–26/AN-RM). The same year, music critic Banning Eyre reports that the Malian government made an unsuccessful attempt to shut down Radio Kayira, a private Bamako based radio station that was fiercely critical of the government (2000, 198), on the grounds of copyright infringement.[21] The following year, global music production house EMI, affiliated with Ou Bien Productions since 1992, closed its operations on the continent (with the exception of South Africa). Ou Bien chief Philippe Berthier, lacking a strong international backer, turned to local entrepreneur and Grammy Award–winning musician, the late Ali Farka Touré (Maillot 2002). With Touré's partnership, a move that bolstered the local legitimacy of this previously foreign-owned company, a new business, Mali K7 (pronounced, in French, *Mali cassette*), was created. Yet, this symbolic act of cultural political control, providing an air of authenticity to Mali's small private record industry, materialized on the margins of a marketplace in which the perceived anarchy of media piracy predominated.

Banning Eyre's account of record producers' dealings with cassette piracy during his six-month research trip to Bamako in 1995–96 describes the industry's extraordinary (and perhaps foolhardy) attempts to negotiate this disjuncture in the production and circulation of commercial culture, asserting control in the midst of anarchy:

> The moment a new cassette goes public, its producer enters a race with time. He must hustle to sell as many legal cassettes as possible before cheaper pirate copies flood the market. The difference between a two-week and a three-week delay can mean thousands of legitimate sales, maybe tens of thousands in the case of a major artist. (2000, 198–99)

Eyre goes on to cite Oumou Sangaré's husband and manager, who presents his own homegrown tactic to combat piracy: "Most of the pirate copies come up from Guinea, and when the rains start, some of the main roads close. That might delay the arrival of pirate copies a week or more" (199).

Such dramatic efforts (timing a release for the onset of the rainy season) might make sense for an artist of Sangaré's stature, who, with domestic media sales in the tens (if not hundreds) of thousands of cassettes and compact discs, has much to lose to counterfeit commerce. For most Malian musicians, however, the media market, from which earnings are either limited or nonexistent, is of far less concern than Bamako's highly competitive live music scene and the possibility for tours and recording contracts abroad, in the music capitals of Europe and the United States. For these artists, local live performances are, at best, a way to promote themselves and their work in hopes of being discovered by industry-connected world music enthusiasts, who, during the past decade, have listened in to Bamako's popular music culture with growing interest (see, for example, Hammer 2005). At worst, such performances represent a recurrent source of personal and professional discouragement.

While living in Bamako in the late 1990s and early 2000s, I worked closely with *kora* virtuoso Toumani Diabaté, whose group, the Symmetric

Orchestra, played every Friday at a popular (but now defunct) nightclub, Le Hogon (see chapter 4). For Symmetric members, the professional significance of these gigs had little to do with earnings (with a nightly take per musician of around ten dollars); more important was the possibility of joining their globetrotting bandleader on one of his many concert tours abroad. Yet, to their recurrent dismay, Diabaté would leave with his Mande Jazz Trio (still together and very popular at the time), fellow *kora* master Ballaké Sissoko (with whom he recorded an album and toured in 1998), or foreign collaborators like blues legend Taj Mahal (whose collaboration with Diabaté in 1999 produced a global bestseller).[22] For Bamako bands, like the Symmetric Orchestra, the tantalizing—though rarefied—ideal of a global music career must be weighed against the harsh reality of making do and getting by at home, scraping out a meager living at nightclubs and local ceremonies, and waiting for the next chance to get out.[23] This is, perhaps, the most salient everyday condition of musical money trouble *(wariko)* and the cultural-economic social position of the professional musician in the late twentieth- and early twenty-first-century Malian art world.

Such professional concerns, which emphasize artistic persons over products in an otherwise depersonalized culture economy, have, since the late 1990s, gone largely unacknowledged by state and industry authorities, for whom control over the media market remains the predominant political and economic issue. Foreshadowing the piracy crises of the mid-2000s (see Skinner 2012a, 730–39), Mali K7, still the sole music production house in the country, announced in December 1999 that it would halt its operations and lay off its employees. Discouraged by what he considered to be the state's failure to take action against the influx of counterfeit cassettes in the Malian marketplace, CEO Philippe Berthier threatened to move his company to neighboring Burkina Faso. Perhaps as a gesture of good faith, the BuMDA, in an act of punctuated police discipline, confiscated and destroyed 60,000 counterfeit cassettes on February 1, 2000 (Cissé and Traoré 2001, 24). Mali K7 reopened its doors the following March. Reflecting on these events, Berthier had the following to say:

> It created a national crisis! I made a televised appearance on the evening news, artists organized a march and went to see the Prime Minister at the time, [and] there was a big national conference

including producers, artists, police, [and] customs agents. This
didn't solve all the problems, but this crisis did raise awareness.
(Maillot 2002)

This "crisis" did, in fact, herald a period, however brief, of greater control
in the Malian culture economy. In September 2000, ordinance 00–042/
P-RM established the BuMDA as a legal entity with autonomous finances
equipped to "organize and represent authors of literary and artistic works
as well as their beneficiaries" (articles 1 and 2). The government thus established a normative institutional framework within which the pecuniary
interests of artists could, in theory, be guaranteed and the revenues derived
from their works managed and accounted for. In 2002, Seydoni (a Burkina
Faso–based record company) opened recording and cassette/CD duplication facilities in Bamako to become the second music production house in
Mali (Traoré 2004). The same year, the BuMDA, building on the experiences of copyright agencies in Ghana, Côte d'Ivoire, and elsewhere on the
continent, introduced a hologram decal designed to distinguish authentic
cassettes and CDs from counterfeits. The stickers would cost sixty CFA
francs (twelve U.S. cents) and be applied to album jackets prior to the duplication of the cassettes or CDs. Producers were expected to pay this fee,
which would finance artists' copyright allowances. They were also encouraged to produce only as many cassettes and CDs as they expected to sell,
given the upfront copyright expense the sticker fees imposed. Yet, despite
repeated televised national campaigns to educate the population about
the ethics of buying marked legal media—with dramatic claims about the
pauperization of artists and the decline of Mali's cultural heritage—the
stickers have not proven efficacious in the marketplace (Figure 19).[24]
    State authorities have, therefore, turned to other modes of enforce-
ment, largely replacing didactic discipline with martial discipline, manifest, in recent years, in periodic confiscatory raids. These acts of commercial sanction serve to dramatize state power while affirming the culture
industry's commitment to normative media production and circulation,
but they do little to curb media piracy; that is, they have little impact on
the nongovernmental culture economy: those performances, broadcasts,
and exchanges that lie outside the purview of official culture, which neither fully accede to assertions of control nor wholly ascribe to accusations
of anarchy. Rather, the most tangible effects of police raids are exacerbated

*Figure 19. Pirate cassette cart. Photograph by the author.*

socioeconomic tensions and sometimes violence between the plaintiffs and enforcers of such actions, artists and police, and their "criminal" targets, media broadcasters and vendors. Politicians, too, are lambasted for their failure to contain and suppress commercial anarchy, or media piracy, when these actions inevitably fail to produce long-term, or even short-term results (see, for example, Skinner 2012a, 734–39). Among these varied casualties of "the war on piracy" (French, *la lutte contre la piraterie*), we encounter, once again, the social, political, and economic distortions— the exacerbated *wariko*—that neoliberal governmentality engenders when applied to the culture economy.

Yet, everyday transgressions of this cultural political hegemony persist, though such persistence should not be confused with outright protest or resistance. In concluding this chapter, I briefly consider those practices of ostensible anarchy that arguably account for most cultural production and circulation in contemporary Mali (see, for a collection of comparative studies, Karaganis 2011), what I am calling "nongovernmental culture." I do so by returning to the Triton Stars concert with which I began this chapter. To hear this band's performance in the context of the history recounted here is to appreciate the essential ambivalence of a political economy that champions legality at the expense of livelihoods, in which a degraded public sector and an unruly private market necessitate a certain amount of creative infringement of the rule of law—that is, nongovernmental culture—in an era of neoliberal governmentality.

## A Nongovernmental Mix

At the end of their set, the Triton Stars invited one of their guest emcees, *animateur* Man Ken, who earlier in the evening had implored the audience to purchase legal copies of the group's new album, to join them on stage for one final song. As a radio and television personality, Man Ken is known for his admiration for and spot-on musical impersonation of Ivoirian reggae superstar Alpha Blondy. *"Reggae-manw bɛ yan wa?"* ("Are there any reggae fans here?"), he asked the crowd, eliciting a collective *"Awɔ!"* ("Yes!") and a volley of applause. As the noise died down, he proceeded to sing the unaccompanied introduction to Blondy's "Silence Houphouët d'Or" (1996)—a tribute to the late Ivoirian President, Félix Houphouët Boigny (1905–93).

| | |
|---|---|
| *Le soleil s'est couché ce matin,* | The sun has set this morning, |
| *et tous les drapeaux* | and all the flags |
| *ont baissés les yeux.* | have lowered their eyes. |
| *Devant ce chart d'assaut,* | In front of this tank, |
| *nos sanglots montent là haut!* | our cries rise up on high! |
| *Et seul, dans son linceul,* | And alone, within its shroud, |
| *Orange, Blanc, Vert . . .* | Orange, White, Green . . . |

With this final, cadenced, and color-coded reference to the Ivoirian flag, repeated twice—orange, white, green—the Triton Stars joined in with the rocking accompaniment—rising and falling between A minor and G Major 7 chords—to Bob Marley's "War" (1976).[25] *"Houphouët! Reveille-toi!"* ("Houphouët! Wake up!"), wailed Man Ken, as the group fell into a sustained reggae groove. *"Sabali! Sabali! Sabali! Sabali!"* Man Ken sang, repeating the Bamana word for "patience and tolerance" over and over again in an improvised verse. Now, with the crowd on their feet, some spilling over onto the stage, the inspired vocalist layered Marley upon Marley, singing, "Get up! Stand up! Stand up for your right!" At this point, it was no longer apparent what song the group was playing, but it didn't matter—or did it? The mix of Blondy's lament and Marley's musical and lyrical calls to arms offered a clear enough commentary on the civil war raging in Côte d'Ivoire at the time (see McGovern 2011), and the energy of the performance delivered this message with a sonic vibe that brought artist and audience together in soulful communion. But, whose song was it exactly?

The Triton Stars' curtain call performance offers a good example of nongovernmental music culture in contemporary Mali. No permissions were sought, nor royalties paid for the copyright-protected sounds and lyrics the group performed. The music and words were likely learned through repeated listening to other unlicensed shows, unauthorized broadcasts on the radio, or playback of cassettes and CDs, themselves copied and recopied at home, or pirated in the marketplace. Yet, this dramatic display of musical and lyrical borrowing, embedding, and layering is haunted by a culture economy that proscribes such practice, an official discourse echoed, ironically, in same group's calls, made earlier in the show, to buy legal cassettes and save artistic livelihoods (their own in particular). So, is this a case of cognitive dissonance, or just plain hypocrisy?

With regard to the history of cultural policy and intellectual property in Mali, I would say "Neither."

When, in the 1980s, the logic of structural adjustment was applied to a postcolonial economy largely divested of its public servants and resources, through gross domestic mismanagement and the global vogue of privatization, the conditions were created for a radical disjuncture between the unregulated free market, on the one hand, and disciplinary state institutions, on the other. In the Malian art world, this division would manifest in the perceived anarchy of the informal marketplace (piracy) and the prescribed control of intellectual property (copyright), resulting in a culture economy of endemic money trouble *(wariko)*. In this context, nongovernmental culture, such as the Triton Stars' reggae jam, routinely refuses the neoliberal dichotomy of anarchy and control, without, however, altogether refuting its governmentality. In a world of *wariko,* in which "everything is tied to money trouble," as singer Karounga Sacko earlier proclaimed, groups like the Triton Stars must continually cross the threshold between the licit and illicit, the formal and informal. There, in the everyday interstices of neoliberal governmentality, commitment to copyright and its performative violation are less conflictual than contrapuntal, keeping multiple means to secure artistic livelihoods, however precarious, at play and in the mix.

This too is an Afropolitan ethics. Read in relation to the subjects of previous chapters, nongovernmental culture in the Malian music economy echoes the Bamako urbanite's assertion that "if it's not mixed up, it will never work out" (chapter 1). It is the cultural-economic expression of artists' socioprofessional interest in maintaining a mutable status and identity (chapter 2). Further, like principles associated with aesthetics and religion, nongovernmental culture is not antithetical to normative (economic) morality, but, like situated expressions of musical style and religious faith, it draws on such normativity selectively, creatively, in the course of performance and in defense of local lifeworlds and global aspirations (chapters 3 and 4). Finally, nongovernmental culture is not (necessarily) antigovernmental. Indeed, the apparent transgressions of nongovernmental culture are frequently bound up with calls for a more assertive and progressive cultural-economic governmentality, as the case study of the Triton Stars presented here suggests. It is in this sense that I turn, in the next and final chapter, to the musical morality of national politics. In particular, I consider what it means to make Malian music in times of national celebration and crisis. As a mode of being that continues to shape African futures, I examine how national affiliation has been mobilized musically to promote (and contest) a variety of political agendas, global and local, elite and subaltern. This, too, is an Afropolitan ethics.

# CHAPTER 6

# Afropolitan Patriotism

## A Matter of Musical Life and Death

Beginning in June 2012, international news reports about the crisis in the West African Sahel frequently gathered around a common theme: what anthropologist Paul Stoller called, in a recent editorial, "the death of music in Mali" (2013). In the context of an aggressive and expansive Islamist occupation of northern Mali, these stories coupled harrowing testimonies of corporal punishment (including public floggings, stonings, and amputations) with personal accounts of the extreme cultural austerity of everyday life in cities like Gao, Timbuktu, and Kidal. We read of the desecration of medieval mausoleums and manuscripts, the strict enforcement of ostensibly "Islamic" modes of dress and behavior, and, with greater and greater frequency, the absolute silencing of a once vibrant music culture. Cell phones with melodious ring tones were confiscated; musical instruments and equipment burned; rituals and ceremonial gatherings prohibited; artists forced into exile through fear and intimidation; and so on.[1] These reports multiplied as varied factions of Jihadists (some with ecumenical aspirations for a greater Islamic orthodoxy, others with more profane affiliations with smuggling rings and kidnapping cartels) displaced a motley crew of secular Tuareg separatists, who had only a few months prior declared an independent ethnic homeland called "Azawad" following an armed uprising that precipitated a military coup in the country's southern capital, Bamako.[2]

As the political geography of ethnicity gave way to the zealous hegemony of religion—when media reports turned from Tuareg nationalism to Islamist militancy—the plight of an occupied and exiled people found voice in narratives of musical loss. The headlines read, "No Rhythm or Reason as Militants Declare War on Music"; "Music Silenced as Islamists Drive Out Artists"; "Mali's Music Has Been Muzzled": and so on. In May 2013, sociologist Sujatha Fernandes, writing for the *New York Times* under

the rubric "The Day Music Died in Mali," reflected on current events in
Mali in an impassioned defense of music as a mode of cultural coherence
in the face of the socially destructive geopolitics of the present.

> One thing that the events in Mali have taught us is that music mat-
> ters. And the potential loss of music as a means of social bonding,
> as a voice of conscience and as a mode of storytelling is not just a
> threat in an African country where Islamic militants made music a
> punishable offense. We would do well to appreciate music's power,
> wherever we live. (2013)

In the same month, Oxfam International, in collaboration with filmmakers from Sahel Calling, released a video titled "Mali in Crisis: The Power of
Music."[3] The video begins with the staggered rhythms and gritty timbres
of *takamba*, a genre of popular music prominent in and around the city
of Gao in northeastern Mali. Images cut between a map of Mali, bound
together by the long arch of the Niger River, and artists in the midst of
performance, resonant icons of the country's social fabric. Statements and
songs of artists fade into scenes of and testimonies from refugee camps.
And, messages of national pride and hope in the country's capital give way
to the filmmakers' own geopolitical statement of purpose: "It is time for
governments to harness the power of Mali's people and work together toward a future of peace and prosperity for all."

Music has long been a privileged signifier of status and identity in
postcolonial Mali, serving as a primary expressive vehicle of nation building and statecraft through successive periods of postcolonial governance
(see Skinner 2012b). With the international success of artists such as Salif
Keita, Habib Koité, Oumou Sangaré, Toumani Diabaté, Rokia Traoré,
and the late Ali Farka Touré (among many others) music has also raised
the international profile of a country more widely known for its extreme
poverty and harsh climate. Through music, live and mediated, global audiences have encountered and celebrated Mali's rich cultural heritage, its
deep sense of history, its principles of social cohesion, and, as many recent articles and opinion pieces have noted, its traditions of tolerant piety.
As Malian rapper Amkoullel affirms, "Mali is a secular country, tolerant,
where everyone declares their religion according to their feeling, and in
any case, they know that a Mali without music is an impossibility" (cited
in Morgan 2013: 82). Malian music has become synonymous, in other

words, with an inclusive and extensive—tolerant and global—sense of morality that equates good sounds with good sociability and, in the world music market, good fortune. To threaten this music is, thus, a menace to culture itself, its virtue and value, and, more specifically, to the nation that culture is called on to imagine, represent, and perform.

## Music as Biopolitical Culture in Contemporary Mali

In this chapter, I propose three things. The first is that we think of the musical morality I have just described, with its strong associations with national identity, as a social position: a normative framework for social action and community formation within a geopolitical sphere shaped by commercial, developmental, and security interests. As such, this musical morality suggests specific parameters of enactment that define what it means to be a Malian artist and make Malian music in the world today. As a mode of transnational identification, this musical morality manifests among artists who actively appeal to a discourse of cultural authenticity qualified by assertions of national provenance in representing their work to audiences at large. It appears in media reports that characterize the music within their purview as Malian, cast within narratives both celebra-tory and, as we observed, anxious. And, it resounds through the rhythms, tempos, textures, and timbres that are presented to listening publics, near and far, as quintessentially Malian.[4] In the words of Grammy-nominated artist Bassékou Kouyaté, uttered above a soundtrack of plucked strings and slapped gourds on the Oxfam video discussed previously, "Mali is known because of its music. Music is the heart of Mali. . . . If someone wants to stop music in Mali, that would be saying he wants to stop the heart of Mali. . . ." Then, the soundtrack to his statement abruptly stops, and he continues to speak amid a seemingly unnatural silence: "Because Mali is known for its music throughout the world."

Second, I suggest that this Malian morality of music represents a spe-cifically biopolitical social position through which populations in the western Sahel assert their right to live in the world. If biopower operates, in Michel Foucault's terms, by creating "caesuras" between social life and political death, between legitimate and aberrant social positions in mod-ern states (2003: 255–56), then the idea of "Malian music" becomes a means by which people may publicly claim their vitality, viability, and, in a neoliberal world order, the marketable value of their lives as essentially cultural—and, more specifically, musical—subjects. In the context of the current crisis in the Sahel, I further suggest that this biopolitical social position has become increasingly conflated with what Achille Mbembe calls "necropolitics," describing

> the various ways in which, in our contemporary world, weapons are deployed in the interest of maximum destruction of persons and the creation of *death-worlds*, new and unique forms of social existence in which vast populations are subjected to conditions of life conferring upon them the status of the *living dead*. (2003: 40, emphasis in the original)

With the increased militarization of the Sahel as "the new front in the war on terror,"[5] populations across the region—in Mali, Niger, Algeria, and Mauritania—have become more and more susceptible to death, and more and more distant from social, political, and economic life.

In the contemporary Malian art world, this conflation of the biopolitical and necropolitical—of musical morality and global security—has created its own sociomusical caesura, between a vital and vocal musical elite and a stagnant and silent artistic underclass. On the one hand are the musical lives of those with access to transnational networks of circulation, for whom tours abroad and an established social media presence offer viable platforms for artistic agency; on the other are those whose creative work remains beholden to local music economies, of nightclub performances, freelance recording, and life-cycle ceremonies—all greatly diminished during this ongoing crisis: provisional work from increasingly precarious lives. My observations of this fragmented music culture, the focus of the final section of this chapter, are admittedly partial, based as they are on my long-standing work with musicians in the south of Mali, and the capital, Bamako, in particular. The desires, struggles, and expressions of artists in northern Mali—before, during, and following the crisis of 2012–13— adds yet another dimension to the politics of belonging and dispossession I elaborate here.[6] Still, the sounds and statements of my Bamako interlocutors do represent an important counterpoint to narratives that tend to equate the apparent "death" of public culture in Mali with the rise of Islamic radicalism in the Sahel. Their music and words bear witness to a broader biopolitics of culture in a necropolitical world, in which the lives and works of Malian artists are deeply implicated, even as they remain divided.

Yet, the story of this biopolitical music culture is not only one of conflict and division, it is also a story of unity and celebration. I turn, thus, to the sounds and images of an apparently proud postcolonial nationalism, appearing in the weeks prior to Mali's fiftieth anniversary of independence from colonial rule (French, *Cinquantenaire*). Through a close reading of two music videos circulated on YouTube in August 2010, I reflect on a particularly patriotic sense of Afropolitanism among Malian musicians—at home and abroad—during a time of nationalist fervor. Seen and heard, however, from the perspective of a country caught in the throes of profound social, political, and economic turmoil—in the wake of the March 2012 military coup and its aftermath—such celebratory works seem to confirm the postcolonial critic's dismissal of patriotic zeal and statist authority within an insufficiently decolonized Africa. Reflecting on my own recent fieldwork in Mali, I acknowledge this criticism, appreciating its tenor while not wholly subscribing to its prognoses. I ask, Is there a place for the nation and a sense of patriotism within an emergent structure of Afropolitan feeling? It is with this question in mind that I return to the reported "death of music in Mali" in 2012–13 to observe a clearly divided and greatly diminished—though not (yet) deceased—national music culture.

Which brings me to my third and final proposition: that current divisions within the Malian art world are best addressed by the artists themselves and the political society of which they are a part.[7] In other words, I suggest an (intentionally provocative) inversion and revision of the thesis proposed by Oxfam: "It is time for Mali's people to harness the power of government and work together toward a future of peace and prosperity for Mali, Africa, and the world." To more expansively mobilize the biopower of Malian music, one must think and act beyond a cosmopolitanism that seeks to intervene in foreign affairs in the interest of ideals deemed universal. For "peace and prosperity for all" to be contingent on "governments" harnessing "the power of Mali's people" rings of a "civilizing mission" that is as untenable as it is unreasonable. Rather, my attention turns to the performances and politics of a more recent cohort of Afropolitan patriots, for whom the nation-state, Africa, and the world do not represent mutually exclusive scales of place, but mutually constitutive spheres of moral concern; who recognize the biopolitical necessity of national identification in the world today, but insist that claims on African states be grounded in the lived and varied experiences of African subjects.

## The Art of Afropolitan Patriotism

It is August 2010, and two music videos appear on the newsfeed of my Facebook account, both commemorating Mali's *Cinquantenaire*, one month before the September 22 national day. Both videos take the generic form of hip-hop, though both gesture beyond this genre in important ways. The first video, "Cinquantenaire du Mali" by the young Malian rapper Iba One, features the music of Sidiki Diabaté, son of *kora* virtuoso Toumani Diabaté. Representing a new generation in an old lineage of instrumental griots (see chapter 3), the video shows Diabaté carrying on his family tradition and pushing its boundaries as he plays his *kora* with beats and backing tracks that he himself has programmed, arranged, and mixed.[8] As I watch the video for the first time, I am deeply moved. Sidiki, whom I have known since he was six years old, when his apprenticeship with the *kora* was just beginning, has become an accomplished musician, a professional title he prefers to the clan-based and artisanal moniker *jeli*, indicating a more broadly defined African art world with which his generation of artists increasingly identifies—not to the exclusion of family heritage, but in addition to it.

The second video, "Mali Debout" ("Stand Up Mali") appeals to a different kind of African heritage, that of the diaspora. Mokobé Traoré, born to Malian parents and raised in France, is a former member of the French hip-hop trio 113. Since the release of his album *Mon Afrique* in 2007, Mokobé has cultivated a successful solo career by drawing attention to and celebrating his African roots, and his Malian heritage in particular. Yet, Mokobé is Malian in much the same way as Sidiki Diabaté is a *jeli*; there's an irreducibility to his identity that embeds his African identity within post-imperial France—a hybrid subject position evoked by notions of *L'Afrance* and *La Françafrique* and located in the segregated urban and suburban social spaces featured in his work (see Mazauric 2007). A third point of reference for Mokobé is hip-hop itself, binding him to the contemporary Black Atlantic and providing him with a playful medium of sonic, linguistic, gestural, and sartorial expression through which his many filiations and affiliations take shape (Figure 20).[9]

*Figure 20. Mokobé. Courtesy of Oumar Diop.*

At first glance, the two videos represent a plurality of what we might call the "qualified cosmopolitanisms" that constitute the modern African world, where an increasingly urbanized and globalized continent meets an increasingly provincialized—decolonized and diasporic—Euro-American North. Broadcasting from African cities at home and abroad, the videos represent what Paul Gilroy has called the "cosmopolitanism-from-below" of urban popular culture, in general (2004), and Manthia Diawara's "home-boy cosmopolitanism" of hip-hop cultural style, in particular (2004). They manifest what Mamadou Diouf describes as the "vernacular cos-mopolitanism" of a deterritorialized social and cultural heritage (2000), and they evoke Kwame Anthony Appiah's "cosmopolitan patriotism" of postcolonial and diasporic pride (1997). It is this qualified—rooted and routed—cosmopolitanism, articulated from a global city in an African world (Bamako) that I have critically elaborated in the present text with the term "Afropolitanism."

Of the aforementioned Afropolitan qualifiers, I am most interested, in this chapter, in the latter "patriotic" sentiment, what Kwame Anthony Appiah describes as a moral concern for the nation, manifest in a com-mon commitment to the institutions and governing principles of the state (1997, 623–24). As expressions of what I will call "Afropolitan patriotism," both videos present multimodal and intergeneric expressions of Malian being in the African world. In them, the artists publicly manifest their international orientations (toward the African world) while still claim-ing intranational solidarities (within African states). They do so by draw-ing on expressive modes of sound, verbal art, gesture, and sartorial style within and beyond hip-hop to evoke what Iba One calls *Maliba*, or "Great Mali." Here, Mali is "great" because of its transnational scope, represent-ing a homeland that exceeds its geopolitical frontiers. Through Diabaté's *kora*, an instrument his family has performed for generations across West Africa, we see and hear the Old Mali Empire, which, from the thirteenth to sixteenth centuries, stretched from the arid plains of the Sahel to the Senegambian coast. And through the expatriate expressions of Mokobé, we perceive the modern postcolony, with its myriad diasporic enclaves the world over.

This greatness is also rooted in Malian values—the patriotic prin-ciples of which Appiah writes so poignantly. As Iba One waits for the beat to drop in "Cinquantenaire du Mali," he stands near the Monument de la Paix in downtown Bamako, formed of two concrete arms supporting a globe on which a dove rests, a symbol of continental peace. Such urban monuments, signs of nation building and Mali's place in a post-colonial world, populate the video. As Iba raps and Sidiki plays his *kora* over a steady reggae rhythm, we see the Mémorial Modibo Keita, in honor of Mali's first president; the Monument de l'Indépendence, a tribute to African sovereignty; the Pont des Martyrs, memorializing the massacre that precipitated the downfall of Mali's authoritarian Second Republic; and the Monument de l'Hospitalité, showing a kneeling woman offering a calabash of water to her onlooking guests—a act of generosity and welcome in western Africa that, among the Mande, is a sign of hope *(jigiya)* that only a good host *(jatigi)* can offer (see Arnoldi 2007).

Patrimonial pride and hopeful hospitality are echoed in "Mali Debout." As the track begins, a Malian speaker, Mamadou Diabaté (aka "21 DG"), prefaces Mokobé's principally French rap with expressive oratory in Bamana and Soninke, a language from Mali's westernmost region and also spoken in Senegal and Mauritania where Mokobé has family ties. "Malians follow their fathers. They follow their mothers," he chants. "God has blessed the children of Mali. We will not be left behind. . . . Hard work is better than no work at all." Throughout his laudatory and didactic speech, reminiscent of the griot's verbal art, a block-party dance beat punctuates a series of portraits that capture the beauty and vitality of Europe's African community and the Malian diaspora in particular. We see men and women carefully groomed and adorned in all manner of haute couture, from colorful kaftans to tailored suits. Women's faces are artfully accented in makeup and embellished in fine jewelry and vibrant headscarves. Juxtaposed with these portraits are scenes from a neighborhood square, where people sing, dance, and socialize in a space that proclaims itself Malian in an otherwise anonymous French suburb *(banlieue)*. "Mali is beautiful," Mokobé tells us.

The two videos' celebratory representation of Mali and its fifty years of postcolonial independence has not been widely shared among contemporary continental critics. On October 19, 2010, two months after the YouTube release of "Cinquantenaire du Mali" and "Mali Debout," historian and cultural theorist Achille Mbembe appeared on the Paris-based radio program *France Culture* to discuss the legacy of a half-century of African sovereignty and promote his new book on the topic, *Sortir de la grande nuit: un essai sur l'Afrique décolonisée* (2010).[10] When asked about the festivities surrounding the African *Cinquantenaire*, Mbembe is un-equivocal, stating "the celebrations lack both symbolic form and content."

Instead of engaging in a broad-based "critical reflection" on and toward
African futures, he says, "we are trying to dress up . . . 'the Shameful State'
in rags." In an earlier article, excerpted from *Sortir de la grande nuit* and
widely circulated online, Mbembe deepens this critique, in a passage worth
citing at length:

> Here we are, then, in 2010, fifty years after decolonization. Is there
> really anything to commemorate, or is it, rather, necessary to start
> all over again? Authoritarian restoration in one place, technocratic
> democracy in another; elsewhere, feeble and easily reversible
> progress; and, more or less everywhere, very high levels of social
> violence . . . of brewing conflict or open war, all on the foundation
> of an extraction economy that, following the mercantilist logic of
> colonialism, continues to favor predation. *Voilà*, with a few excep-
> tions, the landscape as a whole. (2010, 20)[11]

In short, for Mbembe, the *Cinquantenaire* inspires little reason to cele-
brate, particularly as concerns the contemporary state of the postcolonial
nation.

In these recent critiques, there are echoes of Mbembe's earlier indict-
ment of political and popular culture outlined in his essay, "The Banality
of Power and the Aesthetics of Vulgarity in the Postcolony," first published two decades ago (1992). As a postcolonial corrective to Bakhtin's
Rabelaisian vision, Mbembe locates "the grotesque and the obscene" not
among plebeian culture, but "in 1) the places and times in which state
power organizes the dramatization of its magnificence, 2) the displays in
which it stages its majesty and prestige and, 3) the way it offers these arti-
facts to its 'targets' [*cibles*]" (4). Such dramatizations of state power (real
or imagined) are not merely imposed, Mbembe argues; they are also in-
ternalized. In the postcolony, "officialdom and the people share many references in common, not the least of which is a certain conception of the
aesthetics and stylistics of power, the way it operates and the modalities of
its expansion" (13). Mbembe characterizes the postcolonial relationship
of the political and the popular as "promiscuous," calling it "a convivial
tension between the *commandement* and its 'targets'" (5) that has led to
"mutual zombification."

Indeed, there are signs of such promiscuity in the work of the artists we
have thus far considered. Midway through "Cinquantenaire du Mali," an

image appears of a map titled "Le Mali nouveau," in which Sidiki Diabaté and his instrument are superimposed on Mali's southern territory, while Malian soldiers are shown to march across the Saharan north. The graphic reifies the ethnopolitical hegemony of the Malian South. There, a privileged (Mande) cultural heritage and identity finds expression in the griot and his twenty-one-string harp and political authority manifests in a militarized north. This image is doubly troubling with regard to the March 2012 military coup, an event that was preceded by an escalation of armed conflict in northern Mali between Tuareg militants and the Malian Army and followed by the de facto splitting of the country, right where the artist meets his comrades in arms. In "Mali Debout," we are confronted with the "convivial tension" of popular and political culture in the postcolony through images of Mokobé's own rapprochement with state power. The rapper is shown rubbing shoulders with now-deposed President Amadou Toumani Touré after having received the country's highest civilian honor, the Chevalier de l'Ordre National. In another image, contemporaneous with the release of the track, Mokobé wears his flag-ribboned medal on the breast pocket of a dark tailored suit. His gaze is cast stoically outward with hands pressed together in a chiefly gesture—the embodiment of the "aesthetics and stylistics" of presidential portraiture (and power) in the (African) postcolony.[12]

## The Ambivalence of Afropolitan Patriotism

If, at first glance, we perceived the art of what I have called Afropolitan patriotism in "Cinquantenaire du Mali" and "Mali Debout," we are now confronted with its ambivalence, if not its outright antithesis. For as ostensibly vulgar expressions of a glorified state power, the two videos would seem to betray their rooted cosmopolitanism with an underlying commitment to postcolonial provinciality. In my first attempt to synthesize this material, in a presentation to colleagues at The Ohio State University in January 2012 (two months prior to the military coup), I acknowledged this critique, and, weighing it against the otherwise proud performances, asked, "Can one wear 'the flashy rags of power' with pride?" and, "Are postcolonial celebration and criticism mutually exclusive?" My analytic aim was to "develop a concept of Afropolitan patriotism that acknowledges national celebration as it accommodates postnational criticism." I clung to this attempt to reconcile the social critic's anxiety with the popular artist's pride right up until the end of March, when, after a week of violence and uncertainty, it became clear that the Malian state had collapsed.

Perhaps I should have known better. Between national celebration in the fall of 2010 and state crisis in the spring of 2012, I made three trips to Mali. In December 2010, with signs of the *Cinquantenaire* still prevalent—on the radio and television, on street signs and urban landmarks, and on reams of thematized cloth adorning people's bodies—I attended Mali's Biennial Arts and Culture Festival, held in the southern city of Sikasso. At the festival, which features musical, choreographic, and theatrical performances from Mali's nine administrative regions, national pageantry predominated, a celebratory façade that barely masked criticisms of the state's inability to fund its own cultural initiatives. In Sikasso, the festival relied on the provisional efforts of local authorities to make do with paltry resources and the goodwill of foreign benefactors—a cohort represented for the first time at the Biennale by the Malian community in France, on whose remittances the country significantly depends (see Azam and Gubert 2006). A sign of this diasporic reliance, the 2010 Biennale was made possible by substantial support from Franco-Malian entrepreneur Malamine Koné, who, at the festival's opening ceremony broadcast on national television, received lavish praise from one of Mali's celebrated—and, on this night, clearly intoxicated—international divas. On stage and on television screens across the country, the aesthetics of vulgarity were at play in a clientelist drama of laudatory Afropop within an increasingly privatized postcolony, in all its banality.

I returned to Mali in August 2011, at a time when domestic, regional, and international attention was focused squarely on Libya. There, rebel forces continued to make significant gains against regime loyalists along the coast and, by the end of the month, the endgame in Tripoli had begun. Two thousand miles to the southwest, in Bamako, reactions to these events tended toward the negative, with angry criticisms leveled, principally, against France, Mali's former colonizer, and its Western allies for their intervention in Libya's internecine conflict. Indeed, most people I talked to considered the NATO blockade and bombardment to be a neo-colonial power-play, orchestrated by former French president Nicholas Sarkozy to undermine regional stability by targeting one of the continent's most generous benefactors, Muammar Gadaffi.

Evidence of Gadaffi-backed Libyan beneficence was plentiful at the

Figure 21. Malibya, Ségou. Photograph by Tanya Kerssen, Food First/Institute for Food and Development Policy.

time in Bamako. Libya's name decorated the façades of banks and prominent hotels, including the iconic Hotel de l'Amitié, one of the city's few high-rises. A new district of government offices on the city's left bank bore the name "Malibya," a sign intended to inspire a sense of pan-African solidarity, though more than a few saw it as an affront to Malian sovereignty—once again, anxiety mixed with celebration. This was particularly true in the region of Ségou, some 200 miles north of the capital, where "Malibya" signified a furtive bilateral agreement to cede, virtually free of charge, 250,000 acres of land in Mali's prime zone of industrial agriculture, the Office du Niger, to Libya for the development of export crops and livestock (see Whitehouse 2013d, 42) (Figure 21). This was part of a broader—dare I say "neocolonial"?—trend in sub-Saharan of selling (or conditionally conceding) rights to domestic land production to foreign interests (see Martiniello 2013).

Thus, as bombs fell north of the Sahara in August 2011, and as Malians debated the precarious status of their postcolonial alignments, I recalled another ambivalent scene of national celebration presented a year earlier on Malian television. There was Gadaffi, nestled between Malian president Amadou Toumani Touré and his wife—the patron and clients of Malibya—at an event commemorating Mali's *Cinquantenaire* at the presidential palace on Koulouba, Mali's "hill of power." Before the assembled crowd of elite African celebrants, Djeneba Seck, one of Mali's finest vocalists, sang her informal anthem "An Ka Maliba" ("Our Great Mali"). In counterpoint to the opaque, undemocratic clientelism that facilitated the expropriation of Malian territory to Libya, Seck counseled her audience, near and far, to go to their polling stations, listen carefully, and vote for those who inspire confidence and present good ideas for a homeland that belongs to "us," she sang, the children of a great Mali, Maliba.[13]

In February 2012, I was back in Mali, this time to attend a privately sponsored international music festival, Le Festival sur le Niger, in the riverine town of Ségou in Mali's agricultural heartland. Celebration was in the air, but crisis loomed all around. An emboldened ethnic-nationalist insurgency in the north—fueled by heavy weapons that arrived in Mali along with returning mercenaries, ethnic Tuareg men who had fought for Gadaffi before his fall in October 2011 (see Lecocq 2004)—had asserted control over several towns and villages in Mali's vast Saharan territories. The region's major urban centers (Gao, Kidal, and Timbuktu) were threatened as the Malian military struggled to repel rebel advances, often conceding tactical retreats as they complained of a lack of resources, including ammunition and proper shelter in the harsh desert environment. Earlier in the month, a protest movement initiated by the widows of Malian soldiers—whose husbands had died in an apparent massacre at the hands of rebel fighters in the town of Aguelhok, near the Algerian border—seemed to gain popular sympathy in Bamako as participants openly condemned president Touré's management of the conflict, hurling stones and epithets at his residence (Lecocq et al. 2013). People around me spoke of a coup, as yet in the abstract, though with an air of anxiety. One of those people was a musician friend. I attempted to explain to him my current work on the music of Mali's Afropolitan patriots, who, I argued, frequently give voice to a pluralist, worldly, and unified Mali. To this, he replied, simply, "We've had enough of songs about Mali" (French, *"On a trop chanté le Mali"*). One month later, in the throes of a post-coup crisis, with an occupied north and a power vacuum in the south, there was hardly a Mali left to sing about.

## Afropolitanism: Beyond the Nation or Within?

Perhaps, then, it is best, as Achille Mbembe counsels, to start all over again.[14] Indeed, evidence of continental transformation is increasingly apparent. In Mbembe's words,

> Soon Africa will have more than a billion citizens—more than India. . . . We are witnessing the emergence of an urban citizenry unseen in the region's history. The constitution of an enterprising diaspora, especially in the United States. The arrival of new immigrants coming from China and the rest of Asia.

It is in the burgeoning context of this mutual embedding of Africa in the world and the world in Africa that Mbembe calls for a "formidable remodeling of mentalities" and "a new intellectual and political imagination" with regard to African modernity and the prospect of an African renaissance.[15] The promise of such transnational and anti-essentialist shifts in the African episteme "after the postcolony" (to coin a phrase à la Mbembe) is a source, for the African historian and social theorist, of "paradoxical optimism" (compare Mbembe 2001). Mbembe qualifies this new and cautiously hopeful reconfiguration of African space and subjectivity with the term "Afropolitanism."

In many ways, Mbembe's idea of the Afropolitan resonates with Kwame Anthony Appiah's earlier understanding of the postmodern, the latter defined as a space-clearing conceptual tool—something with which to start all over. "Postmodernism can be seen," Appiah writes, "as a new way of understanding the multiplication of distinctions that flows from the need to clear oneself a space; the need that drives the underlying dynamic of cultural modernity" (1992: 145). Mbembe's Afropolitan subject also bears a certain resemblance to Appiah's postcolonial novelist, who is "no longer committed to the nation" and who chooses "instead of the nation . . . not an older traditionalism but Africa—its continent and its people" (152). Further, both Mbembe and Appiah share the ethics of the postcolonial theorist, whose criticism "is based . . . in an appeal to a certain simple respect for human suffering, a fundamental revolt against the endless misery of the last thirty [now fifty] years" (152). But, beyond this point, Appiah's and Mbembe's intellectual paths diverge.

In Appiah's book, *In My Father's House* (a useful bookend to Mbembe's

*Sortir de la grande nuit*), a chapter on the present condition and future prospects of African states follows the aforementioned chapter on the postmodern and postcolonial. There, Appiah observes, "despite all their limitations, African states persist," from which point he is able to envision the possibility of an end to a politics of postcolonial decline. Appiah's observance of the persistent presence of the state suggests a cautionary endorsement of political society within the nation, embedded, as it is, in a broader critical history of the Ghanaian postcolony. Indeed, Appiah rejects the nationalist fervor of the post-independence era (and its subsequent postcolonial revivals), rooted, in Ghana as in Mali, in the racial essentialisms of a pan-Africanist ideal (see Hall 2011). "African unity, African identity," he writes, "need securer foundations than race."[16] But, Appiah is less interested in "starting over" in light of the postcolonial state's apparent (and genuine) failures; rather, Appiah appeals, in a later essay, to what he calls a rooted cosmopolitanism, in which a critical, though no less proud patriotism reflects a commitment "to the conditions necessary for a common life" (1997, 629). In defense of the polis, in Africa as elsewhere, he writes, "What is required to live together in a nation is a mutual commitment to the organization of the state—the institutions that provide the overarching order of our common life" (629).

"Nations matter morally," Appiah writes, "as things desired by autonomous agents, whose autonomous desires we ought to acknowledge and take account of, even if we cannot always accede to them" (624). In the final section of this chapter, I return to the idea that, in the world today, among artists and audiences across multiple scales of place, Malian music (still) matters morally; not as a celebratory expression of a postcolonial artifice, but as an acknowledged mode of African being in the world; not as a vulgar mimicry of state power, but as a vital signifier of popular politics; not as a sign of nativist authenticity, but as a variegated practice of imagining community; not as a static traditional essence, but as a dynamic and resonant Afropolitanism. Though I attend to the agency and desires of the artists who assert the morality of this social position, I also observe the hardships and struggles of musicians whose moral claims on Malian music remain provisional, precarious, and, in a time of regional crisis, proscribed. It is this biopolitics of culture—in which the sounds of political belonging too often conceal the silences of dispossession—that highlights the existential problem of Afropolitan patriotism in contemporary Mali. If Malian music matters morally in Africa (and the world) today, who has the right to speak and sing of it? Does this social position represent an exclusive mode of being—the prerogative a privileged elite—or does it invite a more inclusive moral community? Is the Afropolitan patriot merely a poor imitation of her cosmopolitan counterpart, or is there substance to her claims to human rights, continental renaissance, and national reconciliation?

## Musical Life after Death?

In the afternoon of January 9, 2013, several hundred militants poured into the village of Konna in central Mali, a farming community on the border between the occupied north and the government controlled south. The Malian soldiers stationed to defend the town were caught off guard. Dozens were killed in heavy fighting that lasted into the night. Outnumbered and outgunned, the government lines broke. In retreat, some soldiers discarded their fatigues in an attempt to blend in with local residents; others fled in jeeps to the military base in Sévaré 30 miles to the south, the last major outpost of Mali's armed forces north of the capital, Bamako. On January 10, Interim President Dioncounda Traoré made a desperate plea to his counterpart in France, François Hollande, to intervene or witness the former French colony fall to Islamist rule. France responded. Beginning on January 11, French gunships and fighter jets launched attacks on insurgent positions advancing on the riverine town of Mopti, 7 miles west of Sévaré and 285 miles north of Bamako along a two-lane highway (see Hammer 2013; Whitehouse 2013b).

The following day, the Malian government declared a state of emergency, enabling "the government to take extraordinary measures to deal with the crisis in the North" and setting strict limits to public gatherings in towns and cities across southern Mali.[17] As a result, cities like Kayes, Ségou, Sikasso, and Bamako, already muted by months of political instability and economic uncertainty, fell silent. Whereas the muzzling of public culture in the north elicited loud indignation from foreign observers, with many announcing the "death" of Malian music and culture, the state's crackdown on civil life in the south went largely unremarked; this silence, it seemed, was justified. Meanwhile, with all eyes on France's "Operation Serval," the military mission "to 'eradicate' terrorism in Mali,"[18] ears tuned in to those frequencies where Malian music still maintained an audible presence, on the airwaves and online. On January 16, Malian singer

Fatoumata Diawara, a rising female star on the world circuit, released the track "Mali Ko" via SoundCloud on Public Radio International's nationally syndicated program, *The World*[19] (Figure 22). With its call for national solidarity in the face of a common existential threat—echoing geopolitical condemnations of a radical and militant Islam—"Mali Ko" quickly became an Internet sensation, posted on YouTube under the rubric "Voices United For Mali" with the word "Peace" added parenthetically to its title. In the Western media, "Mali Ko" (meaning, in Bamana, "For Mali," but also "Mali Trouble") became a key cultural counterpoint to the escalating violence in the Malian north. Against the rise of repressive religiosity, here was a call for tolerance and unity; in the face of civil war, here was a call for peace and reconciliation.

Back in Mali, the globetrotting Diawara, recently returned from a tour in the United States (performing at globalFEST in New York City the Sunday prior), organized a press conference on January 17 for the official domestic release of "Mali Ko"—a musical event "For Mali," and, now, for Malians. She, along with several of the forty artists featured on the track (including Ségou bluesman Bassékou Kouyaté, featured on the May 2013 Oxfam video), repeated the message of peace and unity broadcast to international audiences but added a call to arms intended especially for their Malian listeners. "We have found ourselves in a war in which others are fighting each other in our own country, even before we have taken up arms to fight," Diawara told Mali's national television, a reference to France's military intervention against apparently foreign Islamist fighters.[20] This sentiment of patriotic mobilization echoed two other notable online releases from established artists in the weeks surrounding the battle of Konna and France's military intervention in early January.[21]

On December 30, Ivorian reggae star and vocal pan-Africanist Tiken Jah Fakoly circulated the single "An Ka Wili" ("Let's Rise Up"), drawing on references to Mali's precolonial past to urge present-day Malians (and their neighbors) to come together in defense of their country's cultural and territorial integrity. At the outset of the track, Fakoly warns his listeners, "If we don't rise up, Mali will slip away from us." He invokes the names of great regional warriors, conquerors, and kings—from Sunjata Keita and Sonni Ali Ber, champions of medieval empires, to Samory Touré and Babemba Traoré, remembered for their resistance to colonial rule—and asks, "Where have [their] descendants gone?" Sung in Bamana, and addressed to Mali's contemporary citizens, "An Ka Wili" resonates with a

*Figure 22. Fatoumata Diawara. Courtesy of Berthin Coulibaly.*

broader regional significance. As imagined through its pantheon of historical leaders, Fakoly's "Mali" includes precolonial political geographies that encompass much of present-day West Africa. Fakoly is himself a citizen of neighboring Côte d'Ivoire, though he has lived in exile (mainly in Bamako) since 2003, when death threats followed his vocal criticism of the xenophobic "Ivoirité" politics of the Bedié and Gbagbo regimes (see Reed 2012). In "An Ka Wili," Fakoly sings from Mali, as a resident guest, but also (like Diawara) for Mali, as a concerned neighbor. In this way, Fakoly's music exhibits a kind of regional "double-consciousness," rooted and routed in and through Mali, and mediated by a palpable pan-Africanism—sounded through the diasporic rhythms, timbres, and textures of reggae—which is the artist's ideological and generic trademark (see Gilroy 1993).

On January 19, Malian M.C. Master Soumy released "Sini Ye Kèlè Ye" ("Tomorrow Is The Fight"), "dedicated to the Malian army and destined to mobilize the population behind its army."[22] This was the latest of several tracks of pointed political commentary released by the young rapper since the outset of the current crisis. In the weeks following the March 2012 military coup, Soumy joined the ranks of a Bamako-based hip-hop collective known as *Les Sofas de la République* ("The Soldiers of the Republic"). The Sofas were among the first public figures to vocalize a critique of the unfolding social, political, and economic crisis in the country, drawing attention not only to failures of governance among political elites but also to widespread social apathy and acceptance of an entrenched culture of corruption. Expressed through hip-hop and circulated online, their message—demanding political accountability, civic engagement, and collective action to confront Mali's pressing problems—reached a broad listening public (and caught the attention of several international observers), highlighting the relative lack of substantive critical commentary from the local press and political leadership. It is for this reason that Bruce Whitehouse, in his widely read Bamako-based blog (bridgesfrombamako.com), characterized the group as a unique and vital manifestation of civil society in Mali (2012b). In "Sini Ye Kèlè Ye," Soumy speaks in rhymes and over beats from this platform of public criticism and proclaims his call to arms. "In a time of war," he raps, "every Malian should take action as a soldier. . . . Tomorrow is the fight."

Released over three weeks in the midst of intense internecine warfare, "Mali Ko," "An Ka Wili," and "Sini Ye Kèlè Ye" not only shared the common theme of performing the Malian nation in patriotic—even jingoistic— terms, they also represented a resonant and explicitly moral counterpoint to perceptions of a moribund music culture. In Fatoumata Diawara's words, "We artists cannot remain indifferent to what is happening in Mali, we must help to restore a patriotic spirit."[23] For Diawara and others like her, a renewed sense of nationalist urgency would require a revitalized Malian art world. Yet, this world of Malian art resounded from a new location of culture. In addition to their themes and purpose, these tracks also shared a common platform to communicate and circulate their message: social media. Launched on SoundCloud and YouTube and spread through Facebook and Twitter, Malian music, at the moment of its apparent death, seemed to come alive once again, not on stage but online. Older media frequencies spread their sounds as well, on television and the radio, but, as captured by the name of the program that first broadcast "Mali Ko" in the United States, this music "for Mali" arrived via "The World."

Beneath these digitally coded frequencies of musical activity and activism, a quieter, more somber, and more analog art world languished. From

Timbuktu to Bamako, whether by virtue of repressive acts of violence in
the name of religion or checkpoints and surveillance in the name of civic
order, Mali's once-renowned live music culture settled into an anxious silence. In Bamako, the sounds of outdoor dance parties, drumming ceremonies, ambulant chants, and bands playing into the night—sonic emblem's
of the city's renowned musical ethos—became casualties of war and their
purveyors, Mali's urban artists, de facto prisoners of war. While arguments
could be made to justify a reining in of public culture in a time of heightened domestic conflict, many within Bamako's artistic community cast
doubt on and openly criticized the state of emergency, though their grievances attracted little media attention. A rare public criticism came from
the voice of Madina Ndiaye, Mali's most famous female *kora* player and a
vocal advocate of Mali's domestic music culture. In a May 2013 interview
with a Bamako weekly newspaper *(Bamako Hebdo)*, Ndiaye said:

> What the authorities are doing is not honest. I have the impres-
> sion that the state of emergency applies only to artists. If not, how
> do you explain the organization of soccer matches? It is simply a
> means of bringing ruin upon artists, to silence them, to keep them
> from speaking out and denouncing the calamitous governance of
> the state. This is unjust. If you prohibit artists from taking part in
> lifecycle ceremonies or concerts, especially in Mali, how do you
> expect us to live? It's deplorable.[24]

It is important to note that the artists of and for whom Ndiaye speaks are
not those with the international profiles of Fatoumata Diawara and Tiken
Jah Fakoly, or the social media presence of young and generally affluent
rappers like Master Soumy (see Schulz 2012, 134). These are not the artists who spoke and sang in praise of the nation in August 2010, when the
*Cinquantenaire* anthems of Sidiki Diabaté, Iba One, and Mokobé drew
my attention online. Rather, these are artists whose everyday livelihoods
depend on local economies of culture, on public and private patronage
of ceremonial and recreational performance. These are artists who tell
me they've "had enough of songs about Mali," enough of dressing up the
shameful state in rags. These are the sidemen, backing vocalists, and aspiring stars whose music accompanies baptisms and marriages, animates
nightclubs and bars, and, for the past two decades, has captivated the interest of adventure tourists, amateur sound recordists, travel writers, and

ethnomusicologists. Yet, unlike their cosmopolitan peers, their work reflects both the ambiguity and anonymity of their vernacular status and identity.

If these artists play a vital role in serving the social needs of their communities, as ritual participants and entertainers, they must also confront local stereotypes of socioprofessional vagrancy and parasitism. In his reflection on popular musicians who peddle in praise in contemporary Bamako, Manthia Diawara laments that these modern-day griots too often prey upon the pride and passions of their patrons, invoking a traditional artifice that "bar[s] the door to any sense of cosmopolitanism, any profound mixing of cultures" (1997, 27). And, if artists' cultural output represents a draw for international tourism, it is also frequently conflated in popular accounts of Malian music culture. Take, for example, the itinerant observations of a travel article in the *New York Times* from 2006, which begins with the following line: "We were walking down a dirt road in a neighborhood of Bamako with the mellifluous name of Badalabougou, following the rhythmic beating of a bongo drum." Later, the author describes the Malian capital as a "cultural hothouse and melting pot on the Niger River . . . reminiscent of the Mississippi Delta," where "public open-air performances . . . are as much a part of life . . . as pickup games of le football" (Hammer 2005). Here, individual artistry melts away in the swelter of city sounds, producing an essentialist sense of place in which local artists are heard but rarely listened to, in which they sing, but, to paraphrase Spivak, do not speak.

## Toward a Musical Politics of the Governed

Between the months of February and July 2013, I collected seventeen testimonies from Malian musicians, primarily in Bamako, who responded to several questions about the current state of the arts in Mali, the particular difficulties faced by performing artists during the state of emergency (which ended on July 6, 2013), and the prospects for the future of Mali's music culture.[25] In concluding this chapter, I share some of their words:

> Sada, drummer from Mopti: "The state of emergency that the crisis engendered is the worst difficulty of our life. Without work . . . we can't earn anything, so we have nothing to give to our families. In Bamako, I'd say that artists have done better than those of us in the

interior of the country. They've told us to completely stop everything; even the sound of a flat tire is cause for alarm. In Mopti, we live like convicts. It's impossible to organize even a small event because the area is a designated red zone (high terror threat)."

Sékou, guitarist from Bamako: "With the war, there is no leisure, no entertainment. That's why we have been forced to stop playing, for reasons of security. All the same, I want to say that we artists were poorly greeted by this state of emergency. It was like being told to sit and do nothing for three months. Still, it sometimes happens that we hide ourselves to play, but always at home, behind closed doors."

Sadio, a singer and dancer from Kita: "We musicians have suffered a lot because of the coup d'état and state of emergency. To begin with, we've lost the respect of our landlords because we can no longer pay our rent. We don't eat to our fill. Our contracts with our patrons have been broken. We can't travel abroad, and we can't perform for local ceremonies. . . . Only a few clubs have continued to feature live performances during this period, because people are afraid of the security forces. For example, just last week, the police came to confiscate our instruments because we were playing for a fellow artist's baptism in Sabalibougou."

Drissa, a harpist from Bamako: "Some musicians have been about to produce their work abroad. I'm thinking in particular about Salif [Keita], who, during this time of crisis, has been on tour for eight months outside of Mali. Personally, during the same period, I have been to France and Burkina [Faso] with Nahawa [Doumbia]. Let us say that the state of emergency has been especially bad for those musicians who work day to day to make ends meet. For them, it has been a terrible hardship."

Souleymane, pianist from Mopti: "This is a state of emergency in name only. But the artists don't have a choice. They've told us to stop public gatherings, but at the same time, the national soccer championships continue, and the mosques and marketplaces are full of people. Artists have borne the burden of this situation. . . .

We live day to day, but we can't work. So, we're impoverished, and we can't feed our families. In the end, the Malian state has done more harm [to artists] than the Jihadists."

If we consider the musical morality I described at the outset of this chapter as a social position among artists in contemporary Mali, one that stakes a claim on political subjectivity in the world through expressions of cultural authenticity and accrues its moral significance by intimately coupling an idea of nationhood with the globalization of a music culture ("Music is the heart of Mali," Bassékou Kouyaté told Oxfam. "Mali is known for its music throughout the world."), then the testimonies of the Bamako artists I cited earlier suggest a subjectivity that lacks such positionality. In their claims of social and political neglect, hardship, and dispossession, there is a common narrative of biopolitical loss, of a diminished and degraded artistic personhood left susceptible to the expansive necropolitics of the present. Read together, their criticisms argue for a more open and inclusive biopolitics in Africa (and the world) today, one that includes but cannot be reduced to the world of music *for* Mali; one that recognizes the social and professional value of artists as vital agents of musical performance and politics *in* Mali. Closing the gap between these global and local art worlds to pursue a more comprehensive and sustainable biopolitics of culture while resisting the balkanizing and dehumanizing logics of necropolitical hegemony represent, I believe, pressing existential conditions for the projects of national reconstruction and reconciliation in Mali today, to which Malian artists, from all walks of life, have much to contribute.

It is in this sense that I, like Mbembe, maintain a "paradoxical optimism" in observing the contemporary Malian art world and the municipal, national, and transnational spaces of which it is a part. Though I am sanguine about music as a biopolitics of culture—in the potential for a musically motivated politics of the governed—I remain cautiously critical of the particular forms such music takes in Mali today. In ending on a call for greater political accountability, popular engagement, and national unity among artists, I do not mean to suggest that Mali's troubles can be resolved by the populist nationalism of a YouTube video, the cosmopolitan ideals of a world music act, the vocal activism of a hip-hop collective, or the late-night entertainment of a neighborhood dance band. Rather, my focus is on the fact of political subjectivity as a critical object of popular concern (see also Skinner 2012a), and my interest—here and throughout this book—is in the Afropolitan ethics that take shape through the creative expressions and public manifestations of a vibrant and vital urban African popular culture. The current crisis in Mali may persist, and divisions within the country may multiply, but the struggle for viable political communities in Africa, and for a minimum level of stability and security that is critical to a sound sense of self in modern polities (African or otherwise), will continue and, I believe, expand as long as there is a society worth defending and a better future worth fighting for. Such are the beliefs and aspirations of artists who, speaking and singing at home and abroad (in and for Mali), have had enough of exploitation in the guise of globalization, corruption in place of governance, and demagoguery at the expense of democracy. Theirs is the ambivalent art of an Afropolitan patriotism, of which we, their audiences and observers, might be paradoxically optimistic.

# An Africanist's Query

"IS AFROPOLITANISM THE ANSWER?," asks art historian Salah Hassan, pairing this question with the phrase, "rethinking cosmopolitanism" in his Bashorun M.K.O. Abiola Lecture at the 2013 annual meeting of the African Studies Association.[1] Hassan's title raises two related questions: What is the problem posed by "cosmopolitanism" that suggests Afropolitanism as the answer? And, if we entertain the idea of the Afropolitan as an answer—or, rather, as a way of "rethinking cosmopolitanism"—how might we understand this idea, this identity, this mode of being in the African world? In his talk, Hassan explores these questions through the contradictions and ambiguities of diaspora, with what he calls "the privileged Afropolitan . . . and his underprivileged counterpart." He begins with the visual culture of a growing African cohort of "free-spirited and young diasporic artists" whose work is exhibited with greater and greater frequency in European metropoles (though without, he notes, eliciting substantive attention from art critics). He then turns to the experience of clandestine African migrants in Europe, whose precarious lives—characterized by what he calls a condition of "temporary permanency"—trouble the elite social position of the former group. Hassan appeals to the possibility of an "inter-African cosmopolitanism," implying that Afropolitanism, to be usefully employed as a conceptual tool, must negotiate this gap between center and periphery—between the haves and have nots—in the experience of expatriate Africans.

In this book, I have addressed the Afropolitan from a primarily continental perspective, from a world conceived, lived, and perceived from the vantage of an expansive and dynamic urban Africa. Like Hassan's diaspora, my account of urban African public culture has also drawn attention to manifest contradictions and ambiguities. This is an Afropolitan world structurally adjusted by neoliberal economic policy, institutionally shaped by postcolonial political projects, represented through paradigms of difference, and capitalized through cultural commoditization. And, it is a world in which religious practice connects global ecumenes to local life-worlds; public culture draws on myriad diasporic affinities and exchanges; and aesthetic practices—exemplified, in this book, by music—artfully place modernity in a necessary and irreducible dialogue with tradition. By calling these structures, policies, processes, and practices Afropolitan I have not suggested a new totalizing narrative of African-ness. Rather, my intent has been to draw attention to common and coherent patterns of intersubjective negotiation within fields of experience—of which a totalizing "idea of Africa" is one—which bind African urbanites, like the Malian artists whose lives and works I have elucidated in this book, to a wider African world.

In both accounts of Afropolitanism, diasporic and continental, there is an emphasis on creative possibility in contexts of precarity and constraint, of claims to modes of being-in-the-world that artfully reimagine what it means to be urban, African, and worldly, even as such claims must contend with the inequities and exclusions of endemic poverty, corrupt governance, inadequate infrastructure, social prejudice, and what Hassan calls the "Eurocentric Western stronghold." What these correspondences suggest is a conceptual approach to the Afropolitan that productively engages with multiple scales of place and domains of experience in the African world. Further, this extensive, postcolonial and diasporic Afropolitanism invites a more robust Africanist response to, in Hassan's words, "the insufficiency of classic concepts of modernity." To conclude the present text, I would like to return to the categorical concerns suggested by Hassan's titular query: "Rethinking Cosmopolitanism: Is Afropolitanism the Answer?" What critical perspective does Afropolitanism bring to the cosmopolitan episteme? And, what does this conceptual relationship say about Afropolitanism as an idea, a worldview, and a structure of feeling? I contend that the challenge posed by Afropolitanism to a certain kind of cosmopolitanism—and to a certain idea of Africa—is essentially moral, an interrogation of normatively exclusive, essentialist, and divisive categories of being. And, I suggest that Afropolitanism is best understood as a diverse configuration of existential projects in a world embedded in and emergent from an increasingly urban and extroverted Africa. My hope is to locate the foregoing study of Bamako's musical art world within a broader conceptual framework, in which the Afropolitan ethics of a particular music culture may register meaningfully in other places, among other communities within an urban Africa at large.

## Where the Cosmopolitan Meets Africa

"What is an Afropolitan?," asks Hassan at the outset of his lecture. One of the answers he provides is simple enough: "Where the cosmopolitan meets Africa." It is a definition rooted in Afropolitanism's amalgamated morphology: a word composed of two sociospatial signs, "cosmopolitanism" and "Africa," forming a whole that is both the sum of its parts and an implicit critique of those parts. On the one hand, the combining form "Afro-" unsettles as it displaces the cosmos of a universalist cosmopolitanism. Strongly tied to the Kantian ideal of a unified and peaceful world, the "planetary yearnings" of the cosmopolitan are not, in the words of cultural geographer Tariq Jazeel, "geographically innocent." Such yearnings, Jazeel writes, "normalize universality as an extension of Eurocentric modernity" (2011, 78). In other words, the means by which such cosmopolitans address, make claims on, and engage with the world—through the language of global politics, human rights, transnational finance, tourism, humanitarian aid, intellectual property, and so on—assume a hegemonic Western subject position (Hassan's Eurocentric Western stronghold).[4] This echoes Achille Mbembe's recent critique of Universalism (which he opposes to his own more nuanced, post-imperial definition of cosmopolitanism), associated with sentiments of Eurocentric nationalism in postcolonial France. "Universalism à la française is not the equivalent of cosmopolitanism," he writes. "In large part, the phraseology of universalism has always served to conceal the nationalist ideology and its centralizing cultural model: Parisianism" (2010, 105–6).

Indeed, for many postcolonial subjects, the cosmopolitan universal is not easily distinguished from its metropolitan particular, the Mother City of the imperial world. In other words, a universalist conception of cosmopolitanism is strongly tied to a colonial world order. Or, to take the object of Mbembe's critique, however inclusive La Françafrique (the idea of a privileged socioeconomic and political relationship between France and its former African colonies) might be, it will always have Paris at its center. The underlying postcolonial métropolitanisme of the cosmopolitan means that even relativistic efforts to reclaim and decenter the cosmopolitan by multiplying it are fraught with essentialist and, potentially, neocolonialist danger. As Jazeel puts it, "Attempts to pluralize our understandings of cosmopolitanism ultimately serve to reinstantiate the liberalism, rationalities and taxonomies of thought that are tethered to the concept's irredeemably European and universalizing set of values and human normativities" (2011, 77).

Suggestions to qualify such cosmopolitanisms, and thereby link the Eurocentric cosmos to a host of fragmented Others, have also met with cautionary criticism. For anthropologist Charles Briggs, "Hybrid, vernacular, or rooted cosmopolitanisms are no more resistant to dangerous essentialisms—or to elitism and paternalism—than purification practices are" (2005, 95). In other words, to acknowledge the qualified—and, thus, partial—cosmopolitanisms of subaltern communities without, to borrow a phrase from Dipesh Chakrabarty, "provincializing Europe" (2000), or, in Mbembe's terms, "decolonizing oneself" (French, *se décoloniser*), is to merely reinforce existing dichotomies. What is required, Briggs argues, is not a politics of qualification, but of embedding; what he calls a *"cosmocular critical practice"* that locates "the vernacularisms embedded in existing cosmopolitanisms as well as the cosmopolitan underpinnings of existing vernacularisms" (2005, 95; emphasis in the original). It is precisely in this sense of embedded criticism that the "Afro-" of Afropolitanism disturbs and disputes cosmopolitan universality and, in doing so, extends the Du Boisian project of engaging the world and its history from an African vantage (Du Bois [1946] 2003). It does not dispel difference—the Afropolitan is no more "geographically innocent" than the cosmopolitan—but it does engender a new relationality predicated on an-Other's perspective, experience, and mode of being in the world, that of the Afropolitan.

Yet, like the Eurocentric cosmos, the idea of Africa is also unsettled by its global extension. The essentialization of Africa takes many forms, but it follows a common logic (Agawu 2003; Mudimbe 1988): Africa is considered to be an authentic, pure and coherent source of contemporary cultural complexity; it is bound to a rural and traditional ethos; it displaces difference with narratives of changing-sameness; and it continues to conjure fantasies of exoticism and savage desires, caught, as it has been for at least the past 500 years, in the hegemonic gravity of the Western cosmos. From the perspective of the Afropolis—which is to say, many of the fastest-growing urban centers and diasporic enclaves on the planet—this idea of Africa, as a mode of identification and a category of analysis, must be reconceived. There is a need, in other words, to better theorize an increasingly urban, demographically young, internally diverse, widely dispersed, highly productive, intensely creative, and always already modern African World.

## From Afropolitanism to Afropositivism

As a categorical intervention, Afropolitanism rejects the moralizing imperatives of a normative Eurocentric cosmos and an essentialist African ethos. As a cosmocular critical practice, Afropolitanism embraces the manifold moral perspectives that urban Africans actively adopt and adapt in fashioning their lifeworlds. That these lifeworlds encompass common challenges, concerns, styles, and sensibilities has been noted by several observers of contemporary Africa over the past two decades. Arguing for a paradigmatic shift in understandings of contemporary African-ness in the early 1990s, Kwame Anthony Appiah notes, "There is no doubt that now . . . an African identity is coming into being" (1992, 174). The basis of such an identity is not, he argues, the reductive ontologies of "race, a common historical experience, [or] a shared metaphysics," but "the project of a continental fraternity and sorority." It is a project, he claims, of shared cultural and institutional interests. Writing as an exponent of this "continental identity," Appiah further states:

> We share a continent and its ecological problems; we share a relation of dependency to the world economy; we share the problem of racism in the way the industrialized world thinks of us (and let me include here, explicitly, both "Negro" Africa and the "Maghrib"); we share the possibilities of the development of regional markets and local circuits of production; and our intellectuals participate, through the shared contingencies of our various histories, in a common discourse. (180)

Listening in to these lifeworlds, and in dialogue with other scholars of contemporary African expressive culture, I add that these Afropolitans also share a widespread and well-established investment in popular cultural production, performance, and circulation (Barber 1997); they share a sensitivity to and engagement with the politics and poetics of diasporic soundscapes (Monson 2000; Olaniyan 2004); they share a critical awareness of the global currents of an audibly African expressive culture (Ebron 2002; Meintjes 2003); and their artists contribute, in myriad ways, to the (re)production of urban African social life (Perullo 2011; White 2008) and its place in an uneven global order (Erlmann 1999; Weiss 2009) through novel generic innovations (Feld 2012; Shipley 2013), as continental as they are diasporic (Charry 2012).

The stories and sounds related and resounded in this book offer ethnographic substance to this project of socially and sonically signifying
an emergent Afropolitanism. Throughout, I have elaborated the multiple
moralities and ethical projects expressed through the lives and works of
Bamako artists, eschewing reductive typologies that reinscribe "local"
and "global," "traditional" and "modern," "cosmopolitan" and "vernacular"
dichotomies (to which the "African" is too often either the embodiment
or exception). In each chapter, I have emphasized a distinct (though not
exclusive) social position, exploring the intersubjective, spatial, historical,
and, given the aural orientation of the text, sonic parameters of enactment
for that particular mode of being: urban, professional, aesthetic, religious,
economic, and political. Social positions, I have argued, mobilize moral
worldviews. They represent ideological orientations that systematize discourse and agency in everyday life. Being variably co-present, subject to
shifts in moral interest and concern, social positions are also conditional.
In thickly describing these contingent categories of a modular habitus,
I have considered the way Afropolitan artists reflect on, represent, and
reinterpret their social positions, often in the course of musical performance. This is where my analysis of the Afropolitan in Bamako turns from
the social positions of moral personhood to the existential projects ethical
agency, from strategies of social being to the tactics of self-fashioning.
    This turn toward ethics returns us to the contradictions and ambigui-
ties of the Afropolitan lifeworld. Interfering with and impeding ethical
agency in cities like Bamako is an extensive and intensive sense of wildness, a condition defined as much by precarity, by hazard and insecurity,
as by provisionality, what Hassan identifies as a permanent experience
of the temporary ("temporary permanency"). As witnessed within the
Bamako art world, this is the wildness of an inhospitable urbanity, a ma-
ligned professional status, a contested spirituality, an exploitative economy, and a corrupt and divisive politics. It is a wildness that fuels so much
of the so-called Afro-pessimism that pervades accounts of contemporary
Africa. Yet, the stories of Afropolitan artistry I have related in the foregoing pages testify, again and again, to a remarkable and persistent ingenuity,
even amid endemic abuse and instability. As such, I present this study in
the spirit of what historian Gregory Mann calls "Afropositivism": "a real,
empirical and ethical commitment to perceiving African societies . . . as
lived, by Africans, now" (2013). Sustained attention to what I have called
an "Afropolitan ethics" moves critical inquiry beyond anxious accounts

of simply "getting by" and "making do" against all odds to encompass dynamic and transformative potentials of intersubjective agency across multiple domains of place and practice. Such tactical enactments of multiple modes of being across the social space of the African city constitute the empirical core of this work. My particular ethnomusicological intervention has been to argue that such transformative social dynamism resounds in the vibrant urban African music cultures that have garnered increasing attention from academics, journalists, and cultural critics attentive to Africa's twenty-first-century lifeworlds.

## Back to Bamako, and Beyond

And, Bamako *is* a remarkably musical city. Through voice, instrument, loudspeaker, and earphone, *Bamako sounds*. To relate the moralities and ethics of Bamako's urban ethos without recourse the musical, to the urbanely organized sounds of this soundly organized urbanity (to paraphrase Blacking 1973), is, in my opinion, scarcely conceivable. Thus, each chapter of this book may be read as a particular take on a broader theme: the way musical sounds suffuse and produce a complex and coherent Afropolitanism. In Bamako, there is music in the social and material space of the city, giving voice—intoned and inscribed—to the possibilities and constraints of everyday life; in the work of urban artists, amplifying the dynamism of political and professional projects and personae; in performance, embodying an intimate coupling of ethics and aesthetics; in religion, invoking the sacred morality of an increasingly profane public; in the economy, resounding the contradictions of capital in artful counterpoint; and in politics, communicating—through circulating sounds and stifling silences—the ambiguous state of the postcolonial nation. Music is, in other words, a pronounced and privileged sign of a variegated and vital Afropolitan ethics, in Bamako and beyond. As other Afropoles resound, broadcasting their being and becoming to an increasingly African world, we would be wise to listen in, and, wiser still, to learn from what we hear.

# Acknowledgments

THIS BOOK MARKS SIXTEEN YEARS OF EFFORT to explore, study, understand, and represent the varied and dynamic music culture of Bamako, Mali. It is preceded by other attempts in other forms to synthesize the experiences of my encounters with this art world: a children's book; an album; a pair of theses; a handful of articles; and numerous presentations, performances, lectures, and discussions in as many classrooms, concert halls, conference rooms, and coffee shops. And, it will be followed (I hope) by still other expressions of academic, artistic, and deep personal interest in the resonant lifeways of a city, its inhabitants, and the wider world of which they are a part. At this point in such a long-term work in progress, the debts of gratitude I owe are significant. No less significant is my desire to say "Thank you."

To my mentors: Chérif Keïta, who, in his ebullient undergraduate courses at Carleton College, first introduced me (among many other students over the years) to the languages, literature, social thought, and music of Mali and the wider Mande world; Toumani Diabaté, who invited a young, naïve, but ambitious young man from Minnesota to live in his Bamako home, study the *kora*, and share in a rich musical community; Dialy Mady Cissoko, who taught me to play the *kora* and, in the process, gave me innumerable lessons in life (a combination of social and musical edification that eventually led me to the field of ethnomusicology); Aaron Fox, my graduate advisor at Columbia University, whose critically framed, theoretically interested, and ethnographically grounded anthropology of music continues to inform my approach to the field; and Ellen Gray, Brian Larkin, Greg Mann, and Ana Maria Ochoa, who served on my doctoral committee and guided this research project through its early stages.

To my friends, in and out of the field: Fassiriman Dembelé, an extraordinary artist, teacher, research assistant, and travel companion who has contributed to this project—intellectually, practically, and creatively—in myriad ways; Souleymane Eyili, a journeyman from Cameroon and world-class bass player, who taught me a great deal about what it means to be an artist in urban Africa today; the family of Ablo Keita and Djebou Sidibé in Bolibana, my Bamako hosts, who welcomed me into their home and made me a part of it; Gabriel Farrell, whose knowledge, wisdom, and friendship have contributed greatly to this book (and many other projects in life); Dov Stucker, for the fraternal and musical dialogues here, there, and the places in between; Madeleine Fix, who employed her immense artistic and technical talents in designing the website for this book; Brandon County, always a comrade and a fellow student of Mali and the Mande world, whose attention to scholarly detail and composition is second to none; and Johanna Sellman, my most faithful collaborator and life partner, whose intellectual insights are woven throughout this text, and who (along with Brandon) patiently read through successive drafts of this book, from start to finish.

To my colleagues and friends in (and out of) the academy: Franco Barchiesi, Harmony Bench, Graeme Boone, Danielle Fosler-Lussier, Katie Graber, Steven Hyland, Margarita Mazo, Ike Newsum, Lois Rosow, Jennifer Schlueter, Barry Shank, Cheikh Thiam, and Sarah Van Beurden at The Ohio State University; John Baboukis, Bill Evenhouse, and Dave Tawfik at the American University in Cairo; Harry Berger, Alex Dent, Banning Eyre, Fabian Holt, Louise Meintjes, Jeff Piatt, Matt Rahaim, Jesse Shipley, and Gavin Steingo, kindred spirits in the world of musical anthropology; Jeremy Dell, Barbara Hoffman, Hannah Koenker, Jamie Monson, Marie Rodet, and Bruce Whitehouse in the world of African Studies; and Tyler Bickford, Andy Eisenberg, Toby King, Lauren Ninoshvili, Dave Novak, Matt Sakakeeny, and Anna Stirr, cherished interlocutors from a brilliant graduate community in ethnomusicology at Columbia University.

To my research assistants, interlocutors, and editors: Billie Eaves, Matthew Campbell, Erin Allen, Maggie Bissler, Yun Wang, Olivia Wikle, and Austin McCabe Juhnke at OSU, who worked with me to build bibliographies, transcribe field recordings, prepare presentations, track down images, and edit texts; Doug Anthony, Alison Furlong, Michael Goecke, Rachel Wishkoski, and the many other (ethno)musicology graduate students at OSU who have discussed and contributed to the ideas in this book in seminars and office hours; Mady Ibrahim Kanté, Seybou Keita, and Chaka Ndiaye, with whom I have spent many hours listening to recordings, working on transcriptions, and discussing translations; Kalifa

Gadiaga and Tiécoura Traoré, who, in sharing their vast knowledge of Malian social movements and political institutions, helped me navigate the trials and complexities of this current moment in the country's history; Pieter Martin, my editor at the University of Minnesota Press, who has patiently and diligently guided me through the process of publication, all the while nurturing this project with informed interest and insight; and AbdouMaliq Simone and another anonymous reader of the manuscript, whose engaged and incisive comments helped shape and refine this book in its final phase of composition.

To my research affiliates in Mali (2005–8): Gaoussou Mariko, cultural affairs liaison at the American embassy; Oumar Kamara, director of the Institut National des Arts; Mamadi Dembelé and Seydou Camara, assistant director and director of research at the Institut des Sciences Humaines; Aly Yéro Maiga at the Centre National de la Recherche Scientifique et Technologique; Abdoulaye Traoré and Timothée Saye at the Archives Nationales (Hamdallaye and Koulouba branches); Kora Dembelé, director of the Direction Nationale de l'Action Culturelle; and Masamu Welé Diallo, director of music at the Conservatoire des Arts et Métier Multimédia Balla Fasséké Kouyaté.

To the institutions that have supported this work, from the initial fieldwork, through the doctoral research, to the published manuscript: the Fulbright Institute for International Education fellowship (2000–1); Columbia University Institute for African Studies Leitner Family summer travel grant (2005); Social Science Research Council International Dissertation Research Fellowship (2006–7); Wenner-Gren Foundation dissertation research fellowship (2006–7); Columbia University Graduate School of Arts and Sciences dissertation writing fellowship (2007–8); Columbia University Department of Music summer research grant (2008); Charlotte W. Newcombe Doctoral Dissertation Fellowship (Woodrow Wilson Foundation, 2008–9); Whiting Foundation dissertation writing fellowship (2008–9); Quadrant Visiting Scholar Program at the University of Minnesota (2012); OSU College of Arts and Sciences faculty research grant (2010–13); and OSU Arts and Humanities Grant-in-Aid for manuscript preparation (2014).

To my family: Sallie and Stan Skinner, for their creative passions and unceasing encouragement, inspiring me early on and often to explore the world and learn from it; Nicholas Skinner, for the brother he is and for his passionate commitment to the arts of all kinds; Frida and Todd

Brooks and Erik and Eva Sellman, an extended family that is always close to home; Elias and Nils, my greatest inspirations, for their bountiful energy and joy, and for reminding me to play every day; and Jakob Ahlqvist, Bilge Erdemli, Jeremy Kuhel, Kara Lapso, Erika Lauri, and to the wonderful teaching staff at the Columbus Early Learning Center, Saint Joseph Montessori, Clinton Elementary, and Indianola Children's Center, for all those moments when I had to go back to work.

Finally, to all the Bamako bands and artists I have worked with, played with, learned from, and listened to over the years: Amadou & Mariam, Ngou Bagayoko, Mody Cissoko, Drahmane Coulibaly, Fernand Coulibaly, Marus Coulibaly, Issiaka Daman, Panka Dembelé, Kélétigi Diabaté, Ladji Diabaté, Madou Sidiki Diabaté, Mamadou Diabaté, Mohamadou Diabaté, Nfa Diabaté, Sidikiba Diabaté, Tata Diabaté, Nci Diakité, Barou Diallo, Dialyco, Adama "Djo Dama" Diarra, Fatoumata Diawara, Nahawa Doumbia, Les Escrocs, Tiken Jah Fakoly, Amadou Fofana, Groupe Issa Bamba, Iba One, Babily Kanouté, Salif Keita, Ami Koita, Habib Koité, Tata Bambo Kouyaté, Boncana Maiga, Drissa Maiga, Madina Ndiaye, Man Ken, Need One, Moussa Niang, Issa Ouattara, Yacoub "Jimmy" Ouerdraogo, Fanta Sacko, Karounga Sacko, Oumou Sangaré, Ballaké Sissoko, Nana Soumbounou, Master Soumy, the Symmetric Orchestra, the Symphonie de la Kora, Tata Pound, Mussa Tolo, Dialy Mady Tounkara, Sidi Touré, Amadou "Adez" Traoré, Aliou Traoré, Karjigé Laico Traoré, Lobi Traoré, Mokobé Traoré, Rokia Traoré, and the Triton Stars. This book is for them.

# Notes

## Introduction

1. The term "Mande" refers to a broad category of peoples with historical ties to the thirteenth-century Mali Empire encompassing parts of modern-day nation-states of Mali, Mauritania, Senegal, The Gambia, Guinea-Bissau, Guinea-Conakry, Liberia, Sierra Leone, Côte d'Ivoire, and Burkina Faso.

2. Throughout this book, foreign language terms appear in italics. Foreign languages include French, Mali's official language; Arabic, the language of Islam, most commonly articulated in Mali in its classical register; and Bamana (or Bambara), a Mande language and Mali's lingua franca. Bamana is the predominant foreign language employed in this book. When employing French or Arabic terms, I indicate their use either in the text or parenthetically to distinguish them from Bamana terms. In transcribing Bamana speech and song, I follow the orthographic standards set by the Malian National Office of Functional Literacy and Applied Linguistics (DNAFLA). For Arabic, I employ a simplified transliteration system based on the *International Journal of Middle East Studies* (IJMES) guidelines. However, when citing other sources (such as song texts, articles, and books), I follow the spelling conventions employed by the authors.

3. Sidiki Diabaté, interview with the author on December 15, 2010, in Bamako, Mali.

4. "Culture," much debated, contested, and all but dismissed during anthropology's disciplinary critique of the 1980s and '90s (Marcus and Fischer 1986; Dirks 1998)—as "a mystification of material relations of production, an 'effect' of dominant ideology, the product of culture industries and colonial and state bureaucracies" (Fox 2004, 32)—has more recently been given a sophisticated (and, I argue, salutary) reappraisal. "Culture," writes anthropologist Michael Fischer, "is not a variable; culture is relational, it is elsewhere, it is in passage, it is where meaning is woven and renewed often through gaps and silences, and forces beyond the conscious control of individuals, and yet the space where individual and institutional social responsibility and ethical struggle take place" (Fischer 2003, 7). Culture is neither an effect of power nor its condition. It is, rather, "an active and hegemonic (or power-inflected) process of organizing communal experience and social relations" (Fox 2004, 31), in which "power and meaning are not placed

in theoretical opposition but are shown to be intimately linked in an intersubjective matrix" (Biehl, Good, and Kleinman 2007, 14). As Michael Jackson observes, culture is "the field of a dialectic in which the sedimented and anonymous meanings of the past are taken up as means of making a future, and givenness transformed into design" (1996, 11). And, to rephrase the ideas of Fischer, culture mediates the psychosocial tensions between individual agency and institutional responsibility. Such conceptions of culture have strongly shaped the ethico-moral approach to the nested structures and practices of human social life I elaborate in this book.

5. My argument that multiple moralities socially constitute a dynamic and coherent urban African structure of feeling in Bamako resonates with Matt Sakakeeny's observation of the "multiple orientations" toward the soundscape of African American social space in New Orleans. As Sakakeeny argues, "While identity politics bind individuals together according to shared characteristics of race and place in a way that allows us to speak of a community of black New Orleanians, those operating within and across this community construct an individual subjectivity by drawing upon a shifting set of identifications based on their interactions in historical and social context. . . . Soundscapes encompass multiple, sometimes opposing, subject positions, and this is precisely why they have been so critical to the production of locality in New Orleans" (2010, 20–21, 25).

6. This dialectic of social position and existential project resonates with what Judith Butler, in her reading of Althusser's theory of subjectification, terms an "ethics" of the "desire to be," which she posits as being in tension with the socially conditioned, interpellated form of "being," interpreted here in terms of "morality" (1997, 130–31).

## 1. Representing Bamako

1. My interest in the coupling of aural experience and the production of social space has been strongly influenced by the work of Steven Feld. Feld's "sense of place" emerges ethnographically, observing "how spaces are transformed and 'placed' through human action, and, more crucially, how places embody cultural memories and hence are substantial sites for understanding the construction of social identities" (Feld 1996b, 73). Feld is particularly attentive to the sonic dimension of such sociospatial production, an acoustic mode of being-in-the-world he describes as an "acoustemology of place," or "local conditions of acoustic sensation, knowledge, and imagination, embodied in the culturally particular sense of place" (Feld 1996a, 91).

2. In fact, Samory Touré defeated the French at Woyowayankɔ on April 2, 1883, but then abandoned the Niger Valley in favor of eastern territories in Côte

d'Ivoire. Samory was captured in 1898 in Côte d'Ivoire (Brandon County, personal communication on January 15, 2014).

3. In Bamako, several adjoining neighborhoods on the Niger River's left bank include the name "Bolibana." The neighborhood I am describing here is officially known as "Oulofobougou-Bolibana," though it and the other Bolibana districts are collectively referred to as Bolibana.

4. This lyric ("Badenya duman tunbɛ") uses the past imperfect tense and would more literally translate as "Good conviviality has been here." When discussing this and other lines from the track "Bolibana" with the group Need One, however, the present tense was always used in their translations of the Bamana into French. Thus, I use the present tense is to translate the past imperfect has been throughout the track. Further, I have indicated the emphatic adjective duman (pleasant, good, useful) with an exclamation point.

5. Because I did not record this particular encounter with Need One, I recall their words through my field notes, written after the visit. Because the sentiments I ascribe to them are of a general nature, and because I did not note the particular attributions of statements made that evening, I use the third-person plural they as opposed to individual names.

6. The video for Need One's "Bolibana" can be viewed here: http://www.youtube.com/watch?v=FKPgjzw8X1E.

7. Hɔrɔnya describes the state of being "noble" or "free-born" in Mande society. While hɔrɔnya refers to a particular group (free-born nobles, hɔrɔnw) within the Mande social hierarchy, which also includes clan-based artisans (ɲamakalaw) and captives (jɔnw), its use in everyday discourse is more generalized. Anyone may possess hɔrɔnya. Thus, I translate it as "dignity," rather than, say, "nobility" (see Conrad and Frank 1995 and Hoffman 1990).

8. Today, with more than half of the city's population living in so-called spontaneous districts (French, spontanés), describing unregulated shantytowns on the outskirts of the city (Diarra, Ballo, and Champaud 2003, 42, 44–46), one must wonder about the enduring coherence of civil space in the face of unrelenting urban poverty.

9. Tiécoura Traoré, who performs the role of Chaka, worked as an engineer for the Malian railroad, before furloughs as a result of privatization in 2003 led to his dismissal. In addition to screen acting and farming (his current profession), Traoré is the leader of COCIDIRAIL (Collectif Citoyen pour la restitution et le development intègre du rail / Civil Association for the Railroad's Restitution and Sustainable Development), which lobbies on behalf of railroad workers, former railroad workers, and rural communities that had been served by Mali's national railroad before its privatization.

10. This "perceived" space of "appearance" in the (African) city is strongly resonant with Brian Larkin's notion of "immaterial urbanism," defined as "modes

of affect [that] suffuse the bricks and mortar of streets and buildings: the tedium, fear, arousal, anger, awe, and excitement felt as one moves from one space to another or seeks out particular places at particular times." Coupling affect with experience, Larkin observes that "moving through the city means moving through these emotions—praying in the morning, eating, traveling, working, dealing with petty bureaucracies, hanging out with neighbors, reading, and praying again—circumambulating the routes offered by the city and the forms of life that come with them" (2008, 148).

11. Personal communication, April 2, 2013.

12. My reference is to Hannah Arendt, who, in *The Human Condition*, writes, "The remedy for unpredictability, for the chaotic uncertainty of the future is contained in the faculty to make and keep promises. . . . Binding oneself through promises, serves to set up in the ocean of uncertainty, which the future is by definition, islands of security without which not even continuity, let alone durability of any kind, would be possible in the relationships between men" (Arendt [1958] 1998, 237).

13. Need One's "Sabali" can be viewed here: http://www.youtube.com/watch?v=4fAkhoBCNxY.

14. On social stratification and hierarchy in the Mande world, see Bird, Kendall, and Tera 1995; Camara [1976] 1992; Conrad and Frank 1995; Hoffman 1995; and McNaughton 1988.

15. In her study of gendered personhood among the Sana (Mali) Bamana, Grosz-Ngaté cites a proverb that captures the distinct ontological risks associated with shameful behavior among men and women: "If you find a woman in trouble, help her. But if you find her in a shameful situation, leave her because she will get over it. If you find a man in trouble, leave him because he can get out of it on his own. But if you find him in a shameful situation, get him out of it because otherwise he might die" (1989, 171).

16. This means that attempts to discipline another's child may be justified ("The porridge is boiling") but are not sanctioned or blessed ("The stirring spoon is lost") when elders and parents alike are themselves perceived to be uneducated. More generally, the proverb argues that children who are entering adulthood cannot be put on the right path (that is, properly socialized) if their elders lack the moral authority to guide them.

17. This proverbial expression is used to convey a general sense of dismay and desperation. The "horse and her/his master," in this context, may be understood as the child and her/his parents or elders who are exhausted by incomprehension and mutual suspicion.

18. Earlier, I defined the term *sabali* as "patience." I translate the term in the track's chorus as "chill out" to reflect an English vernacular expression closer to the speech of contemporary Bamako youth.

## 2. Artistiya

1. The following history is based on interviews with former Pionnier Jazz members Amadou Traoré, conducted on June 26, 2007, and August 11, 2008, and Karamoko Isiaka Dama, conducted on January 25, 2007, in Bamako, Mali.

2. Quoted from Cutter 1968, 77. I have retained the original Bamana orthography from the citation, though I have amended the translation.

3. The video I consulted on YouTube has been taken down due to "multiple third-party notifications of copyright infringement."

4. I limit my discussion in this chapter to the professional lives and works of musical artists. It is to them that the term *artistiya* most often refers in contemporary Mali, perhaps given popular music's great public appeal, among young women and men (Schulz 2002, 2012), and music's far greater commercial success, locally and globally, over the other performing arts (Diakité 1999).

5. On public/private shifts in radio content, consumption, and broadcast in contemporary Mali, see Mamadou Diawara 1997; Schulz 1999; and Tower 2005.

6. On the social position, roles, identity politics, and local and global expressive culture of Mande *jeliw*, see, among others, Charry 2000a; Ebron 2002; Eyre 2000; Hale 1998; Hoffman 1990; 2000; Knight 1973; 1991; Roth 2008; Schulz 2001; and Skinner 2004.

7. Malians have been very well represented among the recipients of RFI's Prix Découvertes since its inception in 1981. Winners of the prestigious award include Nahawa Doumbia, Amadou & Mariam, Habib Koité, Rokia Traoré, and Idriss Soumaoro.

8. The term *siyɔrɔkɔ*, meaning "bedroom trouble," expresses a whole range of socioeconomic issues, including those of unwed lovers for whom intimate evening encounters must take place in secret and urban migrants who struggle to find stable lodging (*siyɔrɔ*, "a place to sleep") without regular employment.

9. Bob White (2008) notes the musical idiom of *ambiance* expressed in urban popular music in postcolonial Congo-Kinshasa, highlighting its polysemic and thus "poorly defined" character (23). Venturing a definition in the context of Mobutu-era Kinshasa, White writes, "The term generally refers to the city's particular combination of sexuality, spectacle, and dance music" (254n9).

10. Such mixing of regional instruments was made possible by the sociocultural heterogeneity of urban space and the cultural policy of newly independent African states, which sought to bolster "national" culture through the curatorial mixing of "traditional" musical idioms from the countryside (see Mamadou Diawara 1997, 42).

11. Consider the following description of an Ambiance Association event in the mid-1960s: "The afternoon before the evening performance, low-ranking *ñamakala* [artisanal clans, including griots] of the association prepare a large

space in front or near the house of the person who issued the invitation. They drive poles into the ground around a square, and hang a chain of electric lights on all four sides. Loud speakers set at every corner amplify the music of the orchestra. The show begins at night, after dinner" (Meillassoux 1968, 109).

12. Panka Dembelé, interview with author on April 29, 2007, in Bamako, Mali.

13. In his memoir, written with Lilian Prévost, Sorry Bamba (Issa Bamba's father) describes his membership in a musical association known as *goumbé* in the town of Mopti in the late-1940s and '50s. The term *goumbé* referred to a modern dance and musical style that was "all the rage" in contemporary Côte d'Ivoire, perhaps derived from the *gombey* popular dance rhythms of early twentieth-century Sierra Leone (Collins 1989). By the mid-1950s, the Mopti youth association had become a "modern" orchestra with horn and woodwind players, an acoustic guitarist, percussionists, singers, and dancers. In Bamba's words, "The *ambiance* was contagious" during Goumbé performances, adding "that the youth really appreciated our modern music. It was because it gave them a rare occasion to dance, one against the other, like the Whites" (1996, 31–39). Meillassoux's study of Bamako associational life includes a detailed account of similar *gūbe* events in the Malian capital, present in the city from the mid-1930s (1968, 116–30).

14. In a related discussion, Durán notes the vocal timbre preferred by young female griots *(jelimusow)* in Bamako, described as a "high-pitched, shrill nasal sound with a narrow, fast vibrato." "This type of voice," Durán writes, "has been in vogue since the early 1980s. . . . It is a type of vocal production associated with the style sometimes called *'musique d'ambience'* (music for dancing at weddings and other life-cycle celebrations)." Durán suggests that the *ambiant* aesthetic of vocal *jeliya* may have been "created in part by amplification using inferior quality PA systems" (2007, 591).

15. Issa Sory Bamba, interview with author on May 9, 2007, in Bamako, Mali.

16. The term *Bama Nare* is a reference to the city of Bamako, combining the word *bama*, meaning "crocodile," the city mascot, with the family name *Nare* (or Niaré), one of the founding clans of the city.

17. Issa Bamba, interview with author on July 17, 2007, in Bamako, Mali.

18. These plots are located in a part of Ntomikorobougou known as the *cité sportif*, originally designated as a residential area for Mali's national soccer team.

19. Bruno Maiga and Dialy Mady Cissoko, interview with author on August 17, 2011, in Bamako, Mali.

## 3. Ethics and Aesthetics

1. This new recording of solo *kora* music would be released seven years later as *The Mande Variations* (Diabaté 2008).

2. An audible manifestation, perhaps, of what Richard Waterman describes, in an early theorization of form and function in African music, as the "metronome sense": "a theoretical framework of beat regularly spaced in time" and, in the musical elaboration of rhythmic patterns, "of co-operating in terms of overt or inhibited motor behavior with the pulses of this metric pattern whether or not the beat are expressed in actual melodic or percussion tones" (Waterman [1952] 1973, 86–87). While Waterman's representation of what he calls, in essays from the 1940s and '50s, "Negro Music" relies on overly essentialist and general characterizations of African and African-derived musics (see Agawu 2003; Waterman 1991), I have found many of his conceptual insights ("metronome sense," "offbeat phrasing," and "hot music" in particular) relevant to my analysis of Mande popular music in Bamako.

3. Chérif Keïta, conversation with the author on February 18, 2012, in Ségou, Mali.

4. When asked, Toumani Diabaté refers to himself as a musical autodidact, acknowledging the instrumental patrimony he inherited from his father as a kora player but insisting on his self taught mastery of the instrument (interview with the author on September 17, 2000, in Bamako, Mali). The elder Sidiki, who learned to play the kora during his youth in The Gambia, was among the first to perform the kora in southwestern Mali, along with Batourou Sékou Kouyaté, who was also present in Kita in the mid-1940s (interview with Djelimory Nfa Diabaté on November 9, 2006, in Bamako, Mali; see also Charry 2000a, 117–18).

5. All of the Kayiratɔn contemporaries I interviewed in Bamako and Kita in November 2006 and July 2007 spoke of the group's vital presence in 1940s Kita. "Everybody in Kita loved Kayira," Djely Bourama Diabaté, a relative of Sidiki Diabaté and a Kita native, declared, emphasizing community members' strong respect for the group. "If you wanted to get married, and didn't have the consent of the Kayiratɔn, the marriage didn't happen" (November 12, 2006). Djely Mady Diabaté, who was only a child at the time, described how Kayiratɔn musicians would motivate farmers in the fields, singing and drumming during the harvest (November 5, 2006). Others spoke of social and cultural concerns. Kankouba Diawara and Fanta Kanté (July 21, 2007) related how the Kayiratɔn intervened in arranged marriages, decrying such unions as unfavorable without the couple's consent. At one point during my interview with kora player Nfa Diabaté (November 10, 2006), he exclaimed, "In the Kayiratɔn, it was a revolution! Just like the Mamayatɔn was." The "Mamayatɔn" referred to a popular music and dance movement similar to the Kayiratɔn that emerged between the two World Wars in the Guinean city of Kankan (see Kaba and Charry 2000). For an historical analysis of the piece "Kayira," see Camara et al. 2002.

6. In Bamana, the lyric is *"Dondon kana kasi / Fajiri sɔgɔma wuli ka gelen ne ma."* Mohamadou Diabaté, the youngest of Sidiki Diabaté's sons in Bamako,

explained these lyrical interpretations to me during an interview on November 2, 2006, in Bamako, Mali.

7. Bakari Soumano, interview with the author on November 29, 1998, in Bamako, Mali.

8. According to Nfa Diabaté, a native of Kita who came of age as a young observer and participant in the Kayiratɔn, Sidiki Diabaté was the most widely respected *kora* player of his generation. Born to a family of *ngoni* (lute) players, the younger Nfa frequented the elder Sidiki to learn the *kora,* because the instrument was not well known in Kita at the time (interview with the author on November 10, 2006, in Bamako, Mali). Nfa would later go on to join Sidiki in the Ensemble Instrumental National du Mali in the early 1960s (Charry 2000a, 118; Skinner 2009: 69–72). Djeli Bourama Diabaté, a young contemporary of the Kayiratɔn, described Sidiki Diabaté's public rivalry with *kora* player Batourou Sékou Kouyaté, also a founding member of Mali's National Ensemble (interview with the author on November 12, 2006, in Bamako, Mali). Both Djeli Bourama and Nfa recalled a public competition between Sidiki and Batourou Sékou in which the two exchanged solos in a performance of "Kayira" (though Nfa did not specify the piece they performed). For Nfa, Sidiki was the apparent victor; for Djeli Bourama, Batourou Sékou had no equal when it came to "Kayira."

9. In her vocal performance, Nana moves along a continuum of Mande language, using both Bamana and Maninka syntax and morphology. For example, both the Maninka plural ending *-lu* and the Bamana *w* are used, as in the second person plural *alu* (Maninka) and *aw* (Bamana). Though Bamana is Bamako's lingua franca, Nana's use of Maninka, predominant in southwestern Mali and northern Guinea, represents, I believe, an aesthetic choice. For many Bamako artists, Maninka is perceived as the privileged language of sung poetics, perhaps due to the influence of prominent *jeli* vocalists from the Maninka towns of Kita and Kela, such as Kandia Kouyaté and Kassé Mady Diabaté.

10. The term *balimaya* more literally translates as "kinship," describing the condition (indicated by the suffix *-ya*) of being among one's family *(balima).* I translate the term, here, as "fellowship" to encompass the broader sense of "family" Nana invokes among her band mates.

11. Lucy Durán (1978) uses the Mandinka (western Mande) terms *donkilo* and *sataro* to refer to the melodic patterning, thematic content, and metrical periodicity of song and the melodic variability, narrative improvisation, and metrical irregularity of narration respectively; what I call here "chorus" and "recitation."

12. Ethnomusicologist Heather Maxwell offers the following definition of "song" *(dɔnkili)* based on her fieldwork among popular artists in Mali: "The world for song itself is *dònkili,* meaning at once 'the egg or testicles of the dance,' or 'the egg or testicles of knowledge,' depending how one interprets *dòn* (*dòn* is a noun for both knowledge and dance" (2008, 29–30). The consensus among Mande lin-

guists is that the term better translates as "to call to the dance," combining the word "dance" *(dɔn)* with the verb "to call" *(kili)* common to southern and western Mande languages (Maninka and Mandinka, in particular). I, like Maxwell, gesture to the "popular" etymology here out of deference to the artists and audiences in places like Bamako who appeal to a different, polysemic sense of the word in the Bamana language.

13. In Mande cosmology, *nama* refers to the "vital force" found in all animate, inanimate, and esoteric objects, such as human beings *(mɔgɔw)*, iron *(nɛgɛ)*, and speech *(kuma)*. The ability to control the last (speech) is the hereditary claim of griots. On the sociomaterial nature of *nama* in Mande social thought, see Cissé 1973, 160–61.

14. Chernoff's work has been criticized for its essentialist appeal to "African unity," generalizing from particular expressions of rhythm and collectivity among Ewe and Dagbamba communities in Ghana themselves juxtaposed with an equally essentialist rendering of "Western" music culture (see Merriam 1980, for an example of this critique; see also Ebron 2002, 33–53). Yet, African unity is not merely an ethical and aesthetic conceit in Chernoff's work, reliant on sociomusical generalizations; it is also a cultural and political practice of actively negotiating and representing difference, at home and abroad. See, for example, Chernoff's reflections on the florescence of African popular music in the early 1970s, with reference to dozens of bands from across the continent to reveal the growing presence of an identifiably African musical presence in the world (1979, 115–16).

## 4. A Pious Poetics of Place

1. To call such spoken and sung expressions "musical" risks offending those who hold a more doctrinal perspective on Islamic verbal art. From this point of view, blessings, chants, recitations, and prayer calls do not qualify as "music," per se, but as eloquent verbal expressions designed to heighten one's piety through focused listening *(sam')* (see Hirschkind 2006). Music, especially in its popular forms (as performed in concert halls and nightclubs), is said to inspire feelings that rival one's affection for God and, for this reason, should be discouraged or even forbidden among the faithful. While this perspective may be found among certain conservative reformists in West Africa, it is perhaps still more common to encounter those who accept a broader spectrum of musical expression within the context of Islamic practice in their daily lives.

2. It should be noted, however, that this popular confluence of national and religious identity has been profoundly unsettled by the March 2012 coup d'état and its destabilizing aftermath throughout the country. In this context of internecine conflict, to identify oneself as Malian or Muslim has implied tensions—in terms of political subjectivity ("Who belongs to this nation-state?") and public

piety ("Who represents Islam?")—exacerbated in the months leading up to and following the coup (for commentaries on the question of national belonging, see Moseley 2012; on the question of religious identity, see Peterson 2012). Moreover, these political and religious dissonances have been textured, in certain public forums, by a heightened sense of ethnic and racial difference, in which northern grievances are cast in black and white—figuratively and racially (Mann 2012b)— while southern critiques turn toward sectarian prejudice (Baba 2012).

3. While describing what it means to be a Muslim in the Malian postcolony, Benjamin Soares observes that "the public sphere has helped to foster a supralocal sense of shared Muslim identity in Mali, an imagined community of Muslims often linked to the Malian state whose members are to varying degrees attentive to the broader Islamic world that lies beyond the state boundaries" (2005, 238). For Soares, this national sense of Islam represents an important point of orientation among those who have distanced themselves from provincial traditions (such as local Sufi orders) without abandoning a sense of local distinction in their identities as Muslims (238–43). My observations of an Islamic popular culture in contemporary Bamako may be taken as situated expressions of this "postcolonial tradition" of Islamic identification (243).

4. "Marie" is a pseudonym.

5. On the use of the socioaesthetic practice of "sweeping away the dangerous energy of a place" during funerary rites, see Cissé 1973, 175, 175fn131.

6. Djo Dama Diarra, interview with author on December 6, 2006, in Bamako, Mali.

7. Lyrics reprinted with permission of the group Tata Pound. The translation of this particular passage, originally in French, is my own.

8. This has been exemplified, more recently, by the formation of the Malian hip-hop collective *Les Sofas de la République* (The Soldiers of the Republic), including two members of Tata Pound (Ramsès and Dixon), which Bruce Whitehouse describes as a vocal and youthful expression of Malian civil society whose mediated expression (with several tracks released on YouTube) have produced poignant, critical responses to the social, political, and economic crises of the March 22 coup and its aftermath (Whitehouse 2012b).

9. Like those who consume and circulate Islamic cassette sermons on the subaltern margins of urban Egyptian society described in Charles Hirschkind's seminal ethnography, *The Ethical Soundscape* (2006), artists and audiences within Bamako's hip-hop community often "stand in tension with the moral and political exigencies and modes of self-identification of national citizenship," and, again, like their Cairene counterparts, perform this "disjunctive relationship to the public sphere" through pious expressions of the voice and embodied practices of listening (117). Unlike the pious subjects who populate Hirschkind's study, however, established hip-hop artists in Mali are typically affluent members of the Malian

middle class (see Charry 2012, 304) who use their positions of privilege to speak to the broader societal concerns of contemporary African urbanites.

10. By contrast, Michael Ralph has recently examined the absence of sociable discourse in comparable streetside conversational tea circles in Dakar (2008). Ralph analyzes the gaps and silences in everyday speech that draw attention to the impossibility of convivial intersubjectivity in social spaces where poverty is endemic, employment is scarce, and anomie is pervasive.

11. Brandon County, personal communication on May 19, 2011.

12. This lyrical passage is drawn from a transcription made by Lucy Durán and included in the liner notes to the compilation album *Jarabi: The Best of Toumani Diabate, Master of the Kora* (Durán 2001). I have slightly modified the transcription in accordance with Bamana language spelling conventions.

13. Moussa Niang, personal communication on June 30, 2012.

14. I thank my colleague Cheikh Thiam for providing me with a full translation of the Wolof language lyrics to "Tapha Niang."

15. As the principle copyright holder, Diabaté has a particularly strong claim to the content of *Boulevard de l'Indépendence*, including "Tapha Niang," a point of contention that Moussa Niang is quick to point out in his reflections on this song.

16. On the sounds of African alterity, see Agawu (1995) and Ebron (2002).

17. The song can be heard, along with some images from *LittleBigPlanet*, here: http://www.youtube.com/watch?v=zV5ABoAIQFU.

18. Toumani Diabaté, interview with the author on December 22, 2010, in Bamako, Mali.

## 5. Money Trouble

1. In this chapter, I use the term *copyright* in the francophone sense of *le droit d'auteur*, employed in Mali, a former French colony. "The right of the author" includes both moral and proprietary rights (*droits moraux et patrimoniaux*) pertaining to the material publication and exploitation (proprietary rights) as well as the personal attribution and integrity (moral rights) of a work (for a definitional history of French copyright, see Latournerie 2001).

2. For a broad-based ethnographic survey of money—its materiality, uses, and troubling effects—in contemporary Mali, see Wooten 2005. For a more general, comparative discussion of shifting forms and understandings of wealth and value in sub-Saharan Africa, see Guyer 1995.

3. I thank Marc Perlman for bringing my attention to this reference.

4. Panka Dembelé, former member and director of the Orchestre National du Mali, interview with the author on May 3, 2007, in Bamako, Mali.

5. Djelimory Nfa Diabaté, interview with the author on November 9, 2006, in Bamako, Mali; see also Amselle 1978, 343, 348.

6. See, for example, musical selections included on the two-volume release, *Epic, Historical, Political and Propaganda Songs of the Socialist Government of Modibo Keita (1960–1968)* (Various Artists 1977).

7. Ethnomusicologist Graeme Counsel documents a pair of recordings released in 1968 by "Republic *[sic]* du Mali Radiodiffusion Nationale" in his extensive online "Radio Africa" discography (2012). Elsewhere, Counsel writes that "commercial recordings were sporadic until the German label, Bärenreiter-Musicaphon, in conjunction with UNESCO and The Malian Ministry of Information, released over a dozen discs in circa 1971. It wasn't until 1973 that the Malian government first released its own material" (2006, 138). These recordings sought to sample the regional diversity of Malian cultural expression and likely served as tools of promotion, to "perform the nation" (Askew 2002) abroad. Examples of such state-sponsored promotional releases include *Panorama du Mali* and *Regard sur le passé à travers le présent* (Various Artists 1973a and 1973b).

8. Comité revolutionnaire de coordiantion de la JUS-RDA de Bagadadji to Comité Nationale de la Jeunesse (Bamako, December 26, 1967), Archive National du Mali, Hamdallaye, FBPN 52/140.

9. On the late and postcolonial politics of the Union Soudanaise de Rassemblement Démocratique Africaine (US-RDA), which governed Mali as a single-party state from 1960 to 1968, see Hodgkin 1957 and Morgenthau 1964. On the US-RDA's postcolonial politics of culture, see Skinner 2012b. For an artful account of Bamako's unofficial postcolonial youth culture, replete with foreign sounds, see the photographic work of Malick Sidibé (Mangin 1998).

10. Amadou Traoré, former member and director of the Orchestre National du Mali (section B), interview with the author on June 26, 2010, in Bamako, Mali.

11. "Special Clôture," *8ième Biennale Artistique et Culturelle* (1984), edited by the Commission de Presse et d'Information. Unfiled archival document at the Direction Nationale Patrimoine Culturel, Bamako, Mali.

12. In Bamana, *Sanjikɔrɔwɔsi tɛ dɔn.*

13. Mandé Moussa Diakité, adjunct director at the Bureau Malien du Droit d'Auteur, interview with the author on January 20, 2007, in Bamako, Mali.

14. Bruno Maiga, former administrative director of the Théatre National du Mali, interview with the author on August 17, 2011, in Bamako, Mali.

15. Journal Officiel de la Republique du Mali, August 15, 1986, 42–44.

16. Bourama Diarra, the president des Partants Volontaires à la Retraite at the Bourse de Travail (Labor Exchange) in Bamako, states that the VER programs persisted until 1995 (interview with the author on December 16, 2008, in Bamako, Mali). My own inquiries revealed VER legislation pertaining to the "second wave" through 1993 (see Journal Officiel de la Republique du Mali, February 28, 1991, 155–58; March 15, 1991, 167; October 15, 1992, 694; and April 15, 1993, 258).

17. Bourama Diarra, December 15, 2008.

18. Amadou Fofana, former member of the Badema National (Malian National Orchestra) and VER participant, interview with the author on August 15, 2008, in Bamako, Mali.

19. Jeli Magan Diabaté, former member of the Ensemble Instrumental National du Mali and VER participant, interview with the author on November 23, 2006, in Bamako, Mali; Amadou Fofana, August 15, 2008.

20. Mandé Moussa Diakité, January 20, 2007.

21. Ibid.

22. Albums associated with Toumani Diabaté's internationally touring groups in the 1990s include the Mande Jazz Trio's *Djelika* (Diabaté et al. 1995), *New Ancient Strings* (Diabaté and Sissoko 1998), and *Kulanjan* (Diabaté and Mahal 1999).

23. Symmetric Orchestra band members would eventually get their break in the decade that followed, for those who endured the wait, with the group's internationally acclaimed release, *Boulevard de l'Indépendence* (2006).

24. Mandé Moussa Diakité, January 20, 2007.

25. It is worth noting that Blondy recorded his own version of Marley's "War," titled, "La Guerre," on the album *Dieu* (1994), which preceded *Grand Bassam Zion Rock* (1996).

## 6. Afropolitan Patriotism

1. Here is a sampling of headlines from international media reports detailing Islamist violence in northern Mali at this time: "Radical Islamists Stone Adulterous Couple to Death in Northern Mali" (July 30, 2012. theguardian.com); "Mali Crisis: Gao Protests 'Stop Hand Amputation'" (August 6, 2012. bbc.co.uk); "Mali Festival in the Desert Postponed Due to Insurgence" (August 30, 2012. news.bbc .co.uk); "Mali: Rebel Groups Ban Music and Replace Ringtones" (December 6, 2012. bbc.co.uk2012); "Blues for Mali as Ali Farka Toure's Music Is Banned" (December 7, 2012. bbc.co.uk); "La Musique Malienne, En Berne Au Sud, Interdite Au Nord" (January 1, 2013. france24.com); and "Mali's Musicians Defiant in Face of Music Ban" (January 21, 2013. cbc.ca). For a nuanced dialogue about the varied experience of "Islamist" administration in northern Mali during this time, see Hall et al. 2013, especially the section on "Secularism, Political Islam, and Justice." Andy Morgan deals explicitly and extensively with the plight of music culture in Mali following the social and political upheavals of 2012 in his book, *Music, Culture, and Conflict in Mali* (2013), and in his recent freelance journalism (andymorganwrites.com).

2. On March 22, 2012, a military mutiny in Kati, Mali's main garrison town, spawned a military coup, destabilizing Mali's political order, sending its economy into a tailspin, and ushering in myriad parastatal factions that thrust this poor, landlocked nation into the theater of global warfare (Mann 2012a; Soares 2012;

Whitehouse 2012c). The latter issue of armed conflict has not been limited to the rebellion in the North, where a complex mix of ethnic nationalists, territorial separatists, Islamists, and smuggling cartels vie for territorial hegemony (for a historical perspective on this "complex mix," see Lecocq 2010); the southern capital, Bamako, too has witnessed the strong-armed politics of a military junta, compounded by the vigilantism of civilian mobs (Whitehouse 2012d). For a historical account and analysis of the unfolding of these (and other) events in Mali in 2012, see Lecocq et al. 2013.

3. This film can be viewed here: www.youtube.com/watch?v=k16Eoyccip4.

4. The apparent morality of Malian music is, of course, neither universally embraced nor uncontested. It is precisely this social position of "musical Malianness" that groups like Tinariwen have refused, articulating, by contrast (though relatedly), a social position of Tuareg nationalism under the banner of a culturally distinct and politically independent Azawad. See, for an example of this position, the blog post "Tinariwen Speaks on the Coup in Mali" from the website africasacountry.com, published on April 2, 2012. For a critique of this position, see Gregory Mann's commentary on "the racial politics of Tuareg nationalism" from the same website (Mann 2012b).

5. A headline from *Der Spiegel*'s international website on January 21, 2013: "Mali Conflict Opens New Front in War on Terror" (spiegel.de).

6. See, in particular, Andy Morgan's *Music, Culture, and Conflict in Mali* (2013) for detailed accounts of artists, audiences, and the politics of everyday life in northern Mali, related with a historically informed perspective on the current crisis.

7. Here, I echo the insights and interventions of Partha Chatterjee, whose notion of a "politics of the governed" among subaltern populations in postcolonial societies stresses that "the functions of governmentality can create conditions not for a contraction but rather an expansion of democratic political participation" (2004, 76).

8. The video for Iba One's and Sidiki Diabaté's "Cinquantenaire du Mali" can be viewed here: www.youtube.com/watch?v=8vTqHNb_2gs.

9. The video for Mokobé Traoré's "Mali Debout" can be viewed here: www.youtube.com/watch?v=WWnI3z7L2qw.

10. The interview, "L'Afrique 50 ans après les indépendences avec Achille Mbembe," can be viewed on the website franceculture.fr. I first viewed this interview on a blog post by Tom Devriendt ("Achille Mbembe's Africa") on africasacountry.com.

11. An online version of this text was published on April 1, 2010, on courrierinternational.com.

12. This image can be viewed here: www.journaldumali.com/article.php?aid=1976.

13. The video for Djeneba Seck's "Maliba" performed with the Symphonie du Cinquantenaire can be viewed here: www.youtube.com/watch?v=7IO1of_GqMO.

14. The title of the section is a reference to Partha Chatterjee's essay, "Beyond the Nation? Or Within?" (1998).

15. Interview with Achille Mbembe on franceculture.fr (October 19, 2010), as cited by Tom Devriendt in his blog entry "Achille Mbembe's Africa" on africasacountry.com.

16. Mbembe's recent text *Critique de la Raison Nègre* echoes this criticism of postcolonial nativism while also suggesting that the objectified condition of "race" coupled with the idea of "blackness" *(la raison nègre)* has become much more generalized across the globe in the current era of neoliberalism (2013).

17. An announcement of the "state of emergency" was made by the U.S. Embassy in Bamako on January 11, 2013, (mali.usembassy.gov) and reported (for the purpose of clarification) in the Malian press on January 12 (journaldumali.com).

18. This quotation refers to a headline on January 13, 2013 ("France Determined to 'Eradicate' Terrorism in Mali, Official Says") that cites French Defense Minister Jean-Yves Le Drian on cnn.com.

19. The audio file for Fatoumata Diawara's "Maliko" can be streamed here: soundcloud.com/theworld/maliko.

20. For a lyrical transcription and analysis of "Maliko," see Whitehouse 2013c. Fatoumata Diawara's commentaries on the track's release in Mali can be viewed here: youtube.com/watch?v=Hg1f3pBHoPQ.

21. I am thankful to Bruce Whitehouse for bringing my attention to the proximate release of these singles (2013a and 2013c).

22. This statement is quoted from an interview with Master Soumy, "'Sini yé kêlêyé' de Master Soumy bientôt dans les bacs," published via the weekly journal *Bamako Hebdo* on January 19, 2013, on maliweb.net.

23. This statement is quoted from an interview with Fatoumata Diarwara, "'Maliko': le cri de coeur des artistes pour le Mali," published January 18, 2013, on journaldumali.com.

24. This statement is quoted from an interview with Madina Ndiaye, "Madina Ndiaye, unique femme malienne joueuse de la kora," published May 11, 2013, via the weekly journal *Bamako Hebdo* on maliweb.net.

25. Working remotely from the United States, I sent two questionnaires by email to interlocutors within Bamako's artistic community in February and May 2013. Fassiriman Dembélé, a professional musician and music educator in Bamako who has long assisted me, recorded the responses of the seventeen artists who chose to participate in the survey. Seybou Keita, a local journalist, then transcribed the responses and sent them to me electronically in April and July 2013.

## Conclusion

1. I attended this talk on November 23, 2013, in Baltimore, Maryland. Citations from the talk are from my own notes taken during the lecture.

2. In a recent article titled "Rethinking African Culture and Identity: the Afropolitan Model" (2014), Chielozona Eze takes a more accommodating stance toward cosmopolitanism as a framework for understanding contemporary African subjectivities, at home and abroad. Eze critiques exclusive and elitist understandings of the cosmopolitan in favor of what he calls a "normative conception of morality" that fosters an "empathetic imagination." This "new universalism" grounds his account of Afropolitanism "explored within a cosmopolitan context" (243–44). I am drawn to Eze's Afropolitan "reading of the African postcolonial identity as necessarily transcultural [and] transnational" (241), though I think the singular moral compass of his overarching cosmopolitanism may obscure (in its noble aim for a more convivial theory of identity) more than it reveals about worldly (and, in my view, morally multiple) African cultures in the twenty-first century.

# Bibliography

Adorno, Theodor W. 2001. *Problems of Moral Philosophy*. Stanford, Calif.: Stanford University Press.

———. [1951] 2005. *Minima Moralia: Reflections on a Damaged Life*. New York: Verso.

Agamben, Giorgio. 1998. *Homo Sacer: Sovereign Power and Bare Life*. Stanford, Calif.: Stanford University Press.

———. 2005. *State of Exception*. Trans. Kevin Attell. Chicago: University of Chicago Press.

Agawu, Kofi. 2003. *Representing African Music: Postcolonial Notes, Queries, Positions*. New York: Routledge.

Althusser, Louis. 1971. *Lenin and Philosophy and Other Essays*. London: New Left.

Amselle, Jean-Loup. 1978. "Le conscience paysanne: la révolte de Oulossébougou (juin 1968, Mali)." *Canadian Journal of African Studies / Revue Canadienne des Etudes Africaines* 12, no. 3: 339–55.

Appiah, Kwame Anthony. 1992. *In My Father's House: Africa in the Philosophy of Culture*. London: Oxford University Press.

———. 1997. "Cosmopolitan Patriots." *Critical Inquiry* 23, no. 3: 617–39.

Arendt, Hannah. [1958] 1998. *The Human Condition*. Chicago: University of Chicago Press.

Arnoldi, Mary Jo. 2006. "Youth Festivals and Museums: The Cultural Politics of Public Memory in Postcolonial Mali." *Africa Today* 52, no. 4: 55–76.

———. 2007. "Bamako, Mali: Monuments and Modernity in the Urban Imagination." *Africa Today* 54, no. 2: 3–24.

Askew, Kelly. 2002. *Performing the Nation: Swahili Music and Cultural Politics in Tanzania*. Chicago: University of Chicago Press.

Azam, Jean-Paul, and Flore Gubert. 2006. "Migrants' Remittances and the Household in Africa: A Review of Evidence." *Journal of African Economies* 15, no. 2: 426–62.

Baba, Ahmed. 2012. "Pogroms anti-Touregs à Bamako." February 2. jeuneafrique .com.

Bagayogo, Shaka. 1989 "Lieux et théorie du pouvoir dans le monde mandé: passé et present." *Cahier de Science Humaine* 25, no. 4: 445–60.

————. 1992. "Littérature Orale et Légitimation Politique au Mali, 1960–1990." In *Constructions identitaires: questionnements théoriques et etudes de cas,* 31–52. Québec: CÉLAT, Université Laval.

Bailleul, Charles. 2000. *Dictionnaire Bambara-français.* Bamako: Editions Donniya.

Bamba, Sorry, and Liliane Prévost. 1996. *De la Tradition à la World Music.* Paris: L'Harmattan.

Barber, Karin, ed. 1997. *Readings in African Popular Culture.* Bloomington: Indiana University Press.

Barchiesi, Franco. 2012. "Precarity as Capture: A Conceptual Reconstruction and Critique of the Worker-Slave Analogy." October 10. uninomade.org

Bayart, Jean-François. 2000. "Africa in the World: A History of Extraversion." *African Affairs* 99, no. 395: 217–67.

Bayart, Jean-François, Stephen Ellis, and Béatrice Hibou. 1999. *The Criminalization of the State in Africa.* Bloomington: Indiana University Press.

Becker, Howard S. 1982. *Art Worlds.* Berkeley: University of California Press.

Berger, Harris. 2010. *Stance: Ideas about Emotion, Style, and Meaning for the Study of Expressive Culture.* Middletown, Conn.: Wesleyan University Press.

Biehl, João, Byron Good, and Arthur Kleinman. 2007. "Introduction: Rethinking Subjectivity." In *Subjectivity: Ethnographic Investigations,* ed. João Biehl, Byron Good, and Arthur Kleinman, 27–35. Berkeley: University of California Press.

Bird, Charles S., and Martha B. Kendall. 1980. "The Mande Hero: Text and Context." In *Explorations in African Systems of Thought,* ed. Ivan Karp and Charles Bird, 13–26. Bloomington: Indiana University Press.

Bird, Charles S., Martha B. Kendall, and Kalilou Tera. 1995. "Etymologies of *nyamakala.*" In *Status and Identity in West Africa: Nyamakalaw of Mande,* ed. David C. Conrad and Barbara E. Frank, 1–26. Bloomington: Indiana University Press.

Blacking, John. 1973. *How Musical Is Man?* Seattle: University of Washington Press.

Blondy, Alpha, and the Solar System. 1994. *Dieu.* EMI France. Compact Disc.

————. 1996. *Grand Bassam Zion Rock.* EMI France. Compact Disc.

Born, Georgina, and David Hesmondhalgh. 2000. "Introduction." In *Western Music and Its Others: Difference, Representation, and Appropriation in Music,* ed. Georgina Born and David Hesmondhalgh, 1–58. Berkeley: University of California Press.

Bourdieu, Pierre. 2000. *Pascalian Mediations.* Stanford, Calif.: Stanford University Press.

Briggs, Charles. 2005. "Genealogies of Race and Culture and the Failure of Vernacular Cosmopolitanisms: Rereading Franz Boas and W. E. B. Du Bois." *Public Culture* 17, no. 1: 75–100.

Butler, Judith. 1990. *Gender Trouble: Feminism and the Subversion of Identity.* New York: Routledge.

————. 1997. *The Psychic Life of Power: Theories in Subjection*. Stanford, Calif.: Stanford University Press.

————. 2004. *Precarious Life: The Powers of Mourning and Violence*. New York: Verso.

Camara, Seydou, Eric Charry, and Jan Jansen. 2002. "The Mande Praise Song *Kayra* (Peace): Mande Global Perspectives." *Metamorphoses* 10, no. 1: 300–21.

Camara, Sory. [1976] 1992. *Gens de la parole: Essai sur la condition et role des griots dans la société malinké*. Paris: ACCT/Karthala/SAEC.

Cashion, Gerald A. 1984. "Hunters of the Mande: A Behavioral Code and Worldview Derived from the Study of Their Folklore." Ph.D. diss., Indiana University.

Césaire, Aimé. 1983. *Aimé Césaire: The Collected Poetry*. Berkeley: University of California Press.

Chakrabarty, Dipesh. 2000. *Provincializing Europe: Postcolonial Thought and Historical Difference*. Princeton: Princeton University Press.

Chalfin, Brenda. 2010. *Neoliberal Frontiers: An Ethnography of Sovereignty in West Africa*. Chicago: University of Chicago Press.

Charry, Eric. 2000a. *Mande Music. Traditional and Modern Music of the Maninka und Mandinka of Western Africa*. Chicago: University of Chicago Press.

————. 2000b. "Music and Islam in Sub-Saharan Africa." In *The History of Islam in Africa*, ed. Nehemia Levtzion and Randall L. Pouwels, 545–73. Athens: Ohio University Press.

————. 2012. "Music for an African Twenty-First Century." In *Hip Hop Africa: New African Music in a Globalizing World*, ed. Eric Charry, 283–315. Bloomington: Indiana University Press.

Charry, Eric, ed. 2012. *Hip Hop Africa: New African Music in a Globalizing World*. Bloomington: Indiana University Press.

Chatterjee, Partha. 1998. "Beyond the Nation? Or Within?" *Social Text* 56:57–69

————. 2004. *The Politics of the Governed: Reflections on Popular Politics in Most of the World*. New York: Columbia University Press

Chernoff, John M. 1979. *African Rhythm and African Sensibility: Aesthetics and Social Action in African Musical Idioms*. Chicago: University of Chicago Press.

————. 2003. *Hustling Is not Stealing: Stories of an African Bar Girl*. Chicago: University of Chicago Press.

Cissé, Nana Mourkayrou, and Oualy Sékou Traoré. 2001. "Les aspects théoriques et pratiques de la lutte contre la contrefaçon au Mali." Master's thesis, Faculté des Sciences Juridiques et Economiques, Université du Mali, Bamako, Mali.

Cissé, Youssouf Tata. 1964. "Notes sur les Sociétés de Chasseurs Malinke." *Journal de la Société des Africanistes* 34, no. 2: 175–226.

————. 1973. "Signes graphiques, représentations, concepts et tests relatifs à la personne chez les Malinké et les Bambara du Mali." In *Colloques Internationaux du Centre National de la Recherche Scientifique no. 544, La notion de personne en Afrique Noire,* ed. G. Dieterlen, 131–79. Paris.

——. 1994. *La Confrérie des Chasseurs Malinké et Bambara: Mythes, Rites et Récits Initiatiques.* Paris: Nouvelles du Sud/Arsan.

Collins, John. 1989. "The Early History of West African Highlife Music." *Popular Music* 8, no. 3: 221–30.

Comaroff, Jean, and John L. Comaroff, eds. 2006. *Law and Disorder in the Post-colony.* Chicago: University of Chicago Press.

Connor, Steven. 2004. "Edison's Teeth: Touching Hearing." In *Hearing Cultures: Essays on Sound, Listening, and Modernity,* ed. Veit Erlmann, 153–72. New York: Wenner-Gren Foundation for Anthropological Research.

Conrad, David C., and Barbara E. Frank, eds. 1995. *Status and Identity in West Africa: Nyamakalaw of Mande.* Bloomington: Indiana University Press.

Conrad, David C., and Barbara E. Frank. 1995. "Introduction: *Nyamakalaya,* Contradiction and Ambiguity in Mande Society." In *Status and Identity in West Africa: Nyamakalaw of Mande,* ed. David C. Conrad and Barbara E. Frank, 1–26. Bloomington: Indiana University Press.

Cooper, Frederick. 1996. *Decolonization and African Society: The Labor Question in French and British Africa.* New York: Cambridge University Press.

Couloubaly, Pascal Baba. 2004. *Le Mali d'Alpha Oumar Konaré: Ombres et lumières d'une démocratie en gestation.* Paris: L'Harmattan.

Counsel, Graeme. 2006. "Mande Popular Music and Cultural Policies in West Africa." Ph.D. diss., University of Melbourne.

——. 2012. "Discography of Malian Vinyl Recordings." radioafrica.com.au. August 30.

County, Brandon, and Ryan T. Skinner. 2008. "*Faso* and *Jamana*: Provisional Notes on Mande Social Thought in Malian Political Discourse, 1946–1979." In *Mande Mansa: Essays in Honor of David Conrad,* ed. Stephen Belcher, Jan Jansen, and Mohamed N'Daou, 181–92. Münster: LIT Verlag.

Cutter, Charles H. 1968. "The Politics of Music in Mali." *African Arts* 1, no. 3: 38–39, 74–77.

——. 1971. "Nation-Building in Mali: Art, Radio, and Leadership in a Pre-Literate Society." Ph.D. diss., University of California, Los Angeles.

Dabiri, Emma. 2014. "Why I'm Not an Afropolitan." africasacountry.com. January 21.

Dayan, Joan. 1983. "The Figure of Negation: Some Thoughts on a Landscape by Césaire." *French Review* 56, no. 3: 411–23.

de Beauvoir, Simone. [1948] 1976. *The Ethics of Ambiguity.* New York: Citadel.

De Boeck, Filip, and Marie Françoise Plissart. 2004. *Kinshasa: Tales of the Invisible City.* Kinshasa: Ludion.

de Certeau, Michel. 1988. *The Practice of Everyday Life*. Berkeley: University of California Press.

de Villers, Gauthier. 2002. "Introduction." In *Manières de vivre: Economie de la "débrouille" dans les villes du Congo/Zaïre*, eds. Gautheir de Villers, Bogumil Jewsiewicki, and Laurent Monnier, 11–32. Tervuren: Institut africain-CEDAF.

Diabaté, Massa Makan. 1984. "Etre griot aujourd'hui: Entretien avec Massa Makan Diabaté." *Notre Librairie* 75–76: 115–19.

Diabaté, Sidiki, et al. 1970. *Première anthologie de la musique Malienne, Vol. 5, Cordes anciennes* [Ancient strings]. Bärenreiter-Musicaphon. BM 30 L 2505. 33.3 rpm disc.

Diabaté, Toumani. 1988. *Kaira*. Hannibal. HNCD 1338. Compact Disc.

———. 2006. Transcript from the *Musique* Radio Program. *Radio France Internationale*, July 4, 2006.

Diabaté, Toumani, and Ballaké Sissoko. 1998. *New Ancient Strings*. Hannibal. HNCD 1428. Compact Disc.

Diabaté, Toumani, Keletigui Diabaté, and Bassekou Kouyaté. 1995. *Djelika*. Hannibal. HNCD 1380. Compact Disc.

Diabaté, Toumani, and Lucy Duràn. 2006. Liner Notes, In *Boulevard de l'Indépendence*, Toumani Diabaté and the Symmetric Orchestra. Nonesuch.

Diabaté, Toumani, and Ketama, with José Soto. 1994. *Songhai 2*. Hannibal. HNCD 1383. Compact Disc.

Diabaté, Toumani, and Taj Mahal. 1999. *Kulanjan*. Hannibal. HNCD 1441. Compact Disc.

Diabaté, Toumani, and the Symmetric Orchestra. 2006. *Boulevard de l'Indépendence*. Nonesuch. 79953-2. Compact Disc.

Diakité, Mandé Moussa. 2006. "La piraterie des oeuvres usicales dans le district de Bamako: Cas du Dabanani." Master's thesis. L'Institut National de la Jeunesse et des Sports, Bamako, Mali.

Diakité, Moussa. 1999. *La Musique Malienne en tant que Produit Commerciale*. Bamako: Confé…ence des Nations Unies sur le Commerce et le Développement.

Diarra, Balla, Moïse Dallo, and Jacques Champaud. 2003. *Structure urbaine et dynamique spatiale à Bamako, Mali*. Bamako: Éditions Donniya.

Diarrah, Cheick Oumar. 1991. *Vers La IIIe Republique du Mali*. Paris: L'Harmattan.

Diawara, Mamadou. 1996. "Le griot mande à l'heure de la globalization." *Cahiers d'Études Africaines* 36, no. 144: 591–612.

———. 1997. "Mande Oral Popular Culture Revisited by the Electronic Media." In *Readings in African Popular Culture*, ed. Karin Barber, 40–48. Bloomington: Indiana University Press.

———. 2003. *L'empire du verbe et l'éloquence du silence: Vers une anthropologie du discours dans les groupes dits dominés au Sahel*. Köln: Köppe.

Diawara, Manthia. 1997. "The Song of the Griot." *Transition* 74:16–30.

————. 2004. *We Won't Budge: An African Exile in the World.* New York: Civitas.

Diouf, Mamadou. 2000. "The Senegalese Murid Trade Diaspora and the Making of a Vernacular Cosmopolitanism." *Public Culture* 12, no. 3: 679–702.

Dirks, Nicholas, ed. 1998. *In Near Ruins: Cultural Theory at the End of the Century.* Minneapolis: University of Minnesota Press.

Dougnon, Isaïe. 2007. *Travail de Blanc, travail de Noir: La migration des paysans dogon vers l'Office du Niger et au Ghana (1910–1980).* Paris: Karthala.

Du Bois, W. E. B. [1946] 2003. *The World and Africa: An Inquiry into the Part Which Africa Has Played in World History.* New York: International Publishers.

Durán, Lucy. 1995a. "Jelimusow: The Superwomen of Malian Music." In *Power, Marginality, and African Oral Literature,* ed. Graham Furniss and Liz Gunner, 197–207. Cambridge: Cambridge University Press.

————. 1995b. "Birds of Wasulu: Freedom of Expression and Expressions of Freedom in the Popular Music of Southern Mali." *British Journal of Ethnomusicology* 4:101–34.

————. 1998. Liner Notes. In *New Ancient Strings,* Toumani Diabaté and Ballaké Sissoko. Hannibal. HNCD 1428. Compact Disc.

————. 1999. "Stars and Songbirds: Mande Female Singers in Urban Music, Mali 1980–99." Ph.D. diss., London University.

————. 2000. "Women, Music, and the 'Mystique' of Hunters in Mali." In *The African Diaspora: A Musical Perspective,* ed. Ingrid Monson, 136–86. New York: Routledge.

————. 2001. Liner Notes. In *Jarabi: Best of toumani Diabate, Master of the Kora,* Toumani Diabaté. Hannibal. HNCD 1462. Compact Disc.

————. 2007. "Ngaraya: Women and Musical Mastery in Mali." *Bulletin of SOAS* 70, no. 3: 569–602.

Eagleton, Terry. 2009. *Trouble with Strangers: A Study of Ethics.* Oxford: Wiley-Blackwell.

Ebron, Paula. 2002. *Performing Africa.* Princeton, N.J.: Princeton University Press.

Ensemble Instrumental National du Mali. 1977a. *Soundiata: L'épopée Mandingue.* Mali Kunkan. KO 77.04.10. 33.3 rpm disc.

————. 1977b. *Dah-Monzon ou l'épopée Bambara.* Mali Kunkan. KO 77.04.11. 33.3 rpm disc.

————. 1977c. *L'Ensemble Instrumental National du Mali.* Mali Kunkan. KO 77.04.12. 33.3 rpm disc.

Erlmann, Veit. 1999. *Music, Modernity, and the Global Imagination: South Africa and the West.* New York: Oxford University Press.

————. 2004. *Hearing Cultures: Essays on Sound, Listening, and Modernity.* New York: Wenner-Gren Foundation for Anthropological Research.

Eyre, Banning. 2000. *In Griot Time: An American Guitarist in Mali.* Philadelphia: Temple University Press.

Eze, Chielozona. 2014. "Rethinking African Culture and Identity: The Afropolitan Model." *Journal of African Cultural Studies* 26, no. 2: 234–47.

Fanon, Frantz. [1963] 2004. *The Wretched of the Earth.* New York: Grove Press.

Feld, Steven. 1982. *Sound and Sentiment: Birds, Weeping, Poetics, and Song in Kaluli Expression.* Philadelphia: University of Pennsylvania Press.

———. 1984. "Sound Structure as Social Structure." *Ethnomusicology* 28, no. 3: 383–409.

———. 1994a. "Communication, Music, and Speech about Music." In *Music Grooves,* ed. Charles Keil and Steven Feld, 77–95. Chicago: University of Chicago Press.

———. 1994b. "Aesthetics as Iconicity of Style (uptown title); or, (downtown title) 'Lift-up-over Sounding': Getting into the Kaluli Groove." In *Music Grooves,* ed. Charles Keil and Steven Feld, 109–50. Chicago: University of Chicago Press.

———. 1996a. "Waterfalls of Song: An Acoustemology of Place Resounding in Bosavi, Papua New Guinea." In *Senses of Place,* ed. Steven Feld and Keith H. Basso, 91–136. Santa Fe, N.M.: School of American Research Press.

———. 1996b. "A Poetics of Place: Ecological and Aesthetic Co-evolution in a Papua New Guinea Rainforest Community." In *Redefining Nature: Ecology, Culture, and Domestication,* ed. Roy Ellen and Katsuyoshi Fukui, 61–88. Washington, D.C.: Berg.

———. 2000. "A Sweet Lullaby for World Music." *Public Culture* 12, no. 1: 145–71.

———. 2012. *Jazz Cosmopolitanism in Accra: Five Musical Years in Ghana.* Durham, N.C.: Duke University Press.

Ferguson, James. 1999. *Expectations of Modernity: Myths and Meanings of Urban Life on the Zambian Copperbelt.* Berkeley: University of California Press.

———. 2006. *Global Shadows: African in the Neoliberal World Order.* Durham, N.C.: Duke University Press.

Fernandes, Sujatha. 2013. "The Day Music Died in Mali." newyorktimes.com May 20.

Fischer, Michael. 2003. *Emergent Forms of Life and the Anthropological Voice.* Durham, N.C.: Duke University Press.

Foucault, Michel. 2003. *"Society Music Be Defended": Lectures at the College de France, 1975–1976.* New York: St. Martin's Press.

———. 2007. *Security, Territory, Population: Lectures at the Collège de France, 1977–1978.* New York: Palgrave Macmillan.

Fox, Aaron. 2004. *Real Country: Music and Language in Working-Class Culture.* Durham, N.C.: Duke University Press.

Frith, Simon. 1996. "Music and Identity." In *Questions of Cultural Identity,* eds. Stuart Hall and Paul du Gay, 108–27. London: Sage.

Gikandi, Simon. 2010. "Foreword: On Afropolitanism." In *Negotiating Afropolitanism: Essays on Borders and Spaces in Contemporary African Literature and Folklore*, ed. Jennifer Wawrzinek and J. K. S. Makakha, 9–11. Amsterdam: Rodopi.

Gary-Tounkara, Daouda. 2008. *Migrants soudanais/maliens et conscience ivoirienne: Les étrangers en Côte d'Ivoire (1903–1980)*. Paris: L'Harmattan.

Gilroy, Paul. 1993. *The Black Atlantic: Modernity and Double Consciousness*. Cambridge: Harvard University Press.

———. 2004. *After Empire: Multiculture or Postcolonial Melancholia*. London: Routledge.

Graft, Kris. 2008. "Muslim Group Condemns LBP 'Censorship.'" next-gen.biz. October 20.

Gray, Lila Ellen. 2013. *Fado Resounding: Affective Politics and Urban Life*. Durham, N.C.: Duke University Press.

Grosz-Ngaté, Maria. 1989. "Hidden Meanings: Explorations into a Bamanan Construction of Gender." *Ethnology* 28, no. 2: 167–83.

Guilbault, Jocelyne. 2007. *Governing Sound: The Cultural Politics of Trinidad's Carnival Musics*. Chicago: University of Chicago Press.

Gupta, Akhil, and James Ferguson. 1992. "Beyond 'Culture': Space, Identity, and the Politics of Difference." *Cultural Anthropology* 7, no. 1: 1–23.

Guyer, Jane, ed. 1995. *Money Matters*. Portsmouth, N.H.: Heinemann.

Hale, Thomas A. 1998. *Griots and Griottes*. Bloomington: Indiana University Press.

Hall, Bruce. 2011. "Bellah Histories of Decolonization, Iklan Paths to Freedom: The Meanings of Race and Slavery in the Late-Colonial Niger Bend (Mali), 1944–1960." *International Journal of African Historical Studies* 44, no. 1: 61–87.

Hall, Bruce, et al. 2013. "Mali: Which Way Forward? A Chat with Bruce Hall, Baz Lecocq, Gregory Mann, and Bruce Whitehouse." africanarguments.org. May 14.

Hall, Stuart. 1980. "Cultural Studies: Two Paradigms." *Media, Culture, Society* 2: 57–72.

———. 1985. "Signification, Representation, Ideology: Althusser and the Post-Structuralist Debates." *Critical Studies in Mass Communication* 2, no. 2: 91–114.

Hammer, Joshua. 2005. "The Siren Song of Mali." *New York Times*, April 2, Section 5, 10–11.

———. 2013. "When the Jihad Came to Mali." nybooks.com. March 21.

Heidegger, Martin. 1962. *Being and Time*. Trans. John Macquarrie and Edward Robinson. Oxford: Basil Blackwell.

Hellweg, Joseph. 2011. *Hunting the Ethical State: The Benkadi Movement of Côte d'Ivoire*. Chicago: University of Chicago Press.

Hirschkind, Charles. 2001. "The Ethics of Listening: Cassette-Sermon Audition in Contemporary Egypt." *American Ethnologist* 28, no. 3: 623–49.

————. 2006. *The Ethical Soundscape: Cassette Sermons and Islamic Counter-publics*. New York: Columbia University Press.

Hodgkin, Thomas. 1957. *Nationalism in Colonial Africa*. New York: New York University Books.

Hoffman, Barbara. 1990. "The Power of Speech: Language and Social Status among Mande Griots and Nobles." Ph.D. diss., Indiana University.

————. 1995. "Power, Structure, and Mande *jeliw*." In *Status and Identity in West Africa: Nyamakalaw of Mande*, ed. David C. Conrad and Barbara E. Frank, 36–45. Bloomington: Indiana University Press.

————. 2000. *Griots at War: Conflict, Conciliation, and Caste in Mande*. Bloomington: Indiana University Press.

Hopkins, Nicholas S. 1972. "Persuasion and Satire in the Malian Theatre." *Africa* 42, no. 3: 217–28.

————. 1997. "Memories of Griots." *Alif: Journal of Comparative Poetics* 17:43–72.

Ivaska, Andrew. 2011. *Cultured States: Youth, Gender, and Modern Style in 1960s Dar Es Salaam*. Durham, N.C.: Duke University Press.

Jackson, Michael. 1996. "Introduction: Phenomenology, Radical Empiricism, and Anthropological Critique." In *Things As They Are: New Directions in Phenomenological Anthropology*, ed. Michael Jackson, 1–50. Bloomington: Indiana University Press.

————. 1998. *Minima Ethnographica: Intersubjectivity and the Anthropological Project*. Chicago: University of Chicago Press.

Jansen, Jan, and Clemens Zobel. 1996. "Kinship as Political Discourse: The Representation of Harmony and Change in Mande." In *The Younger Brother in Mande: Kinship and Politics in West Africa*, ed. Jan Jansen and Clemens Zobel, 1–7. Leiden: Research School CNWS.

Jazeel, Tariq. 2011. "Spatializing Difference beyond Cosmopolitanism: Rethinking Planetary Futures." *Theory, Culture and Society* 28, no. 5: 75–97.

Jézéquel, Jean-Hervé. 1999. "Le 'théâtre des instituteurs' en Afrique Occidentale française (1930–1950): Pratique socio-culturelle et vecteur de cristallisation de nouvelles identités urbaines." In *Fêtes urbaines en afrique: Espaces, identités et pouvoirs*, ed. Odile Goerg, 181–200. Paris: Karthala.

Johnson, John William. 2003. "The Social Setting." In *Son-Jara: The Mande Epic*, John William Johnson and Fa-Digi Sisòkò, 8–21. Bloomington: Indiana University Press.

Johnson, John William, and Fa-Digi Sisòkò. 2003. *Son-Jara: The Mande Epic*. Bloomington: Indiana University Press.

Jones, James. 2002. *Industrial Labor in the Colonial World: Workers of the Chemin de Fer Dakar-Niger, 1881–1963*. Portsmouth, N.H.: Heinemann.

Kaba, Lansiné, and Eric Charry. 2000. "*Mamaya*: Renewal and Tradition in Maninka

Music of Kankan, Guinea (1935–1945)." In *The African Diaspora: A Musical Perspective*, ed. Ingrid Monson, 187–206. New York: Routledge.

Kanouté, Oumar. 2007. *Le théâtre malien (tome 1) de 1916 à 1976*. Bamako: EDIS.

Karaganis, Joe, ed. 2011. *Media Piracy in Emerging Economies*. New York: Social Science Research Council.

Keïta, Cheick M. Chérif. 1990. "Fadenya and Artistic Creation in Mali: Kele Monson and Massa Makan Diabaté." *Research in African Literatures* 21, no. 3: 103–14.

———. 1995a. *Massa Makan Diabaté: Un Griot mandingue à la rencontre de l'écriture*. Paris: L'Harmattan.

———. 1995b. "*Jaliya* in the Modern World: A Tribute to Banzumana Sissoko and Massa Makan Diabaté." In *Status and Identity in West Africa: Nyamakalaw of Mande*, ed. David C. Conrad and Barbara E. Frank, 182–96. Bloomington: Indiana University Press.

———. 2009. *Salif Keïta: L'ambassadeur de la musique du Mali*. Brinon-sur-Sauldre: Éditions Grandvaux.

Kelley, Robin D. G. 2012. *Africa Speaks, America Answers: Modern Jazz in Revolutionary Times*. Cambridge, Mass.: Harvard University Press.

Knight, Roderic. 1973. "Mandinka Jaliya: Professional Music of The Gambia." 2 vols. Ph.D. diss., University of California, Los Angeles.

———. 1991. "Music Out of Africa: Mande Jaliya in Paris." *World of Music* 33, no. 1: 52–69.

Konaré, Adame Ba. 2006. *Quand l'ail se frotte à l'encens*. Paris: Présence Africaine.

Konè, Kassim. 1995. *Bamanankan Danyegafe*. West Newbury, Mass.: Mother Tongue Editions.

———. 1996. "Bamana Verbal Art: An Ethnographic Study of Proverbs." Ph.D. diss., Indiana University.

Kruger, Loren. 2013. *Imagining the Edgy City: Writing, Performing, and Building Johannesburg*. New York: Oxford University Press.

Laing, Dave. 2004. "Copyright, Politics, and the International Music Industry." In *Music and Copyright*, 2nd ed., ed. Simon Frith and Lee Marshall, 70–88. New York: Routledge.

Larkin, Brian. 2008. *Signal and Noise: Media, Infrastructure, and Urban Culture in Nigeria*. Durham, N.C.: Duke University Press.

Latournerie, Anne. 2001. "Petite histoire des batailles du droit d'auteur." *Multitudes*. multitudes.samizdat.net. May 5.

Lecocq, Baz. 2004. "Unemployed Intellectuals in the Sahara: The *Teshumara* Nationalist Movement and the Revolutions in Tuareg Society." *International Review of Social History* 49, no. 12: 87–109.

———. 2010. *Disputed Desert: Decolonisation, Competing Nationalisms, and Tuareg Rebellions in Northern Mali*. London: Brill.

Lecocq, Baz, et al. 2013. "One Hippopotamus and Eight Blind Analysts: A Multi-vocal Analysis of the 2012 Political Crisis in the Divided Republic of Mali." *Review of African Political Economy* 40, no. 137: 343–57.

Lefebvre, Henri. 1991. *The Production of Space.* Cambridge: Blackwell.

Lessig, Lawrence. 2004. *Free Culture: The Nature and Future of Creativity.* London: Penguin Books.

Levtzion, Nehemia, and Randall L. Pouwels, eds. 2000. *The History of Islam in Africa.* Athens: Ohio University Press.

Luke K. 2010. "Religion, Atheism, and Videogames (Nihilistically Ever After)." criticalgamer.co.uk. July 22.

Maillot, Elodie. 2002. "Mali K7, l'usine à rêve." rfimusique.com. January 17.

Maingard, Jacqueline. 2010. "Screening Africa in Colour: Abderrahmane Sissoko's *Bamako.*" *Screen* 51, no. 4: 397–403.

Mangin, André. 1998. *Malick Sidibé.* Berlin: Helvetas.

Mann, Gregory. 2012a. "The Mess in Mali." *Foreign Policy.* foreignpolicy.com. April 5.

———. 2012b. "The Racial Politics of Tuareg Nationalism." April 7. africasacountry.com.

———. 2013. "Afropositivism." culantl..org. 16 June.

Marcus, George, and Michael Fischer. 1986. *Anthropology as Cultural Critique: An Experimental Moment in the Human Sciences.* Chicago: University of Chicago Press.

Marley, Bob, and the Wailers. 1976. *Rastaman Vibration.* Island. 33.3 rpm disc.

Martiniello, Giuliano. 2013. "Land Dispossession and Rural Social Movements: The 2011 Conference in Mali." *Review of African Political Economy* 40, no. 136: 309 20.

Maxwell, Heather A. 2002. "Destiny's Divas: Wassolu Singing, Music Ideologies, and the Politics of Performance in Bamako, Mali." Ph.D. diss., Indiana University.

———. 2003. "Divas of the Wassoulou Sound: Transformations in the Matrix of Cultural Production, Globalization, and Identity." *Consumption Markets and Culture* 6, no. 1: 43–63.

———. 2008. "Of Youth-Harps and Songbirds: The Sweet Music of Wasulu." *African Music* 8, no. 2: 26–55.

Mazauric, Catherine. 2007. "Les rappeurs de l'Afrance: de la negotiation identitaire auz pistes didactiques?" *Synergies: Afrique Centrale et de l'Ouest* 2: 175–85.

Mbembe, Achille. 1992. "The Banality of Power and the Aesthetics of Vulgarity in the Postcolony." *Public Culture* 4, no. 2: 1–30.

———. 2001. *On the Postcolony.* Berkeley: University of California Press.

———. 2003. "Necropolitics." *Public Culture* 15, no. 1: 11–40.

————. 2010. *Sortir de la grande nuit: Essai sur l'Afrique décolonisée*. Paris: Editions La Découverte.

————. 2013. *Critique de la Raison Nègre*. Paris: Editions La Découverte.

McGovern, Mike. 2011. *Making War in Côte d'Ivoire*. Chicago: University of Chicago Press.

McNaughton, Patrick R. 1988. *The Mande Blacksmiths: Knowledge, Power, and Art in West Africa*. Bloomington: Indiana University Press.

McLaughlin, Fiona. 1997. "Islam and Popular Music in Senegal: The Emergence of a 'New Tradition.'" *Africa* 67, no. 4: 560–81.

Meillassoux, Claude. 1968. *Urbanization of an African Community: Voluntary Associations in Bamako*. Seattle: University of Washington Press.

Meintjes, Louise. 2003. *Sound of Africa! Making Music Zulu in a South African Recording Studio*. Durham, N.C.: Duke University Press.

Melly, Caroline. 2010. "Inside-Out Houses: Urban Belonging and Imagined Futures in Dakar, Senegal." *Comparative Studies in Society and History* 52, no.1: 37–65.

Merleau-Ponty, Maurice. [1962] 2002. *Phenomenology of Perception*. London: Routledge.

Merriam, Alan. P. 1980. "Review of *African Rhythm and African Sensibility: Aesthetics and Social Action in African Musical Idioms* by John Miller Chernoff." *Ethnomusicology* 24, no. 3: 559–61.

Michaels, Sean. 2008. "Toumani Diabaté 'Disappointed' over Koran Song Ban." guardian.co.uk. October 24.

Modic, Kate. 1996. "Song, Performance, and Power: The *Bèn Ka Di* Women's Association in Bamako, Mali." Ph.D. diss., Indiana University.

Monson, Ingrid, ed. 2003. *The African Diaspora: A Musical Perspective*. New York: Routledge.

Moorman, Marissa J. 2008. *Intonations: A Social History of Music and Nation in Luanda, Angola, from 1945 to Recent Times*. Athens: Ohio University Press.

Morgan, Andy. 2013. *Music, Culture, and Conflict in Mali*. Copenhagen: Freemuse.

Morgenthau, Ruth Schachter. 1964. *Political Parties in French-Speaking West Africa*. Oxford: Clarendon Press.

Moseley, William G. 2012. "Azawad: The Latest African Border Dilemma." aljazeera.com. April 18.

Mudimbe, V. Y. 1988. *The Invention of Africa: Gnosis, Philosophy, and the Order of Knowledge*. Bloomington: Indiana University Press.

Muller, Carol Ann, and Sathima Bea Benjamin. 2011. *Musical Echoes: South African Women Thinking in Jazz*. Durham, N.C.: Duke University Press.

Novak, David. 2010. "Cosmopolitanism, Remediation, and the Ghost World of Bollywood." *Cultural Anthropology* 25, no. 1: 40–72.

————. 2013. *Japanoise: Music at the Edge of Circulation.* Durham, N.C.: Duke University Press.

Ntahokaja, l'Abbé. 1963. "Réunion africaine d'étude sur le droit d'auteur. Brazzaville, 5–10 août 1963." *Le Droit d'Auteur* 76:250–59.

Nuttall Sarah, and Achille Mbembe, eds. 2008. *Johannesburg: The Elusive Metropolis.* Durham, N.C.: Duke University Press.

Olaniyan, Tejumola. 2004. *Arrest the Music! Fela and His Rebel Art and Politics.* Bloomington: Indiana University Press.

Olukoju, Ayodeji. 2004. "'Never Expect Power Always': Electricity Consumers' Response to Monopoly, Corruption, and Inefficient Services in Nigeria." *African Affairs* 103, no. 410: 51–71.

Orchestre Régional du Mali, Mopti. *Les meilleurs souvenirs de la 1ère Biennale Artistique et Culturelle de la Jeunesse.* Bärenreiter-Musicaphon. BM 30 L 2602. 33.3 rpm disc.

Osborn, Emily Lynn. 2011. *Our New Husbands Are Here: Household, Gender, and Politics in a West African State from the Slave Trade to Colonial Rule.* Athens: Ohio University Press.

Pauthier, Céline. 2012. "La musique guinéenne, vecteur du patrimoine national (des années 1950 à 1984)." In *L'Afrique des saviors au sud du Sahara (XVIe-XXIe siècle): Acteurs, supports, pratiques,* ed. Daouda Gary-Tounkara and Didier Nativel. Paris: Karthala.

Perullo, Alex. 2008. "Rumba in the City of Peace: Migration and the Cultural Commodity of Congolese Music in Dar es Salaam, 1968–1985." *Ethnomusicology* 52, no. 2: 296–323.

————. 2011. *Live from Dar es Salaam: Popular Music and Tanzania's Music Economy.* Bloomington: Indiana University Press.

Peterson, Brian J. 2012. "Mali: Confronting 'Talibanization'— the Other Ansar Dine, Popular Islam, and Religious Tolerance." allafrica.com. April 25.

Piot, Charles. 2010. *Nostalgia for the Future: West Africa after the Cold War.* Chicago: University of Chicago Press.

Plageman, Nate. 2013. *Highlife Saturday Night: Popular Music and Social Change in Urban Ghana.* Bloomington: Indiana University Press.

Porcello, Thomas, et al. 2010. "The Reorganization of the Sensory World." *Annual Review of Anthropology* 39:51–66.

Ralph, Michael. 2008. "Killing Time." *Social Text* 26, no. 4 97: 1–29.

Reed, Daniel B. "Promises of the Chameleon: Reggae Artist Tiken Jah Fakoly's Intertextual Contestation of Power in Côte d'Ivoire." In *Hip Hop Africa: New African Music in a Globalizing World,* ed. Eric Charry, 92–108. Bloomington: Indiana University Press.

Rodney, Walter. 1974. *How Europe Underdeveloped Africa.* Washington, D.C.: Howard University Press.

Roth, Molly. 2008. *Ma Parole s'Achète: Money, Identity, and Meaning in Malian Jeliya*. Berlin: LIT Verlag.

Sakakeeny, Matt. 2010. "'Under the Bridge': An Orientation to Soundscapes in New Orleans." *Ethnomusicology* 54, no. 1: 1–27.

———. 2013. *Roll with It: Brass Bands in the Streets of New Orleans*. Durham, N.C.: Duke University Press.

Said, Edward. 1978. *Orientalism*. New York: Vintage Books.

Samuels, David, et al. 2010. "Soundscapes: Toward a Sounded Anthropology." *Annual Review of Anthropology* 39: 329–45.

Sanankoua, Bintou. 1990. *La chute de Modibo Keïta*. Paris: Editions Chaka.

Sartre, Jean-Paul. [1956] 2001. *Being and Nothingness: A Phenomenological Essay on Ontology*. New York: Citadel.

Schulz, Dorothea. 1999. "'In Pursuit of Publicity': Talk Radio and the Imagination of a Moral Public in Urban Mali." *Afrika Spectrum* 34, no. 2: 161–85.

———. 2001. *Perpetuating the Politics of Praise: Jeli Praise Singers, Radio, and Political Mediation in Mali*. Köln: Rüdiger Köppe Verlag.

———. 2002. "'The World Is Made by Talk': Female Fans, Popular Music, and New Forms of Public Sociality in Urban Mali." *Cahier d'Études Africaines* 42, no. 4: 797–830.

———. 2012. "Mapping Cosmopolitan Identities: Rap Music and Male Youth Culture in Mali." In *Hip Hop Africa: New African Music in a Globalizing World*, ed. Eric Charry, 129–46. Bloomington: Indiana University Press.

Shain, Richard M. 2009. "The Re(Public) of Salsa: Afro-Cuban Music in *Fin-De-Siècle* Dakar." *Africa* 79, no. 2: 186–206.

Shipley, Jesse Weaver. 2013. *Living the Hiplife: Celebrity and Entrepreneurship in Ghanaian Popular Music*. Durham, N.C.: Duke University Press.

Simone, AbdouMaliq. 2001a. "Straddling the Divides: Remaking Associational Life in the Informal African City." *International Journal of Urban and Regional Research* 25, no. 1: 102–17.

———. 2001b. "On the Worlding of African Cities." *African Studies Review* 44, no. 2: 15–41.

———. 2004. *For the City Yet to Come: Changing African Life in Four Cities*. Durham, N.C.: Duke University Press.

Sissako, Aberrahmane. 2006. *Bamako*. New Yorker Films.

Skinner, Ryan T. 2004. "Determined Urbanites: Diasporic *Jeliya* in the 21st Century." *Mande Studies* 6: 139–62.

———. 2008a. *Sidikiba's Kora Lesson*. Minneapolis: Beaver's Pond Press.

———. 2008b. "Celebratory Spaces Between Homeland and Host: Politics, Culture, and Performance in New York's Malian Community." In *Migrations and Creative Expressions in Africa and the African Diaspora*, eds. Toyin Falola, Niyi

Afolabi, and Adérónké Adésolá Adésànyà, 279-98. Durham, N.C.: Carolina Academic Press.

——. 2009. "*Artistiya*: Popular Music and Personhood in Postcolonial Bamako, Mali." Ph.D. diss., Columbia University.

——. 2010. "Civil Taxis and Wild Trucks: The Dialectics of Space and Subjectivity in *Dimanche à Bamako*." *Popular Music* 29, no. 1: 17–39.

——. 2012a. "Artists, Music Piracy, and the Crisis of Political Subjectivity in Contemporary Mali." *Anthropological Quarterly* 85, no. 3: 723–54.

——. 2012b. "Cultural Politics in the Post-Colony: Music, Nationalism, and Statism in Mali, 1964–1975." *Africa* 82, no. 4: 511–34.

Smith, Margit Cronmueller. 2011. *The Mande Koru: A West African System of Thought. Collected Writings, Essays, and Interviews*. Augusta: University of Maine.

Smitherman, Geneva. 1997. "'The Chain Remain the Same': Communicative Practices in the Hip Hop Nation." *Journal of Black Studies* 28, no. 1: 3–25.

Soares, Benjamin. 2005. *Islam and the Prayer Economy: History and Authority in a Malian Town*. Ann Arbor: University of Michigan Press.

——. 2012. "On the Recent Mess in Mali." *Anthropology Today* 28, no. 5: 1–2.

Stollei, Paul. 2013. "The Social Life of Music—in Mali." huffingtonpost.com. May 21.

Tata Pound. 2002. *Cikan (Le Message)*. Mali K7 SA. Compact Disc.

——. 2006. *Revolution*. Mali K7 SA. Compact Disc.

Thompson, Robert Farris. 2011. *Aesthetic of the Cool: Afro-Atlantic Art and Music*. New York: Periscope.

Totilo, Stephen. 2008. "'Little Big Planet' Musician Defends Controversial Song to MTV, Muslim Experts Assess Whether Song Is a Problem." multiplayerblog .mtv.com. October 21.

Touré, Younoussa. 1996. "La Biennale Artistique et Culturelle du Mali, 1962–1988: socio-anthropologie d'une action de politique culturelle africaine." Thèse de doctorat de 3e cycle, École des Hautes Études en Sciences Sociales, Marseille.

Tower, Craig. 2005. "'Arajo Efemu': Local FM Radio and the Socio-Technical System of Communications in Koutiala, Mali." *Radio Journal: International Studies in Broadcast and Audio Media* 3, no. 1: 7–20.

——. 2008. "Radio Ways: Society, Locality, and FM Technology in Koutiala, Mali." Ph.D. diss., Northwestern University.

Traoré, Richard. 2004. "Music Industry in Burkina Faso and Mali—The Case of Seydoni Production." In *Sounds of Change: Social and Political Features of Music in Africa*, ed. Stig-Magnus Thorsén, 197–219. Stockholm: Sida.

Triton Stars. 2006. *Immigration*. Self-released album. Compact Disc.

Tuakli-Wosornu, Taiye. 2005. "Bye-Bye Barbar." thelip.robertsharp.co.uk. March 3.

Turino, Thomas. 1999. "Signs of Imagination, Identity, and Experience: A Peircian Semiotic Theory for Music." *Ethnomusicology* 43, no. 2: 221–55.

————. 2000. *Nationalists, Cosmopolitans, and Popular Music in Zimbabwe*. Chicago: University of Chicago Press.

Tveit, Marta. 2013. "The Afropolitan Must Go." africasacountry.com November 29.

Various Artists. 1973a. *Panorama du Mali*. Mali Music. Mali 1002. 33.3 rpm disc.

Various Artists. 1973b. *Regard sur le passé à travers le présent*. Mali Music. Mali 1001. 33.3 rpm disc.

Various Artists. 1977. *Epic, Historical, Political, and Propaganda Songs of the Socialist Government of Modibo Keita (1960–1968)*. Vols. 1 & 2. Albatross. VPA 8326. 33.3 rpm disc.

Warner, Michael. 2002. *Publics and Counterpublics*. New York: Zone Books.

Waterman, Christopher. 1991. "The Uneven Development of Africanist Ethnomusicology: Three Issues and a Critique." In *Comparative Musicology and Anthropology of Music*, ed. Bruno Nettle and Philip V. Bohlman, 169–86. Chicago: University of Chicago Press.

Waterman, Richard A. 1948. "'Hot' Rhythm in Negro Music." *Journal of the American Musicological Society* 1, no. 1: 24–37.

————. [1952] 1973. "African Influence on the Music of the Americas." In *Mother Wit from the Laughing Barrel: Readings in the Interpretation of Afro-American Folklore*, ed. Alan Dundes, 81–94. Jackson: University of Mississippi Press.

Weiss, Brad. 2009. *Street Dreams and Hip Hop Barbershops: Global Fantasy in Urban Tanzania*. Bloomington: Indiana University Press.

Werbner, Pnina. 2006. "Understanding Vernacular Cosmopolitanism." *Anthropology News* 47, no. 5: 7–11.

White, Bob W. 2002. "Congolese Rumba and Other Cosmopolitanisms." *Cahiers d'Études Africaines* 42, no. 168: 663–86.

————. 2008. *Rumba Rules: The Politics of Dance Music in Mobutu's Zaire*. Durham, N.C.: Duke University Press.

Whitehouse, Bruce. 2012a. *Migrants and Strangers in an African City: Exile, Dignity, Belonging*. Bloomington: Indiana University Press.

————. 2012b. "Fighting for the Republic, with Beats and Rhymes." bridgesfrombamako.com. June 5.

————. 2012c. "What Went Wrong in Mali?" *London Review of Books* 34, no. 16: 17.

————. 2012d. "The Force of Action: Legitimizing the Coup in Bamako Mali." *Africa Spectrum* 47, no. 2: 93–110.

————. 2013a. "An Ka Wili." bridgesfrombamako.com. January 1.

————. 2013b. "Merci François!" bridgesfrombamako.com. January 13.

————. 2013c. "Malian Voices United (Mostly)." bridgesfrombamako.com. January 21.

————. 2013d. "'A Festival of Brigands': In Search of Democracy and Political Legitimacy in Mali." *Strategic Review for Southern Africa* 35, no. 2: 35–52.

Williams, Raymond. [1961] 2001. *The Long Revolution*. Peterborough, Ontario: Broadview Press.

Wooten, Stephen, ed. 2005. *Wari Matters: Ethnographic Explorations of Money in the Mande World*. Münster: LIT Verlag.

Yúdice, George. 2004. *The Expediency of Culture: The Uses of Culture in the Global Era*. Durham, N.C.: Duke University Press.

# Index

RYAN THOMAS SKINNER is assistant professor of ethnomusicology in the School of Music and Department of African American and African Studies at The Ohio State University.